God's Girls

Finding the Freedom to Become the Women God Created Us to Be!

Susan Slone Dantzler

AmericaHouse
Baltimore

First printing

ISBN: 1-59129-240-9
PUBLISHED BY AMERICA HOUSE BOOK PUBLISHERS
www.publishamerica.com
Baltimore

Printed in the United States of America

Acknowledgments

I thank my dear Lord for giving me the vision for God's Girls. As I obeyed Him in writing this book, He has been faithful to direct me throughout the entire process. His loving–kindness and tender mercies toward His girls never cease to amaze me. To God be all the Glory for the things He has done!

I thank my husband, Brad, who is my very best friend, my lover and my life soul–mate. He encourages and supports me in every area of my life, and for this I am truly grateful. I thank Brad for encouraging me to share stories from our life with all who read God's Girls. (What a brave man.) Knowing Brad has made me a better person. I am so thankful to God for divinely placing this wonderful man in my life. He and our two sons have made my life rich beyond words. Thank you, sweetie. I love you.

I thank my precious sons, L.B. and Blake, who have so graciously shared me with our computer during the months it took to write God's Girls. I thank God for blessing me with these two great little guys, who continue to bring joy, laughter, and excitement to my life. I thank them for allowing me to share some of their personal stories in God's Girls. I have been so blessed by their sweet prayers for me and the book. L.B. prayed, "Dear God let somebody buy Moms book…I mean, please, let lots of people buy Moms book all over the world." Because it really bothers Blake when he thinks people might be laughing at him, he prayed, "Dear God, please don't let anyone laugh at Mommy's book, and let her be real famous too."

I thank my dear friend, mentor, and sister in Christ, Millie Farthing. She is a gifted teacher of the Word, who's devotion to God has inspired many of women to grow closer to their Heavenly Father. I thank Millie for so graciously helping with the editing of God's Girls for which I am truly grateful.

Dedication

To my Heavenly Father, who has so lovingly offered His hand to me to walk with through life, reminding me that I am His little girl. I stand in awe as He has revealed to me that He created me so He could spend time with me. He is not only an important part of my life, but He has become my life, and I never ever want to live without His sweet, precious life–changing presence.

To my Mother, Lori Slone, who literally poured her life into me, teaching me by her example that the most important role I'll ever have in life is being a child of God. She is a true woman of prayer, and her prayers are a priceless treasure which are greatly to credit for who I am today.

To my sisters, Jane Pfleiderer and Leslie Coscia, who have taught me that there's only one way to love…and that is unconditionally, through laughter and sometimes tears. Though we are uniquely individual, we remain united as one team, weathering the storms of life side by side, sisters forever.

To my closest friend, Becky Coscia, who God divinely placed in my life to teach me about His gift of friendship to women. Our spirits have become one, connecting us at the heart forever. Becky has influenced my life in every single area, always encouraging and supporting me, while pointing me to Christ.

To my dearest girlfriends, (you know who you are) whom God has so graciously place in my life. God has used your strengths, talents and life experiences, which are uniquely yours, to sharpen, strengthen me, making me the woman I am today.

To every woman in the world, this book celebrates the blessed truth that we are daughters of God, created by God for the purpose of knowing God. No matter where you live or what your life circumstances are…He loves you just the way you are.

Table of Contents

Chapter 1
God's Girls! 9

Chapter 2
Life Is How You Change It! 21

Chapter 3
Putting First Things First 29

Chapter 4
The Ultimate Interior Designer 41

Chapter 5
Little Red Sports Car 53

Chapter 6
Heads Up, Girls! 63

Chapter 7
I Will Trust You! 79

Chapter 8
He Will Make A Way 91

Chapter 9
Café Mocha with Whipped Cream, Please! 105

Chapter 10
Fitness Unlimited 125

Chapter 11
You Go, Girl! 143

Chapter 12
Girlfriends! 159

Chapter 13
Taking Control of Busyness 175

Chapter 14
Free! Free To Be...God's Girl! 197

Appendix A
Take Your Wellness Temperature 217

— 1 —

God's Girls!

I have come that you might have life and have it more abundantly... John 10:10

"*For I know the plans I have for you,*" *declares the Lord,* "*plans to prosper you and not to harm you, plans to give you hope and a future...*" Jeremiah 29:11

I thank God for creating me a woman. I thank Him for the beautiful women He has so graciously placed in my life. God created women with such endless potential to bring rays of sunlight, fresh breezes of fragrance and rainbows of color into the lives of those they love. Woman are uniquely designed to be the bearers of many gifts that enrich our lives. Women can add excitement, energy, tenderness, laughter, warmth, courage, strength, perspective, healing, and so many other good things to our lives. Simply by being created a woman, we have been given the awesome opportunity to impact the lives of those around us for the better.

I imagine God sitting back after the creation of the world, proudly surveying all that He had created...then smiling...and saying, "This is very good." I also imagine Him thinking of some really precious gifts He wanted to give to His creation. I imagine God taking all of these wild and wonderful qualities and attributes I mentioned above and packaging them up in the beautiful design He called 'woman.' Yes! God's first gift to His created world...to man...was the *gift of women.*

A friend was sharing with me about a conversation she recently had with her daughter. She had explained to her, "We are women by birth, but it takes extra effort and discipline to become a lady."

Women by birth, and ladies by choice. How true, I thought. God creates us "women," and we must make a conscious choice to become all that He has designed us to be.

Women have strengths that amaze men. Women brave the storms of life with courage. They are God's only vehicle for bringing new life into the world. Women are thankful for a calm, peaceful sunrise, a gentle breeze blowing through open windows, and a favorite old–faithful sweatshirt. Women allow the simple joys of life to sooth their souls; a child sweetly sleeping, quiet time with a good book and favorite cup of tea, the cozy warm feeling that comes from a burning candle, gentle kisses from little ones, and a picture perfect rainbow.

Women appreciate the basic things in life like a perfectly ripe banana, a piece of warm chocolate chip cheese cake, a delicate clear glass vase filled with freshly cut roses from your garden, a great sale and a perfect cup of coffee in a favorite coffee mug. Women spice up life by slow dancing in the kitchen with their husbands, and rehearsing the tango with their sons.

Women treasure love notes from close friends, an 'I love you' from her husband, a prolonged period of silliness and exuberant laughter with sister or friend and a simple 'thanks Mom.' Women recognize a value in a promptly delivered epidurals, nursing pads, disposable diapers, relaxed fit jeans, bathing suit cover–ups, ideal car cup holders, and American made toilets. (If you've ever had the opportunity to visit one of the uniquely designed ladies restrooms in Paris, London, or Rome, you understand exactly what I'm referring to. There were several styles that I never could figure out how to utilize.)

Women vote for the person that will do the best job for family issues. They walk the extra mile for their friends, family, and those in need. Women slip love notes in their husbands sock drawer, in the lunch boxes of their children and on the dressers of their beloved girlfriends. Many times women do without essential items, so their children can have what they need.

Women are quick to come to the aid of a friend in crisis, driving her to an important doctors appointment, praying with her, and many times simply lending a listening ear, which allows her friend to bare her heart and soul.

Women love unconditionally, passionately, and openly. They are honest, loyal, considerate, and forgiving. Women can provide a safe place for other women to share their inner most thoughts with, as they walk together through life.

Women are intelligent and intuitive. They strive to season their delivery of words with kindness, while never compromising the truth. Women want to be the best for their families, their friends, and themselves.

Women are teachers, mothers, attorneys, and doctors. They are wives, sales clerks, friends, managers, writers, and grandmothers. Some women are fitness trainers, dentists, nurses, and executives, while others are biker babes, Sunday school teachers, gardeners, and professional athletes. Women make excellent speakers, chefs, construction workers and coaches.

Women wear everything from business suits to swim suits. They wear funky denim skirts, elegant evening gowns, hospital scrubs, and police uniforms. Some women sport cowboy boots, while others prefer go–go boots. Women wear sweat pants, leather pants, khaki pants and silk pants. They wear running shoes, high heel shoes, leopard skirts, and floral shirts. Some wear baseball caps, shower caps, and even fancy feathered hats.

Women cry when their children feel pain, and rejoice when their children excel. Women cheer when their friends prosper and do well. They are genuinely happy when they hear about a birth, a marriage, and a new house. (Hopefully, even when the house is much bigger than their own.) Their hearts break when someone dies, a marriage is dissolved, or a friend faces treatment for cancer. Women find strength when they think there is no strength left.

One of my favorite movies is Steel Magnolias. It exemplifies feminine strength at every turn, and is a very heart warming movie. Six women with different personalities, qualities, strengths, and individual life circumstances; each commit to walk through life together, embracing each moment as though they were walking arm in arm and side by side.

I am encouraged and empowered as I watch these women courageously face the daily issues of one another's lives. From the births of babies to the deaths of loved ones, they walk together courageously, supporting one another. They laugh together and cry together, growing stronger as they walk through each situation that life brings. By sharing their unique God given talents and strengths, they amazingly complete and enhance one another's lives.

I thank God for my close friend Caryl Brown and her family, who we have been so very blessed to have as neighbors for the past six years. She and her family have become like family to us, making our daily family life richer now than before we knew them. Our annual trips to Marco Island over the past six years have given us priceless memories that both our families will treasure forever, while bonding us together in a very special way.

Last week, Caryl was unexpectedly faced with saying 'goodbye for awhile' to her mother, as she changed her address from earth to heaven. After Caryl called to tell me her mother had taken her last breath on earth, I wanted to just scoop her up into my arms and make the pain go away, but I knew I could not and should not try to take away this pain that comes from the natural transition of life from this world to the next. My role in her life was to simply walk with her through this difficult time, and lighten the load as much as I could.

I knew exactly what God wanted me to do. I called our mutual friend Michelle, along with others, to rally together and encircle Caryl and her family with love, comfort, and support during this difficult time. We began not only to lift Caryl and her family up in our prayers, but we also planned and coordinated the entire reception for her, so she would be free to focus on the celebration service she and her sisters wanted to plan in memory of their mother, May.

The event celebrated May's life here on earth and her graduation into heaven. It is a priceless treasure…to have women in our lives to walk us through each season of life whatever it may bring.

Women are as fragrant and beautiful as a magnolia flower, yet strong and resilient like steel. The term 'steel magnolias' is an appropriate description of women, which shows their strength and resiliency perfectly blended with their beauty and passion.

My dear friend and mentor, Jan, has lived her life as an exceptional example of a 'steel magnolia.' Raised in a loving home by a Jewish mother and a Catholic father, Jan was married at the early age of 18, which was very common during that era. Throughout the early years of their marriage, Jan gave birth to three boys, and a girl.

As a young mother, she realized that she could not always protect her children from harm, but she could rest knowing that God was completely capable of caring for them. Jan recalls the day when her five and three year old sons decided to light a match in their small tack room, while holding a gasoline can. When the match fell onto the gasoline can, the flame ignited, burning the face of her five year old son. Mysteriously, the flame that in all reality should have exploded that little tack room full of inflammable contents, was blown out by someone other than her two little guys. Jan knows in her heart that God's angels had guarded her sons that night, protecting them from an explosion that would have taken their lives.

In 1978, Jan's husband, Bill, was in a tragic plane crash, which took his life. Yes, Jan's husband's heart actually stopped beating in that emergency room, only to be revived moments later. Although Bill's heart would fully recover, he would have to have both of his legs amputated at the knees.

While Bill was in the hospital with Jan by his bedside, a priest stopped by to visit him, but hesitated in the doorway because he saw an angel standing in Bill's room that day. Just another sign to Jan that her God was sending His angels to care for both her and her family.

Over the next fifteen years, Jan enjoyed raising her children, courageously facing all of the issues that come with raising three boys and a girl.

After devoting the many years to raising her children, Jan decided to return to the workforce, accepting a position at a wellness center for women. One early morning, in 1992, on her way to open the wellness center, Jan stopped at a traffic light only to find herself in the middle of a car jacking.

Before she knew it, four large men had overtaken her, one placing a gun to her head, while shoving her into the back seat of her car. As the car began to move, she knew that if she didn't escape now, she would not live. Her only thought was that she wanted desperately to be at her daughter's upcoming wedding, and she would not allow these men to take her life from her.

Although there was nothing in the car floor for her foot to push off of, she pushed against something, and miraculously propelled her body out of the moving car. Jan escaped those men that morning, convinced that once again, God had sent His angels to protect and rescue His little girl. It pays to know people in HIGH places, if you know what I mean!

I was blessed to work with Jan at the wellness center for about seven years, gaining so much from her both professionally and personally. She became much more to me than my manager. She became my dear friend, confidante, role model, and mentor, whom I grew to love. Sharing the wisdom she had gained throughout her life, Jan greatly impacted my life in powerful ways. I am truly a better woman today because I had the opportunity to walk, side–by–side, with Jan for a season.

Jan is an amazing women, who passionately lives life with a positive attitude that is simply contagious to those around her. She lives what she teaches…a balanced, healthy lifestyle, placing God and family first.

At 56 years old, Jan is the picture of health, exuding confidence in being comfortable with who she is becoming in life. Jan is my hero, a true 'steel magnolia,' who keeps the faith through thick and thin, pressing on with everything in her.

Like Jan, there is a 'steel magnolia' in each of us, just waiting to bloom, bringing both hope and courage to those who walk with us, as well as, those who will come behind us.

Women are wonderful gifts from God each with qualities and life circumstances unique to themselves, committed to walk hand in hand comforting, encouraging, and challenging one another to become the women God has created us to be.

I recently had the privilege to spend a few hours with some extraordinary women who had gathered to pray and begin planning the first annual Celebration of Grace Women's Retreat at Cypress Gardens in Winter Haven, Florida.

As we enjoyed an elegant brunch together at the famous Chalet Suzanne Restaurant in Lake Wales, Florida, I looked around the table in awe. My first impression of this picture perfect and beautifully balanced group of successful looking women seated in this fancy chalet, hugging and laughing and drinking coffee and tea was that they couldn't possibly have a care in the world, let alone have any idea of any painful issues others may be facing in life.

Well, as usual, first impressions are rarely accurate. These women are ordinary women, much like you and me, who have realized that they have an extraordinary God who loves them and cares about the tiniest details of their lives. These women understand the power that comes from knowing that they are God's daughters, and that He has promised to hold their hand and safely walk them through every storm and every struggle that they will face on their journey.

I listened as each woman shared intimate details about her life. My eyes filled with tears of sympathy and joy at the same time, as they shared the heart breaking issues that they had faced on their individual journeys through life, and how God had brought good things from each painful experience.

The struggles of depression, anxiety, death of children and husbands, addictions, obsessions, fears, disease, illness, cancer, family distention, failed marriages, lack of self–esteem, parental challenges, weight issues, abuse, and living in bondage in all areas of life were addressed.

Becky, wearing a bright melon silk blouse, white linen Capri pants, accented with silver jewelry with melon, lime green, and lilac stones, looked elegant as always. Her shoes were delicate silver sandals with a one inch heel. Becky's stylish short hair is the darkest brown which blends beautifully with her dark brown eyes, and striking features. Becky was chosen Mrs. Florida 1980, so you know she's a beautiful woman. Becky is my closest friend in all the world.

Her story is one of a girl who took the wrong road for a season. The road that she found herself on in her late teen age years included drugs, alcohol, teen pregnancy and more. Becky's life is a testimony to the unconditional love that our Heavenly Father has for His girls. With a fragmented life, she called out to God, and He rescued her. He was right there waiting for her to call on Him. He gently picked His little girl up, and loved her back to health. He blessed her with her soul–mate and husband,

Steve, four wonderful sons, four beautiful daughters–in–law, and six precious grand–children.

Becky's life so beautifully illustrates how God is just waiting for His girls to invite Him into their lives. We are all His Cinderella's. He promises to take all of our rags and turn them into something beautiful. Becky is a perfect example of a girl who found herself lost on a lonely road to no where, with no fairy god–mother in sight. She called out to God, and, thus, begun her Cinderella transformation. She now enjoys an abundant life, rich in family, friends, and the wisdom and peace that only comes from God. Becky is a recording artist, a speaker, and an aspiring writer.

Over the past several years, Becky has shared the following letter of testimony with hundreds of teenage mothers, providing them with hope for a bright future which comes from God's transforming love being invited into our lives.

Dear Young Moms,

I am writing you today for several reasons, but basically this note is for encouragement and hope for a bright future.

When I was 16 years old, I became pregnant. It seemed as though the rest of the world went on without me. My friends continued with school functions, cheerleading, proms, and dates…and I was thrown into being a Mother. I did not have a support system. I was encouraged to have an abortion or marry the father.

I could not abort (now I understand why), but I did marry the father and was divorced within 18 months with a baby to take care of and all of the overwhelming feelings of failure, embarrassment, and hopelessness, I turned to alcohol and drugs. During this time, I encountered many personal tragedies and had absolutely no hope for my son or myself. I had truly hit bottom, and by the time I was 21 years of age, my health was wrecked. We lived where we could and all I felt was total despair.

One day I was invited to go to church. I continued going because for the first time in my life, I felt hope. I not only went to church, but I opened my heart and life to Christ. I began a personal relationship with Him. Christ met me where I was.

I married a man who had two sons and a few years later he adopted my son. Michael will be 27 soon, and was married this year to a beautiful young woman who has twin girls. Michael has been an extraordinary blessing in my life. He is a beautiful person and he loves the Lord. Some how, some way, by the Grace of God, I now have a wonderful family and hope everyday of my life. I encourage you to trust God because He has promised us hope for a successful future if we follow His way in life.

Affectionately,

Becky

That sunny morning in January, I wore a casual pale yellow dress with a matching mini sweater made of the softest cotton t–shirt fabric, that delicately ruffled just above my knees. My friend, Karen, said that I looked pretty in the yellow with my new stylish, short blonde hair cut. I think she was just excited to see me without my baseball hat on, or my hair in a ponytail. My eyes are a light shade of hazel green that can be seen through my small brown eye glasses.

My story is one of a first born child, who lived much of her life trying to please everyone. I was raised in a middle class Christian home. My parents taught me wonderful truths about my Heavenly Father. My life's desire was to set a good example for my two younger sisters, make my parents proud, and please God.

I was the girl, who wore the "One Way to Jesus" patch on her home–made denim purse back in the seventies. The home–made denim purses were in, but the patch was considered to be something a "Jesus freak" would buy. I didn't care. I was determined to stand for my God. I guess I was a bit strong–willed even back then.

I chose to get married to a nice young man whom I knew in my heart was not God's perfect choice for me. "I could make it work," I thought. Needless to say, I found myself in a marriage that I did not want. My life had taken such a turn; a detour I'd never planned on taking. After my failed marriage, I moved to Florida to start a new life. No one knew me here, so there were no expectations for me to live up to. For the first time in my life I felt complete freedom to do whatever I wanted to do, living however I wanted to live.

The lifestyle that I had chosen began to distance me from God. I'll never forget the day I received "the letter" from my Dad. I began to tremble when I realized that it was his handwriting on the envelope. I didn't tremble out of fear of my Dad. I trembled because I knew in my spirit that I was not living the life God had planned for me, and God had told my Dad of this fact. You must understand two important points. First, my Dad had never mailed me a letter before that day, and second, over the years God would speak to my Dad in his dreams, giving him insight to his daughters lives and their activities. This was not something over which a daughter would always 'jump for joy.'

My Dad's letter briefly described a dream he had. He was standing by a beautiful lake, and to his surprise the lake was filled with quick sand. He look out into the middle of the lake of quick sand to see me, his daughter. He said that I was laughing and partying, completely oblivious to my sinking state in the quick sand. Dad looked across the lake, and behind a tree he spotted the devil. The devil laughed and called out to my Dad saying, "You can't help her. She's going down, and she doesn't even know it. I've got her now."

You can just imagine the shock that surged through my body. I knew in my very spirit that my life was at stake, realizing that God Himself had sent this message of warning to me, His girl. I know the Bible tells us that Satan is real, he is active on our earth, and his goal is to keep us from a personal relationship with God. Satan gave up his chance to know God, and he wants to steal our chance, as well.

I've always been aware of Satan's existence on the earth, but never feared him because I am well aware of the fact that my God is bigger than he is. I understand that Satan is absolutely powerless when God's on the scene. What frightened me about this dream was that I had stepped into the quicksand, and was choosing to stay there. I had no idea that my lifestyle was leading me down a road that didn't lead to God.

Day after day, I would stand in the shower in a miserable state of mind, tormented by the truth that I was living a life that was not moving me closer to God, and knowing that I was choosing to walking further away from Him, instead. Mondays were the worst because I'd always attempt to convince myself that my lifestyle and activities which I had participated in over the weekend weren't 'all that bad,' when I knew deep down in my heart that my choices were leading me away from the God who loved me and who had always walked by my side.

I'll never forget the night I fell flat on my face before God, feeling ashamed and totally unworthy to even kneel before Him, I laid there in my tiny studio apartment sobbing for what seemed to be hours.

After a time of violent crying which seemed to come from the deepest part of my stomach, hardly able to speak a word, through tears I began to thank my Heavenly Father for never giving up on me or leaving my side, but lovingly and probably with great sadness in His heart, He allowed me the freedom to step away from Him if that was what I chose to do.

Then, I begged His forgiveness for choosing to engage in activities and a lifestyle that didn't include Him at the center. I pledged my life to Him that night, and asked Him to hold me tight and surround me with people and things that would strengthen my relationship with Him. I vowed to never walk away from Him again, but instead I would continue to step closer and closer for the rest of my life on earth.

The life He gave me as a gift, I gave back to Him that day, as I continue to do every day, and asked Him to overhaul it. Thus, began my journey back towards God.

I wanted to know what His perfect plan was for me here on earth. I didn't want to know a religion or a program; I wanted to get to know God in a personal way. I knew the Bible said that God created me because He wants fellowship with me; He wants to spend time with me. So I began to spend time alone with God. I picture myself walking through life, holding my Heavenly Father's hand while skipping along beside Him. That's just where I want to stay.

The more time I spend with Him, the more I am changed. It is not possible to spend time in the presence of Holy God, and remain the same. Since that time, God has been revealing Himself to me continually, and changing me from the inside out. I am not the same girl that I once was. I am experiencing a new found freedom; freedom to be the girl God created me to be; His girl. I just want to be God's girl.

God blessed me with my wonderful husband who loves God first, and me second. Brad and I were blessed with two precious sons. L.B. is ten years old, and loves baseball. Our six year old son is Blake, and he loves critters of every kind.

God brought beautiful women into my life who began to mentor me. He continues to shower me with women who love God, and are committed to know Him intimately. They encourage me, edify me, and challenge me to allow God to work in my life. I am rich! I am rich in God's blessings of these women.

Each struggle shared that day served only as a spring board to the victory that followed. My heart was filled with joy as I listening to the testimonies of how each woman became an over–comer. These were ordinary women with an extra–ordinary God. A God, who promises His girls, (that's you and me), that He will bring good things from every life situation if we love and trust Him. To put it simply, our loving Heavenly Father is known for making the very best lemonade out of the most bitter lemons that life could possibly bring our way. He loves to make the sweetest pink lemonade for His girls!

It was interesting how the word 'hope' continued to be spoken throughout our time together that day. We all agreed that women in all the world are in need of 'hope.' Hope in the midst of our struggles; hope for a better tomorrow; hope for a bright future.

God never planned for us to live in bondage to anything or anyone! His plans for us are clearly stated in Jeremiah 29:11, *"For I know the plans I have for you (my daughters), declares the Lord, "plans to prosper you and not to harm you, plans to give you* ***hope*** *and a* ***future****. Then you will call upon me and come and pray to me, and I will listen to you. You will seek me and find me when you seek me with all your heart."*

Women give so much hope to others. Sometimes we get so involved in meeting the needs of others that we forget to take time to refresh and care for ourselves. Consider for a moment the speech that the flight attendants recite just before takeoff. It goes something like this, "In the event of a loss of cabin pressure, an oxygen mask will automatically be lowered. If you are sitting beside a child, first secure your own mask before applying the child's."

Why would they advise you to do that? Are they promoting an "adults over children" philosophy? Hardly. They realize that unless you as the adult are getting the oxygen you need, you'll be of no help to the child, and you will both perish. Do you get my point, girls? It's so very important that we take time to refresh ourselves, to nurture ourselves.

The purpose of this book, God's Girls, is to inspire women with…the ***strength*** to weather their storms of life, the ***courage*** to make changes that will improve the quality of their daily life, and the ***hope*** that a healthier, happier life will become a reality. My desire for every woman who reads this book is that they ***discover freedom*** to celebrate the uniquely beautiful, strong woman God created her to be.

As we walk together through the next thirteen chapters, I invite you to join me in a quest to learn more about God's original plan for His girls to enjoy life abundant and free. Along the way, if anything I say strikes you as odd, simply tuck it away in your back pocket, and open it up when you're alone with God, asking Him to show you His truth concerning the matter. He will show each of us how to apply His truths to our specific life circumstances. If we simply ask Him for understanding, we will receive it.

I pray that every woman will be able to look into the mirror and in all honesty say, "I like who you are, who you are becoming, the choices you are making, and the life that you're striving to live." May we will learn to ***care for ourselves…spiritually, physically, emotionally, socially***

and intellectually realizing that this is the best gift we can give to ourselves, to those we love, and to our Heavenly Father.

My prayer is that women in all the world will experience the freedom that comes from knowing that their Heavenly Father loves them just the way they are…and that we each were created for the sole purpose of being God's Girls!

Never let the sense of the irreparable cause you to despair. Give your mistakes to the Lord and allow Him to 'make all things new.'

—Gigi Graham Tchividjian, Weather of the Heart

— 2 —

Life Is How You Change It!

Your attitudes and thoughts must be constantly changing for the better. Yes, you must be a new and different person, holy and good. Clothe yourself with this nature.
Ephesians 3:23–24 NIV

Recently, I saw a bumper sticker that declared, IF NOTHING CHANGES, NOTHING CHANGES! "Amen, Sister! Amen," I said.

Think about it. If you keep on doing what you've always done, you'll keep on getting what you've always gotten. If I really want something to change in my life, I must make changes. If you are not making changes in your daily life, this could mean that you're completely satisfied and content with your life at the present time.

When someone is content, they may seem to have no reason to complain. Right? The word complaining means to express dissatisfaction. So…if you speak words that express your dissatisfaction with your present life, it would be accurate to say that you would like to change your life. Sounds like common sense in it's simplest form.

Two years ago, I realized that my family's morning routine was out–of–control. I am not proud to share that my boys would probably be in line for receiving the "most days tardy" award from our school. We could not get out of the door on time or on a positive note.

We'd get up at 6:30 a.m., and the race would begin. My boys would linger in bed until about 7:00. Only after hearing my stern, "GET OUT OF BED, NOW," would they crawl out of bed. Then, my two little sleepy heads would mosey into the kitchen for breakfast, where I was frantically packing lunches. They were often distracted from eating their breakfast by the cartoons or ESPN blaring on the television.

We had a mysterious intruder who would, unknown to us, break into our home each night, and hide the boys school shoes. Sometimes this intruder would even hide their lunch boxes and backpacks, too. This confused intruder would amazingly hide these items instead of stealing them. Imagine that! It never failed that seconds before walking out the door L.B. or Blake would be shoeless.

What usually happened next? You guessed it. I would begin to lecture everyone on how things had to change in our morning schedule as I was walking them to my husbands truck. I would kiss them each good–bye, and say my "I love you's;" and I'd always end with promising to do better tomorrow.

Before school started in August of 1999, I decided it was time to put legs on my words. If the Dantzler morning routine was to change, I would be the girl to initiate the change. The morning television was the obvious first deterrent to have to go. No more would the boys turn on the television before leaving for school.

Next, our mysterious intruder had to be captured and rehabilitated. We did this by designating a spot in the kitchen to keep back packs, lunch boxes and school shoes, which ended the activities of our intruder.

Needing to give my family my full attention during this hour before school, I decided I wouldn't do anything for myself until they were on their way to school with Brad. This change in itself made a huge impact on our morning routine. I would get up between 6:15 and 6:30, open the blinds throughout the house, and kiss my boys good morning. I would begin packing lunches right away in the peace and quiet of the new morning.

Then, after finishing the lunches, I calmly walk to their bedrooms and turn their lights on, deliver early morning snuggles and "I love you's," and lovingly tell them, "It's time, guys!" I also rearranged their uniforms in designated areas in their closets, so now it is very easy for them to get dressed each morning. After getting dressed for school, the boys make their beds, and come to the kitchen for breakfast.

Breakfast time is usually pretty calm now, void of the television noise. L.B. reads the sports page, and Blake reads the cereal box or a book from the bowl full of books that I keep on the breakfast bar. After breakfast, it's time to pray. The four of us hold hands in our kitchen, and Brad prays for our day. Our new routine has helped immensely to transform our exit from our home each day from hectic and crazy to calm and pleasant, and I am happy to report that our boys haven't been tardy for school at all this year, and it's already January.

Needless to say, our mornings have changed for the better. Once in awhile, a crazy morning happens, and I lose it, but that's the exception rather than the norm in our home anymore. I am so thankful that I heard what I was saying when I would complain of our hectic, disorganized morning routine. After realizing our need for change, we made changes in our home. These changes have impacted our family in wonderful, positive ways.

Change, though not easy, is inevitable. With life, comes change. Life's a journey; and the drive is always the best part. Once we realize and accept that life is going to change each day, we can choose to embrace the opportunities change brings to our lives. As women, we make choices every day concerning change. Consciously or subconsciously, we choose to ignore change or embrace it, by the way we live each day.

Changing on a daily basis is definitely an important part of God's perfect plan for our lives. The Bible leaves no question about the truth that God desires us to be continually changing; becoming more like the image of Christ. Because God desires our very best, He wants us not only to tolerate change, but also to welcome it with excitement in our hearts. Change is not something to dread or fear. Much to the contrary, change can be a gift of opportunity. Change is a privilege. It's God's invitation to join Him in the designing process of our lives. He wants us to live a fuller, richer life each day.

Do I really mean that we should actually *look forward to change*? Yes, exactly because that's what God wants from His girls.

As a mother and a wife, I realize that the choices I make daily directly affect my family. As I make small changes in my life, my family benefits. If I choose to remain in my comfort zone, my family will be influenced by my complacency.

I once heard the role of a woman in the home compared to the pieces in a chess game.

The king is the most important piece, but the queen has the most moves; the most power; the most potential for influence. Now, hold on just a minute. I'm not saying that the man of a home is more important than a woman. I'm simply saying that the potential for influence of those living in the home is greater for the woman. The power of influence that a woman has in her home is immeasurable.

If you don't understand what I'm saying, just observe how your attitude and words affect your family each morning. I know in my home that when my attitude is bad and I'm stressed in the morning, my guys feel it. I take my role as morning coordinator very seriously because I've seen the impact my words, actions, and attitudes have had on my three guys. I can help them begin their day on a positive note, or I can be a grouch and send them into their day on a stressful note. A friend gave me a little plaque that reads, "If Mama Ain't Happy, Ain't Nobody Happy!" Country wisdom at it's best!

I don't know about you, but I don't want to look back in 20 or 40 years and regret that I didn't make a few changes to make my life better. Whether it's simplifying your lifestyle, spending more time with your children, working different hours, eating healthier, exercising regularly, watching less television, spending time with friends or having more sex with your husband, make the commitment to work towards the changes you desire.

There's no quick and easy way to make positive changes that will impact you and your family's lives. It takes commitment and discipline. No excuses, just commitment and discipline to take little steps that will bring great rewards.

Ask yourself, "If I did commit to make this change in my life, what difference would it make and what would I see when I look back on my life in 20 years?" I ask myself this question often and it helps me to see the potential there is in my life. ***Life is How You Change It!***

It's the little choices in life that can make a lifetime of difference. Just a little salt added to every meal may be okay for now, but 30 years of salting your meals may lead you to high blood pressure problems. We have been given 24 hours of opportunity each day to choose how we will live our lives and spend our time, and small changes can add freshness to how we look at life.

For the past several years, I've committed to complete most of my Christmas shopping in November, having it wrapped and under the Christmas tree on the day after Thanksgiving. I understand that this might sound a bit compulsive, but I actually have a really great reason for doing such an unheard of thing.

When the majority of my Christmas shopping is finished, my mind is free to relax into the true spirit of the season, and become more sensitive to the presence of God during His birthday month. Each year during the months of November and December the Lord seems to draw very close to me directing my thoughts to the New Year and all of it's wonderfully fresh opportunities to change our lives for the better.

I don't believe in New Year's resolutions because for the most part...they simply have never worked for me. Every year I would make this long list of the craziest, most unrealistic goals which might only have come to pass if I live at Disney World and changed my name to Snow White.

New Year's resolution lists aren't taken seriously most times; instead, they become glorified wish lists written simply to honor an annual tradition, which allows each of us a moment to dream of the life we'd like to live. We make a big long list of 'stuff' we want to change, most of which have been carried over from years past (especially the exercise more and eat healthier ones) and who has ever been successful at changing twenty things in their life beginning all on the same day? Not me, that's for sure!

The only part of the New Year's resolution lists that I actually can appreciate is the fact that they are usually written in invisible ink, which conveniently fades away into the atmosphere somewhere around the months of February or March.

Each year during November, I begin to ask the Lord to show me the specific areas in my personal life that He wants to change in me during the New Year. I ask God to lead me to the scriptures that represent the principles He wants to work in me during the New Year. I also ask Him to direct me to the specific daily devotional book He wants me to follow for the next twelve months.

You may be thinking that these seem to be such trivial requests to bring before a great big God, but God wants us to talk with Him about every detail of our lives. Proverbs 3:5–6 instructs us to do just this thing. *Trust in the Lord with all thine heart; and lean not unto thine own understanding.* ***In all thy ways acknowledge Him,*** *and He shall direct thy paths. (KJ)*

Last year my scriptures dealt with allowing God's wisdom to guide my words. One scripture was Proverbs 31:26, *She openeth her mouth with wisdom; and in her tongue is the law of kindness. (KJ)* Now, my sons couldn't say that the law of kindness was always in my tongue, especially when I'd become frustrated with their constant bickering and lose my cool.

James 3:1–18 is a power–packed scripture that the Lord directed me to last year, as well, *but the wisdom that comes from heaven is first of all pure and full of quiet gentleness. Then it is peace–loving and courteous. It allows discussion and is willing to yield to others; it is full of mercy and good deeds. It is wholehearted and straightforward and sincere, and those who are peacemakers will plant seeds of peace and reap a harvest of goodness. (LB)*

Do you see why I referred to this scripture as being power–packed? I've grown to love and cherish this scripture, as it digs into my natural personality, holding me accountable at every turn. I'll probably never remove this scripture from the sun visor of my car or my bathroom mirror because it has served me well as a needed reminder of the awesomeness of the wisdom of God.

Last year I also had several habits that the Lord began to bring to my attention. A couple of bad habits that simply needed to go, while a few good habits needed to be implemented. He directed me to two specific scriptures which accurately addressed these changes. The first scripture is Hebrews 12:1–2, *Let us strip off anything that slows us down or holds us back, and especially those sins that wrap themselves so tightly around our feet and trip us up; and let us run with patience the particular race that God has set before us. Keep your eyes on Jesus, our leader and instructor. (LB)*

The second scripture is found in 1 Corinthians 9:27, *Like an athlete I punish my body, treating it roughly, training it to do what it should, not what it wants to. Otherwise I fear that after enlisting others for the race, I myself might be declared unfit and ordered to stand aside.*

Over the past twelve months God divinely worked these scriptures into my life, helping me to implement healthier habits while leaving those that were hindering me behind.

God also hinted at my spending habits. Ouch! Did that hit home with anyone out there? Well, it was as though He just tossed this on in at the tail end…just to get me started on the road to acknowledging the fact that my spending habits weren't exactly what He wanted them to be.

God did include many scriptures in the Bible that instruct us concerning our financial wellness, and Proverbs 31:17–18 were the two He brought to my attention, which say, *"She is energetic, a hard worker, and watches for bargains. She works far into the night!"*

This scripture may not strike a cord with you, but it sure hit the spot with me. For you see, I didn't know nor did I actually care what a gallon of milk, loaf of bread, bunch of bananas or bag offresh green beans cost at the grocery store. I just knew that these were staple food items that my family needed in our home every day, so why did it matter what they cost.

I've never been a big fan of coupon clipping either, unless the coupon was for fifty–cents or more and didn't involve the purchase of additional products that the company is promoting. If I'm buying peanut butter, I simply want to buy peanut butter. I don't want someone attempting to convince me to buy two boxes of their new pop tarts by offering a whopping twenty cents off coupon on the purchase of the jar of peanut butter.

Most coupons are a hassle to me, so I've learned to compromise by buying a cheaper brand of certain foods (not my favorites, of course), rather than carrying around paper coupons in my wallet for days, weeks and months. God is helping me to continue to make progress in my financial wellness category and so many other areas of my life, as well.

After talking with Him about my personal life, I ask Him to show me the specific areas in our family and home life that He desires to change. Again, I ask Him for specifics with scriptures to back it up, and He never fails to deliver the goods to the front door of my heart.

Last year, after each of our family members shared what God had brought to their attention to work on during the upcoming year, we discussed them and decided which scriptures would be best suited for each family member. I would post each family member's scriptures in their bedrooms, as a daily reminder of the change that God desired to make in them during the New Year.

Just last week my oldest son shared with me what he felt God wanted him to work on for the year 2002, and he asked me to make him a sign like the one already hanging on his wall. He explained to me how he reads it every night while lying in bed and it helps him remember his commitment. You can imagine how great that made me feel to know that these little reminders which God directed me to place on my son's wall...served HIS purpose well.

Each December, as we recall the year's events, we're gratefully amazed to see how God has led each of us to change in specific areas, changing our lives so that we are not the same as we were the year before. Change is a blessing and a privilege that God places before us daily as an option, an opportunity to grow in Him and live a better life.

As you travel through this book, I want to encourage you to evaluate your own life. My hope is that the chapters ahead will help you interrupt the hustle and bustle of your daily routine for a moment to find out if you are really living life and spending your days doing what is most important to you. If there are changes you need to make, be brave...be optimistic...and begin today working towards making them a reality. You can do it. Believe in yourself because God believes in you. You're the only one who can change your life, you and a great big God. One step at a time will help you lead the life you want to lead. No one else can decide how you live your life day to day; no one else; just YOU.

Erma Bombeck's writing, *If I Had My Life to Live Over*, always leads me into a moment of soul searching and life evaluation.

If she had her life to live over again, Ms. Bombeck would never insist the windows be rolled up on a beautiful, breezy summer day simply because she had just had her hair styled. She would have invited her friends to dinner even if the carpet was stained or the sofa was faded, and she would have eaten popcorn in the 'good' living room. She would have used her fancy pink candle before it melted in storage, and sat in the grass with her children, not worrying about grass stains. She would allow her children to kiss her impetuously instead of saying, "Later, now go get washed up for dinner." Ms. Bombeck declares, "There would have been more 'I love you's'—more—'I'm sorry's'—but mostly, given another shot at life, I would seize every minute—look at it and really see it—live it—and never give it back."

Quite thought provoking, isn't it? Every time I read this writing, I realize just how far I have come. I also can't help but make my own mental list of the things I still want to change. I want to play ball with L.B. more, and jump on the tramp with Blake more often. I want to sit and enjoy a movie with my boys without folding clothes or doing something else at the same time. I want to meet my husband for lunch once a week, and take more family walks after dinner this summer. I want to invite the people we love to our home more often.

Make your list, and begin to make changes. No matter what age you are, there's great news. You're life isn't over yet, and the best is still to come; God says so. Where there is life, the opportunity for change exists. I love what Oprah said about change. "The real work of our lives is never complete—the very nature of our existence involves the privilege to evolve. Each of us is a person in process, an ongoing masterpiece that grows richer and fuller with each rendering.

There is no such thing as a 'finished' person; whatever your circumstances are, it is your challenge to keep asking yourself the tough questions that will move you forward in your life."

A change in attitude doesn't necessarily take physical action. An attitude can be changed by simply adjusting the way you perceive life. List the thoughts that just surfaced in your mind as you read Erma Bombeck's writing. After finishing your list, make a commitment to yourself to change the way you live, so you will not be writing the same list (only in regret form) at the end of your life. Whether it's getting the pink candle sculpted like a rose out of storage and using it, or lowering your expectations of housecleaning so you can enjoy unexpected visits from friends, begin making the changes now. Remember…if nothing changes, nothing changes. Life Is How You Change It!

Don't just dream of the person you would like to be or the life you would like to live. Become that person and live that life. Life is change. Growth is optional. Choose wisely!

—Anonymous

— 3 —

Putting First Things First

To EVERY thing there is a season, and a time to every purpose under the heaven... Ecclesiastes 3:1

Life is a continuous balancing act. We reach balance in one area of our lives just to find another area needing to be balanced. The key to living a balanced life, which yields inner peace, is to always make time for those things which are of the highest priority to you. God's divine plan for His girls involves **Putting First Things First** and allowing Him to help you balance the rest.

We are all jugglers in life as we juggle crystal balls and rubber balls. Picture yourself juggling little rubber balls of different colors and crystal balls much like delicate Christmas tree ornament balls. The rubber balls are fairly resilient and will bounce back if we drop them. The crystal balls, however, are fragile. They will not bounce back. As you're picturing yourself juggling, where is you're focus? You're main concern is for the crystal balls, right? You automatically know that if you drop a rubber ball…it's no big deal…but if you drop a crystal ball…it may shatter into thousands of tiny pieces.

The crystal balls represent our highest priorities; those things closest to our hearts, such as our families and dearest friends. The rubber balls represent everything else in our lives. We must make a conscious effort to focus on our priorities, our crystal balls of life. We have all heard that we should put first things first; this sounds like a logical thing to do, but do we do it? Do the crystal balls in your life come first before all rubber balls?

If you allow yourself to overlook them, you may drop one; it may crack or break; and you may lose it from your life forever. Sounds drastic, I know. This juggling act of life is a serious matter that needs to be addressed by each of us. It is necessary to establish priorities and re–evaluate them on a regular basis. It is very easy to become over committed even for a good cause. Unfortunately, in many cases, it is your crystal balls (the ones most precious to you) that will pay the price of your over–committed schedule. Before making any decisions about accepting any additional responsibilities, we must evaluate our priorities and the effect our choices will have on them.

Take a moment and write down your highest priorities…your crystal balls in life. You may only have two or three things in your life that you consider to be crystal balls, so don't feel pressured to fill in all four blanks.

1. ______________________________

2. ______________________________

3. ______________________________

4. ______________________________

Now that you've written down what's most important to you, ask yourself if the way you live each day reflects the importance of these things. I encourage you to take a look at your calendar and your check book. Many times, we find clues concerning our priorities by how we spend our time and our money.

Sometimes, we may also gain helpful insight through what others see in us. I always encourage women to do what my friend Rachel did. She asked her twelve year old son the question, "What do you think is the most important thing in Mom's life?" To her dismay, her son answered by saying, "Eating fat–free foods." This was quite a shock to my friend because she had no idea that her words and actions were projecting this message. In her heart and mind, her relationship with God was the most important thing in her life. Then, her family came next.

Rachel had been a water skier at Cypress Gardens for many years. A sleek physique with a low body weight was imperative to all Cypress Gardens skiers if they wanted to keep their jobs, so counting calories and fat had become an integral part of Rachel's life. She had not realized that the constant pressure to stay thin had become a state of mind for her. This painful insight from her twelve year old son became a turning point in Rachel's life. She became much more aware of her words and actions. She didn't want the physical dimension of her life to take priority over the spiritual one.

Today, Rachel still skis at Cypress Gardens one day a week. She has also temporarily retired from her career as a Personal Trainer, so she can home–school two of her three children. She rests in knowing that the way she's living her life accurately reflects what's most important to her. This was a life lesson that Rachel will neither forget, nor will she regret making the change.

Just last week I met Rachel and a group of our girlfriends for dinner and she shared with us how the Lord is teaching her about total surrender of everything in her life to God: her husband, family, friendships, and the details of each daily situation and issue that she and her family face. I sensed that she was in a new place spiritually, learning how God wants His girls to put Him first and surrender everything else in our lives to Him.

That evening as we updated each other concerning the summer activities and adventures of our families, there was a common thread that seemed to take us from one topic to the next. God and His obvious presence in our lives was as a beautiful, strong thread that ran through every life situation that our families were experiencing. Our conversation refreshed my spirit; it seemed to be saturated with praises to God for His never ending presence and power in our lives, families, and homes.

The following morning when I opened my Experiencing God daily devotional book to read that days devotion entitled 'Where Your Treasure Is,' I found that Luke 12:34 was the scripture for the day, *"For where your treasure is, there your heart will be also."* The authors Henry T. Blackaby and Claude V. King emphasize the fact that "whatever dominates your conversation is what you treasure and what others know you for is a good indication of what your treasure is." They pointed out how "most Christians are quick to claim that God is their first priority, yet often their actions reveal that their treasure is not God but things of this world." They also assert that "some Christians find it difficult to discuss their relationship with God, but they can chatter easily about their family, friends or hobbies. Some find it impossible to rise early in order to spend time with God, but they willingly get up at dawn to pursue a hobby. Some boldly approach strangers to sell a product, yet they are painfully timid in telling others about their Savior. Some give hundreds of hours to serve in volunteer organizations but feel they have no time available to serve God."

Reflecting on what we enjoy thinking about and discussing will lead us to where our treasure is. The topics of the majority of our conversations will serve as a mirror, reflecting the treasures which lie in your heart of hearts. Identify the conversations you engage in, and you'll have a pretty good idea of where your treasure (priority) lies.

Last week, my six year old son Blake, completed a little Mother's Day description of me, his Mom. It read like this.

Blake's Mom

Name:..........Susan
Age:..........38
Height:..........6 or 5 feet

Weight: .... 110 pounds
Hair color: .... Blonde
Favorite color: .... Blue
Favorite food: .... Chocolate
Favorite drink: .... Coffee
Favorite T.V. show: .... Oprah
Favorite thing to wear: .... Bathing suit
Favorite thing to cook: .... Pancakes
Favorite thing to do: .... Play with her kids
I love my mom because: .... She is my mom
My mom loves me because: .... I'm her kid

The only thing I would add to this kindergarten list would be, Most Important Thing in Mom's Life. Now that's a loaded question that could bring loads of insight.

I will confess to one major exaggeration of the truth concerning Blake's description of me, only because I'd like for you to get an accurate picture of me. Blake was a little low on the 'weight' estimate, but I'll never tell, and my bathing suit is definitely, without a doubt, NOT my favorite thing to wear.

This little kindergarten description of me gave me insight to what Blake sees in me. What he sees me doing is who he perceives I am. He sees me drink coffee every morning, so of course, that's my favorite drink in his little eyes. I love to make him his favorite breakfast of pancakes, so they became my favorite thing to cook.

Blake doesn't see me watch television unless I turn Oprah after school or Bill O'Reilly in the evening, so that's an obvious answer for him based on his perception. He doesn't know that my favorite TV show is really the Today Show with Katie, Matt, Al, and Ann. Why doesn't he know this? It's because he is at school when I watch my 30 minutes of the Today Show.

I must admit, since reading this little description of me, I have been evaluating what my actions are saying to my children. Does the way I live my life support what I say is the most important to me? I want this to be the case, so I have made several adjustments since reading my son's assessment of me.

I want to challenge you to be courageous and ask the significant people in your life, what they think is the most important thing in your life? And after asking, you might want to take a seat because children and spouses can be painfully honest. The people we love the most get not only the very best we have, but also, unfortunately, the worst, as well. This might give you some insight as to what your actions are saying about what's important to you. We all remember the elementary phrase 'actions speak louder than words.' What do your actions reveal about the crystal balls in your life?

Although crystal balls may vary from woman to woman depending on specific life circumstances unique to each woman, God has included clear instructions in the Bible concerning our priorities.

Throughout the Bible, God declares to us that His place in our lives is to be first place above all else, including family, friends, church, jobs, and hobbies. The first and second commandments that God gave to Moses, recorded in Exodus 20:3–5, clearly define that God not only desires the first place in our lives, He demands it. *"You shall have no other gods before me. You shall not make for yourself an idol in the form of anything in heaven above or on the earth beneath or in the waters below. You shall not bow down to them or worship them; for I, the Lord your God, am a jealous God, punishing the children for the sin of the fathers to the third and fourth generation of those who hate me, but showing love to a thousand generations of those who love me and keep my commandments."*

Throughout his New Testament teachings, Paul declares to us that Christ is not only to be a priority, but the priority in our lives. In Philippians 1:21, he boldly declares, *"For to me, to live is Christ and to die is gain."* He is telling us that His very existence on earth is all about Jesus Christ, and death would be even better because he would then be living in Heaven in the very presence of God Himself.

In Philippians 3:7–12, Paul expounds on his commitment to give Christ first place in his life when he says, *"But all these things that I once thought very worthwhile—now I've thrown them all away so that I can put my trust and hope in Christ alone. Yes, everything else is worthless when compared with the priceless gain of knowing Christ Jesus my Lord. I have put aside all else, counting it worth less than nothing, in order that I can have Christ, and become one with Him, no longer counting on being saved by being good enough or by obeying God's laws, but by trusting Christ to save me; for God's way of making us right with Himself depends on faith—counting on Christ alone. Now I have given up everything else—I have found it to be the only way to really know Christ and to experience the mighty power that brought Him back to life again, and to find whatever it takes, I will be one who lives in the fresh newness of life of those who are alive from the dead. I don't mean to say I am perfect. I haven't learned all I should even yet, but I keep working toward that day when I will finally be all that Christ saved me for and wants me to be."*

What a godly example Paul has set before us. I appreciate the fact that he lived his life in such a transparent way, allowing everyone to clearly see that Christ was his priority in life, and everything else fell in line after Christ.

In the last portion of the above passage, Paul's honesty concerning his imperfection is comforting to me considering I am constantly having to check my priorities and readjust my life to keep God in His rightful place. Just as Paul admits his imperfection without allowing himself to surrender to failure or defeat and commits to keep striving to do better, we can too. We can accept that when life has become off balance and out of kilter, we've not failed, we simply need to refocus by revisiting our priorities and promptly adjusting our lives to once again support them.

After your relationship with Christ, if you are married, your husband is to be your second priority in life. Genesis 2:18, 21–24 tells us, "*The Lord God said, It is not good for the man to be alone. I will make a helper suitable for him. The Lord God caused the man to fall into a deep sleep; and while he was sleeping, he took one of the mans ribs and closed up the place with flesh. Then the Lord God made a woman from the rib He had taken out of the man, and He brought her to the man. The man said, 'This is now bone of my bones and flesh of my flesh; she shall be called woman, for she was take out of man. For this reason a man will leave his father and mother and be united to his wife, and they will become one flesh.'*"

When I read this passage, I realize that when God removed a rib from man he became incomplete in a sense, and this rib that once completed the man was now in the form of a woman. This makes perfect sense that the woman God created to be man's helper was created to complete the man, as the rib once did.

Our husbands are to be our top priority after God, the most important person in our lives. After my Parallel Bible, my copy of Stormie Omartian's book The Power of a Praying Wife gets the most use, as God has begun to reveal to me that the most important thing I can do to help my husband and impact his life is to pray for him in the specific areas of his life on a daily basis. I don't consider praying for my husband a bonus, but a fundamental God given responsibility for me as his wife.

As we obey God by putting our husbands first (only after God) in our lives, making prayer for him a priority, God will begin to show us specific ways in which we can better complete our husbands fulfilling our role in their lives.

In Titus 2:4, after Paul addresses the husband's responsibility as the spiritual leader of the home, he explains how the older women can teach the younger women to live by saying,

"Then they can train the younger women to love their husbands and children;" The women were to be taught to love and care for their husbands first and then to love and care for their children. If a woman has children, they are to be her third priority in life, unless, of course, she is not married and then they should come second in priority…just after God.

The most important responsibility of a parent to a child is a commitment to consistently pray for the child. The Bible tells us and God promises us that through prayer to God we can have an impact on the lives of our loved ones. Lamentations 2:19 teaches us to *"Pour out your heart like water before the face of the Lord. Lift your hands toward Him for the life of your young children."* On Wednesday mornings at 7:45 a.m., I meet with a group of precious mothers to pray for our children, their school and the entire school community, as we obey the instruction given to us in Lamentations 2:19.

Stormie Omartian's book *The Power of a Praying Parent* has been a powerful and extremely helpful tool for me to use when praying for the specific areas of need in the lives of my sons. Along with scriptures for various needs, Stormie includes prayers that she prayed for her children, which serve as a guide for me when I simply am at a loss for words to begin my prayer time.

As we strive to give God first place in our lives, our husbands second place and our children third place, God promises to honor our obedience by blessing us with abundant life. What a beautiful life God has planned for His girls if we will only grasp on to His divine plan for us, obey it, then we will reap the benefits as He has intended.

I have had the privilege to share Balancing Life principles with many different groups of women in which I always share my personal priorities; (the crystal balls in my life.) It's amazing. Every single time I list my priorities to a group, I fail to include my own personal care. I thought, "If I am teaching wellness and balancing life…and I forget to include personal care when listing my highest priorities, I bet women, in general, will overlook their own personal care, too."

I have found that many women often tend to provide the very best care for those closest to them while overlooking the importance of their own personal care. Women seem to have the tendency to give priority to the family, work, laundry, housecleaning, school and work projects, meal planning, and other home and family maintenance tasks, instead of setting aside any time for themselves.

The truth is, if we fail to take care of ourselves, in any area of our lives, the care we provide for our families may be affected in a negative way. I've noticed this in myself in different areas of my life. When I go running into my day without taking time for my devotional reading and my morning prayer, which helps me to refocus my attention on Christ and dedicate my day to Him, I am less peaceful in my spirit, and my family can sense it.

I've also learned that when I skip meals and deprive my body of needed nutrients and fuel, my blood sugar levels fluctuate and I don't handle stress very well. In other words, I become very grouchy, and snap at my family unnecessarily. When I neglect my morning jog for prolong periods, I definitely notice that it affects the way I deal with the normal stresses of family life, as well as, impacting my energy level. When I go days without exercise, I become fatigued both physically and mentally, keeping me from giving my best to the care of my family.

You may be asking yourself, "If I put God first, my husband second and my children third, where is there time or room for making my own self–care a priority?" Good question. Jesus answers this question for us in Matthew 6:33 where He promise us saying, *"But seek ye first the kingdom of God, and His righteousness; and all these things shall be add unto you."* In this scripture Jesus is promising that if we give God first place in our lives, He will add all things unto us.

In Proverbs 4:20–22, we are instructed to *"pay attention to what I say; listen closely to my words. Do not let them out of your sight, keep them within your heart; for they are life to those who find them and health to a man's whole body."* Wow! As we give God first place in our lives, making prayer and His Word priority, He will grant us health to our whole body; mind, spirit and body. It's amazing how God actually multiplies the benefits of my workouts and the time involved in every day tasks, when I spend time with Him first thing in the morning.

At this time, feel free to make any changes or adjustments to your list of priorities, and if you didn't include your personal care as one of your priorities above, add it under the heading of 'relationship with God' since we now understand that as we place God first He will help us to care for ourselves in all areas.

After establishing your crystal balls, you'll need to list all of the rubber balls in your life. Yes, all of them. You'll want to take your time and include every single time commitment; committees, organizations, school, work, church and community responsibilities, etc.

Then, establish the importance of each rubber ball in your life. You can do this by placing a 1, 2, 3, or 4 by each of the items.

1 = very important to me
2 = important to me
3 = a good thing for me to do
4 = I just said, “yes” when I was asked to do it.

Rubber Balls:

1. ______________________ __________
2. ______________________ __________
3. ______________________ __________
4. ______________________ __________
5. ______________________ __________
6. ______________________ __________
7. ______________________ __________
8. ______________________ __________
9. ______________________ __________
10. ______________________ __________
11. ______________________ __________
12. ______________________ __________
13. ______________________ __________
14. ______________________ __________
15. ______________________ __________

As you look over your list of rubber balls, you’ll probably notice that every single commitment can be deemed as a worthy cause. In most cases, our lives are filled with really good causes. We’re not choosing between the good and bad. We’re choosing between the good and the best.

After you rate each item, consider the 3's and the 4's. Be brave. You must decide if these items should be weeded from your life. Some items you’ll want to remove from your life for a season; some you may need to remove permanently due to their failure to line–up with your priorities and goals in life.

Let me give you an example. After I became a mother, my priorities (crystal balls) changed dramatically. This precious little sweetie that God had blessed my husband and me with had become the center of our lives. I decided to resign from my position in several women's organizations in our community.

At the time, I had planned that my leave of absence would be temporary; but decided later that these rubber balls were not what was best for me and my family. They were fine organizations that provided many honorable services and opportunities for our community, but it wasn't where I was to be spending my time. Guess what? That's just ok.

Looking back, I'm so thankful that I mustered up the courage to do what was best for my family and me. I didn't cave in to the peer pressures of what other woman thought I should do or expected me to do. I must give credit where credit is due. I was blessed with a wonderful sister–by–marriage, who modeled the healthy practice of saying "No" to things that just didn't line up with her highest priorities, God and her family. Watching her confidently say "No" without feeling guilty, gave me courage. It was like the permission that I seemed to need to say "NO" to clubs, committees, and other competitors for my time. Thanks, Julie.

Yes! I did it! I said, "No." And I have NO regrets. Tell me. How can such a tiny little word be so difficult to speak? We must become friends with this little guy, for you see, he is going to be instrumental in helping to save us and our families from losing precious moments together. Go ahead. Say it right now. NO! NO! NO! Good job! Bravo sisters!

Every time you say No to a request on your time…rest in knowing that you're saying YES to protecting your time with those who are most precious in your life. I encourage you this day, give yourself permission to say 'No' to things that threaten your priorities. Be confident in your choices, and refuse to surrender to the guilt that saying 'No' sometimes brings.

At the end of life, I bet very few women, if any, will regret that they didn't work more, join more civic organizations, or sit on more committees at church. What we will regret is that we didn't spend more time with those we love. We must constantly guard against over–commitment, remembering that even worthwhile and enjoyable activities become damaging when they consume the last ounce of energy or the remaining free moments in the day.

Consider your juggling act before you say "yes" to additional commitments. Always ask yourself the question, "Is this potential rubber ball important enough that I should add it to my juggling act of life?" I want to caution you to be very careful when you add a rubber ball because if you don't remove an existing rubber ball from the juggling act, you may put your crystal balls at risk.

Recently a friend of mine, who had previously resigned from her professional career after having her two children, decided that she was to enter back into the work force. After much thought and prayer, she was certain that this was best for herself and her family, knowing that this was exactly what God had impressed upon her to do.

She knew that she would need to delete several extra curricular activities from her weekly schedule, so she began to pray about what should go. As she evaluated her rubber balls, listing each one, God led her to a decision of which two needed to be discarded.

In spite of some friendly opposition from several friends who wished she'd stayed at home with her children, she courageously followed her heart, obeying the way she believed God was leading her in her life for her life circumstances. I really admire her for her commitment to seek God for advice, and trust Him by obeying despite what others say or do in their lives. I hope you're inspired by this woman's example to ask God to direct you in deciding what activities and responsibilities you should allow in your daily life.

If you're having a 'little hard time' (as I used to say to my boys when they were tiny) removing unnecessary rubber balls from your life, while learning to say 'No' to inviting more rubber balls into your life, take a quick trip to the McDonald's play land in your town. Picture yourself sitting in the middle of all of those brightly colored plastic balls. (Of course, they're not clean. They're sticky, dirty, and disgusting…and our kids love them.)

So, you're sitting there with your four year old son or daughter, and you just keep saying, "Yes," to more and more of these bright colored balls. And, before you know it…you can't even see you child's head. But you haven't learned to say the word 'No' yet, so guess what? The balls keep on filling up the bin. Before you know it, you can't see anything except balls because there are so many balls that they are covering your head, too. Not only are you suffering from your failure to say NO, but your child is suffering, too.

The moral of this story is, either you learn to say 'No' to protect yourself and those you love, or I'll just have to personally escort you to your local McDonald's Play Land, and insist that you sit in with those disgusting, sticky balls until you learn to say, "NO!" Now, we wouldn't want that, would we?

I want my life to be a shrine to God not a shrine to Susan Dantzler. I don't want people to look at my life and simply see what I've accomplished for me, my family, my community or country. I want them to see what I've accomplished for God. I want them to see Jesus in the way I live and the way I speak.

My desire is to live my life as though I am building a shrine to God with each decision and choice that I make. I want people to describe and define my life with words that say, "Jesus."

Christ is the silver lining which guided my every step. My purpose in this lifetime is not to reach a level of success in man's eyes, but to exemplify Christ in all I do and say.

In the Bible, along with other women, Esther, Ruth, and Rahab, each found favor in the eyes of God. Could their love for Him and faith in Him, which they are well–known for in the Bible have had something to do with that favor? Maybe. Only God knows the answer to that question.

Esther was an ordinary girl who's love and faith in her God lead her down a path to become a queen, bringing safety to her people. Ruth, also, was an ordinary girl who's love and faith in God lead both she and her mother–in–law to safety and security in the midst of great loss. Then, there is Rahab, another God's girl, who simply took the wrong road ending in prostitution, but turned her heart back to God, exhibiting such strong faith that God included her in the faith chapter in the Book of Hebrews.

God's favor is not based on our perfection, but our love, obedience, and faith in a Holy God. God never emphasized the faults, sins, and failures of His girls, but quite the contrary. He highlights their obedience to Him, their love for Him, and their faith in Him.

Our God is a merciful God who continues to show tender mercies and loving kindness to His girls, while extending His hand of forgiveness and restoration to us. These women were building their lives as a shrine to their God, living each day with the goal of serving and exemplifying their Heavenly Father. This, too, is my heart's desire, to live my life as building a shrine to God.

Making a few positive changes can greatly impact your life, and the lives of those you love. As you examine your priorities and begin to live your life as though your building a shrine to God, commit to protect your crystal balls, evaluate your rubber balls, and always strive to *put first things first.*

The reason most major goals are not achieved is that we spend our time doing second things first.

—Robert J. McKain

— 4 —

The Ultimate Interior Designer

But Christ is faithful as a son over God's house. And ***we are His house****, if we hold on to our courage and the hope of which we boast.* Hebrews 3:6

For ***we are His workmanship****, created in Christ Jesus unto good works, which God hath before ordained that we should walk in them.* Ephesians 2:10

God is a good God. He has always desired His girls (that would be you and me) to live free, well and in the abundance of all good things. A healthy balance in all areas is God's desire for our lives, which John describes in John 10:10, "*I am come that they might have life, and that they might have it more abundantly.*" Every woman who knows God has eternal life, not every woman experiences abundant living in their daily lives. Abundant life is the process of Christ transforming us and filling us to overflowing in every area of our lives, and any lack we experience is not on His part in giving, but our part in seeking, believing, obeying and receiving.

If you were to purchase a baby seat to attach to your bicycle, would you refer to the manufacturer's instruction manual? Of course, you would because the life of your child would be at risk if you didn't. God manufactured you and I, and then, He wrote His manufacturer's instruction manual for us to follow to ensure that we would live a long life of abundance in all areas.

Manufacturer's manuals always begin by stating in big bold letters, 'READ THE INSTRUCTION MANUAL BEFORE BEGINNING TO ASSEMBLE.' When was the last time you read an entire instruction manual prior to assembling something? I must confess, I don't believe I ever have actually read a manufacturer's instruction manual from cover to cover.

After reading an instruction manual, we are instructed to carefully follow the step–by–step instructions to ensure safety, success, and the quality of performance from the merchandise.

The Word of God is our instruction manual that will direct us safely and successfully through life, if we believe this to be true and read it as if our lives depended on it. God promises health and success in every area of our lives when we treasure God's words and direct our hearts and minds toward His wisdom.

Our Lord's words of wisdom to Joshua are His words of instruction to us, as well. *"Be strong and very courageous. Be careful to obey all the law my servant Moses gave you; do not turn from it to the right or to the left, that you may be successful wherever you go.* ***Do not let this Book of the Law depart from your mouth; meditate on it day and night, so that you may be careful to do everything written in it. Then you will be prosperous and successful. Have I not commanded you? Be strong and courageous. Do not be terrified;*** *do not be discourage, for the Lord your God will be with you wherever you go."* Joshua 1:7–9.

God gave us this incredibly detailed instruction manual for life. Isn't it funny how we sometimes take this awesome gift for granted and struggle along in life without consulting the handbook.

In His handbook, the Bible, God is telling us that if we meditate on His Word day and night, we will live a full and prosperous life. Meditating on the Word is so important because it is our instructional manual for life which God wrote through the hands of His chosen men. 2 Timothy 3:16 tells us, *"Every Scripture is God–breathed (given by His inspiration) and profitable for instruction, for reproof and conviction of sin, for correction of error and discipline in obedience, and for training in righteousness (in holy living, in conformity to God's will in thought, purpose, and action.)"*

In the fifteenth chapter of John, Christ promises His girls that *"If we abide in Him, He will abide in us,"* which means that the Holy Spirit actually takes up residency in us, if we live in Him. This is how we become the temple of God described in 1 Corinthians 6:19–20. *"What? Know ye not that your body is the temple of the Holy Ghost which is in you, which ye have of God, and ye are not your own? For ye are bought with a price; therefore glorify God in your body, and in your spirit, which are God's."* The five dimensions of a woman are like five rooms in God's Temple, which include **spiritual**, **physical**, **emotional**, **social,** and **intellectual**. The drawing below shows the importance of the spiritual dimension as the foundation and basic structure of our lives, while the other four dimensions function within the spiritual dimension.

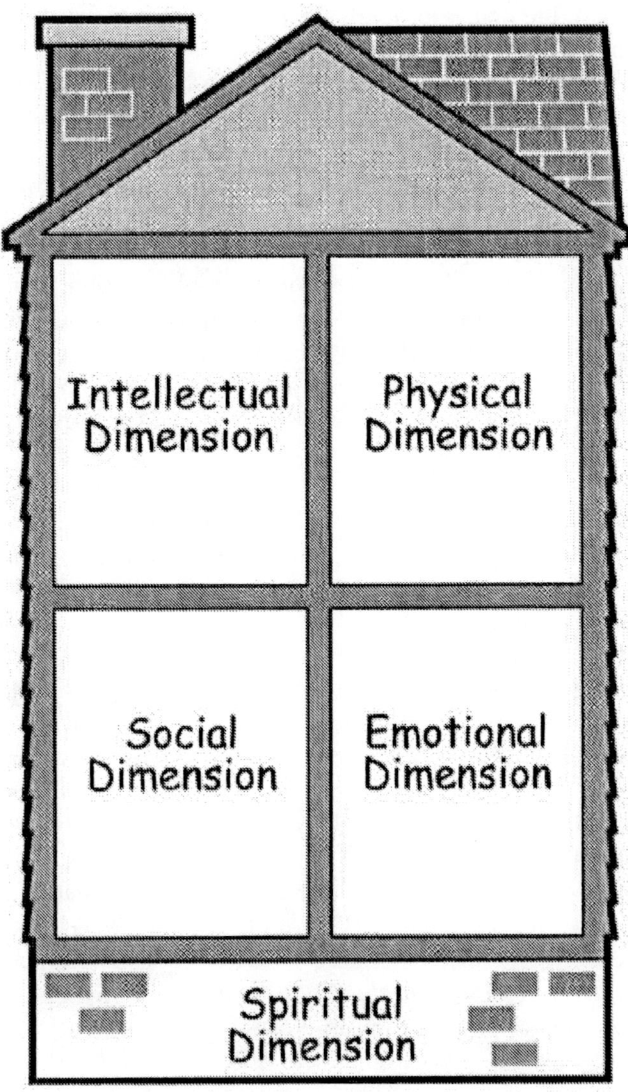

Artwork designed by Doug Heminger

It's difficult for me to comprehend that God created me so He could not only fellowship with me, but live in me in the form of His Holy Spirit. My life is meant to be His home, thus, I want to build my life as though I'm building it as a shrine which honors a Holy God.

Just as the one who lives in the home is of greater importance than the home itself, the one who builds the home, is also of greater importance than the home itself. Hebrews 3:3–6 records this truth, *"Jesus has been found worthy of greater honor than Moses, just as the builder of a house has greater honor than the house itself. For every house is built by someone, but God is the builder of everything. Moses was faithful as a servant in all God's house, testifying to what would be said in the future. But Christ is faithful as a son over God's house. And* ***we are His house****, if we hold on to our courage and the hope of which we boast."*

When we refer to our instruction manual, we find God's specific step–by–step instructions for a woman to follow when building her life, which is His house. Proverbs 14:1 *says, "A WISE woman builds her house."* We shouldn't simply expect our lives to fall into place or just happen, rather, we are to take it's building process very serious, considering who we are building it for.

We, our lives, body, mind, and spirit, are God's house, and the choices we make each day determine the state of His house.

The foundation of a house as defined by Webster as 'the whole masonry substructure of a building,' and is obviously the most important feature of a house considering that it's base support depends on the firmness of it's foundation.

The spiritual dimension of a woman's life is her personal relationship with God, and is the actual foundation of her life, which represents God's house. The state of a woman's personal relationship with God determines the condition of the foundation of her life, and this is the reason that a girl's relationship with her Heavenly Father must be cared for first, above the other four areas.

Put the wellness of your spirit first…and you'll be better equipped to address all other areas of your life. In Matthew 6:33, Jesus is instructing us to do this exact thing when He says, *"Seek ye first the Kingdom of God, and His righteousness, and all these things shall be added unto you."*

Just as the condition of the foundation of a house affects the entire structure, the condition of a woman's relationship with God, affects every area in her life. Jesus addresses the importance of building our lives on a firm foundation, which He refers to as 'the rock' in Matthew 7:24–27. *"Therefore everyone who hears these words of mine and puts them into practice is like a wise man who built his house on the rock. The rain came down, the streams rose, and the winds blew and beat against that house; yet it did not fall, because it had its foundation on the rock. But everyone who hears these words of mine and does not put them into practice is like a foolish man who built his house on sand. The rain came down, the streams rose, and the winds blew and beat against that house, and it fell with a great crash."*

In Psalms 18:1–2, David declares to the world that his 'rock' is the Lord, when he says, *"I love you, O Lord, my strength. The Lord is my rock, my fortress and my deliverer; my God is my rock, in whom I take refuge."* As we place God first in our lives, making our relationship with Him the most important factor in our lives, we are choosing to build our lives on the same firm rock that David referred to as His Lord, and the other rooms in our home will be affected in a healthy, positive manor.

In Proverbs 24:3–4, the Bible describes HOW a wise woman is to build her house, *"Through skillful and godly Wisdom is a house (**a life**, a home, a family) built, and by understanding it is established [on a sound and good foundation]. And by knowledge shall its chambers [of every area] be filled with all precious and pleasant riches," Proverbs 24:3–4 (AMP).*

James 3:17–18 describes in detail the heavenly wisdom of God that a woman is to use to build her house. "But *the Wisdom that comes from heaven is first of all **pure** and full of **quiet gentleness**. Then it is **peace–loving** and **courteous**. It **allows discussion** and is **willing to yield** to others; it is full of **mercy** and **good deeds**. It is **wholehearted** and **straightforward** and **sincere**, And those who are **peacemakers** will **plant seeds of peace** and **reap a harvest of goodness**." (LB)*

God placed these two verses on my heart several years ago to use as my New Year's scripture, so I began to pray them daily, asking God to work His Wisdom in me. Every time I pray this scripture it still 'wow's' me because it's overflowing with God's very own character traits.

In Ephesians 3:17, Paul talks about Christ taking up residence within our hearts as we place our trust in Him, saying, *"I pray that Christ will be more and more at home in your hearts, living within you as you trust in Him. May your roots go down deep into the soil of God's marvelous love."* The Lord, who is the Ultimate Interior Decorator, wants to redecorate each room in His temple (that's us), and transform them to reflect Him. Dear Lord, Please empty me out, and fill me with Your Holy Spirit...and use me as a suit of working clothes to accomplish Your work and will this day, and every day. Give me your eyes, your hands, your mouth, your words, your mind, your heart, your touch, your attitude, and your perspective on the issues that arise in this life.

Years ago, one sunny afternoon, I had just put my two young sons down for a nap, L.B. was four years old and Blakie was one, and I found myself with about ten minutes to spare before the baby sitter came. Wow!

Ten whole minutes. I'm dressed for my luncheon and my boys are sleeping, so what shall I do in these precious ten minutes.

As I walked into my kitchen and looked down at our worn white linoleum floor, and had this fleeting thought of… "Maybe I'll sweep the kitchen floor." (I couldn't help but think my mother's presence must have been in my kitchen that day…sending me those subliminal messages all the way from Ohio, "Sssswwwweeeepppp yyyooouuurrr kkiittcchheenn fflloorr, mmmyyy Deeaarr.")

While trying to decide whether or not to sweep my kitchen during these free ten minutes or wait until later, I began to evaluate it's condition, thinking to myself that…"it didn't look too dirty. I really could wait and sweep tonight." Did I end up sweeping my kitchen floor that day? Well…you guessed it…I couldn't think of anything else to do during these extra minutes, so I began to sweep my kitchen floor.

After only a few sweeps of my straw broom, I began to see just how dirty my kitchen floor was. In no time at all I had accumulated an enormous pile of dirt. As I continued to sweep, my heart felt God's gentle touch, and tears began to stream down my face, as He began to gently show me how sweeping this kitchen floor was much like sweeping the floor of my life; His temple.

Many times we don't even realize that there is dirt on the floor of our lives that God wants to remove until He, ever–so gently, reveals it to us by beginning the sweeping process at our request.

I thank God that in His Wisdom He helps us to sweep the floors of our lives, molding us little by little, revealing only one or two areas at one time that He wants to change in us.

Oswald Chambers said, "You are not where you thought you were." Just like my kitchen floor experience, as I perceived the floor to be fairly clean until I began to sweep it and the dirt was revealed to me. Many times we go along in life thinking we're living the way we should live, and then, God reveals to us, something He wants to change in us. He ever–so–gently, in His wisdom, reveals some unhealthy habit or trait that is preventing us from living the free, abundant life He has planned for us, and suddenly our eyes are opened, and sin is not a pretty sight to see, especially when it's in our own lives.

I find myself inviting God to redecorate the rooms of my life as I pray Psalm 139:23–24 often, *"Search me, O God, and know my heart; point out anything in me that makes you sad, and help me to change it; and lead me through life to everlasting life."* (Author's paraphrase)

In 1986, shortly after moving to Florida, I was interviewed on a local talk show known as "Inside Tampa Bay" to discuss 'Fitness for the

New Year.' At the particular time in my life, I was not living a God–centered life; instead I was calling all the shots, doing what Susan wanted to do. I was definitely trying out the drivers seat in my car of life, choosing to ignore the instruction manual for life that God had given to me in the Bible. This was the darkest time in my life, in which I felt very much alone in my spirit because I had chosen to step away from my God and His plan for my life.

About eight years after this interview, one of my friends watched it on video, after laughing hysterically with her husband, Karen called me late that evening. She just had to know if I had gone through plastic surgery because she noticed that on the video I looked and acted completely different from the Susan she now knows. She kept insisting that I had plastic surgery on my nose because my face looked so different than it does now.

I explained to her that while she did not know me during that time in my life when I was not filled with Christ, I was operating on my own strength and wisdom. My spirit, which was engineered to be connected to God's spirit, seemed to be functioning on auto pilot, void of any divine light glowing inside of me. Instead of a spirit full of life and God's light, my spirit was only filled with a light that I could create, as a human being, lacking in the divine light breathed into a life only by their Creator God. I said, "Karen, I did say that I didn't have plastic surgery, but I actually did."

I began to explain to her how Jesus performed surgery on my heart, penetrating every area of my life, making me new in every way. As Jesus transforms the inside of us, the outside cannot remain the same. In Philippians 2:13, Paul describes this internal transformation that God desires to work in each of His girls by saying, "*For it is God who is at work within you, giving you the will and the power to achieve His purpose.*" (Phillips)

God continues to perform surgeries on me, removing all sorts of ugly habits and attitudes that are not Christ–like, transforming me to be more like Christ…and I'd have it no other way.

Years ago, I watched a documentary about a little bear whose story seemed to be much like mine, and I'd like to share it with you, and maybe it will sound familiar to you too.

The Little Bear

There once was a little bear. He had been found wandering deep in the woods with a chain attached to his leg. The bear obviously had been dragging his chain around for a very long time.

The people who found him could tell this because the chain had become embedded in the bears skin.

The tissue had actually grown over parts of the chain because it was so tight.

The chain had to be surgically removed which was a painful process, but a necessary one. During the healing process, the bear began to adapt to living his life without the heavy chain attached to his leg.

His care–givers noticed that there were a number of times that he would actually forget that the chain was not attached to his leg. He would begin to drag his back leg again, just like he did when the chain was attached.

Due to the duration and intensity that the bear lived dragging the chain around, the surgery left him with a very noticeable scar. A scar that would always remind the little bear...not of his captivity, but of his freedom.

We experience this same four step process, as the Lord begins to reveal and detach the chains that bind us, hurt us, and slow us down. The four steps are, acknowledging the chain, detaching the chain, healing and adapting to life without the chain and living with the scar of the chain. Chains can attach themselves to any area of our lives, becoming embedded in any of the rooms of our being, our temple.

We need the power and Wisdom of our Creator and Ultimate Interior Designer when it comes to declaring war on the chains which exist in our lives. We all have different chains that bind us, and our enemy, Satan, will use anything in our lives to bind us if he can; addictions to food, nicotine, alcohol, sex, pornography. He'll use pride, money, gossip, exercise, success, and bad attitudes because his goal in this world is to take the things that God created perfect for our enjoyment on earth and pervert them, causing them to bind us with the purpose of tripping us up in life, ultimately keeping us from living the abundant life God intended us to live.

In Hebrews 12:1, Paul implores us to allow God to free us from all of the chains that bind us, keeping us from the plan that God has for our lives, when he says, *"Let us strip off anything that slows us down or holds us back, and especially those sins that wrap themselves tightly around our feet and trip us up; and let us run with patience the particular race that God has set before us."*

As I continue to pray Psalm 139:23–24, I am asking the Lord to, "Please, expose the chains that are binding me, as well as, the dirt on the floor of my life. Reveal to me anything that needs to be removed from my life, and help me remove it." Without fail, God begins by making the chain know to me, and after I acknowledge it and express my desire to change and to be molded into the image and character of Christ, the Lord ever–so–gently surgically removes the chain. He, then, holds my hand while I heal just like He promises He will do in Isaiah 41:10, where He says, "*Fear not; for I am with you; be not dismayed; for I am your God; I will strengthen you; yes, I will help you; yes, I will uphold you with the right hand of my righteousness*."

He holds me up as I adapt to life without the chain, and if I revert back to my previous behaviors, He reminds me of my freedom from the chain. While some women choose to see an ugly scar, remembering a painful experience, I choose to see my freedom from that chain, remembering how God rescued me, freeing me from my bondage. God promises in Romans 8:28, *"to work all things for the good for those who love Him and live for Him,"* and this is how He can turn the scars of divorce, addiction, anxiety, and abuse into powerful milestone reminders of His Power in our lives to free us from all that binds us…and keeps us from enjoying the fullness of a life lived in abundance and freedom.

Millie Stamm, the author of Be Still and Know and other daily devotional books, describes this transformation process by comparing it to the sewing of a piece of clothing. When sewing a garment, a woman selects a pattern suitable for the fabric, then she places the pattern on the fabric, proceeding to cut, sew, and fit it to the person, adding finishing touches to complete the garment.

God has a life pattern for us and as He begins to fit it to the fabric of our lives, some rearranging may be necessary to make the pattern fit. Some attitudes, desires, or motives may have to be adjusted, as He begins to cut the fabric. While others will require cutting out completely, some will only need to be trimmed. This process may hurt, but it is necessary in order to complete the garment for His good pleasure.

In Romans 8:28, Paul teaches us that the pieces of our lives have to be fitted together to complete His purpose when he says, "*Moreover we know that to those who love God, who are called according to His plan, everything that happens fits into a pattern for good*." (Phillips)

God continues to add finishing touches to bring out His beauty in our lives. No two lives are designed alike; He has His own special pattern for each of His girls.

To make the garment, it took the pattern, fabric, scissors, thread, and the trimming. Yet not one of them had the power to cut, fit, or sew that garment, but it took the power of the seamstress. We cannot make our lives according to God's pattern because it takes His power. In Ephesians 2:10, Paul reminds us of this truth when he says, "*For we are His workmanship, created in Christ Jesus unto good works, which God hath before ordained that we should walk in them.*"

One of my favorite worship choruses Lord, Prepare Me expresses so beautifully my heart's desire to become a sanctuary appropriate for the Holy Spirit to live in. Oh, Lord, please prepare me to be your sanctuary, pure and holy, tried and still true, and I will be thankful…counting it a privilege…to be a living sacrifice just for You.

At the end of my life, I truly want people to see Jesus living in me, rather than simply a good person with many notable accomplishments. My desire is to dedicate my life on earth to knowing God more intimately and allowing Him to make me a sanctuary, pure and holy, for Him. I want to build my life as building it unto God, as a love offering to Him for all He has done for me, and simply because of who He is.

Thank You, Dear Heavenly Father, for caring about the details of our lives. We're so grateful that you created us in the unique design called woman. Thank you, for giving us your instruction manual, The Holy Bible, to live ,by. You truly are the Ultimate Interior Designer that all women so desperately need. While the best designers of the fashion world charge high fees for their expert design services, the Ultimate Interior Designer, Almighty God, requires an unbelievably high fee, as well.

He requires that we surrender everything in our lives to Him, excluding not one tiny item in any area. His cost is high, as it should be. He gave His only Son to die on an old rugged cross so that we might have the opportunity to be saved from our sins and adopted back into His family, so why should we give less than our lives for Him.

Dear Lord, we surrender our lives to you this day, asking you to forgive us of our sins, knowing that Christ died in our place on the cross, we invite you into our lives, asking you to resign and redecorate your home, which is us, preparing our lives to be sanctuaries, pure and holy, for You. We thank You in advance for all you are going to do in our lives as The Ultimate Interior Designer of all life.

I am only a pencil in God's hand...God writes through us, and however imperfect instruments we may be, God writes beautifully.

—*Mother Teresa, Blessed Are You*

— 5 —

Little Red Sports Car

I am the vine, ye are the branches; He that abideth in me, and I in him, the same bringeth forth much fruit; for without me ye can do nothing.
John 15:6

He that dwelleth in the secret place of the most High shall abide under the shadow of the Almighty.
Psalm 91:1

In an earlier chapter I mentioned that the spiritual dimension of women is the foundation and basic structure of our lives; our very existence. In the beginning of time, God created us spirit and flesh. Our spirit is the part of us that will live on for eternity. Our flesh,(our physical bodies), however, will die. This truth, in itself, tells us that the spirit of a woman is the most important dimension of her existence.

Picture the spirit of a woman as an umbrella, under which the other four dimensions function. The physical, emotional, intellectual, and social dimensions in a woman's life are all greatly impacted by the condition of her spirit.

It is so easy to allow our physical dimension to become the umbrella because that's the part of us we can visibly see. Unless we are physically blind, it is virtually impossible to see a person's spirit before we see their physical bodies. This is the simple reason that our society has become so easily obsessed with the physical exterior of a woman.

Our physical health is so important to our quality of life and longevity; however, it's not as important as our spirit. It is our spirit–man that will live on forever, so why would we spend our entire lifetime focusing only on our physical bodies, when we will eventually say good–bye to our physical bodies.

In Romans 8:6, Paul addresses the spirit and the flesh issue, when he says, "*To set the mind on the flesh is death, but to set the mind on the Spirit is life and peace.*" Our flesh will die, but our spirit will live on forever. It makes perfect sense that we should set our minds on things of the spirit, instead of things of the flesh.

When God created our spirits, He engineered us with a "God Spot" that only He can fill. It's a special place where His spirit communes with our spirit. This is the only way we can receive divine power in our lives.

As human beings, we cannot bring this divine power to our own lives because God is divine, and we are human. God is God, and we are NOT! God did create us in His own image, but this does not mean we are as God Himself. We are His created children. I was born in the image of my earthly parents. I have some of their traits, but I would never think for a moment that I could be them. I am me, and they are my parents.

Many women have shared with me over the years that although they are generally happy, there is something missing from their lives.

As I enjoyed a cup of coffee with a new friend, she revealed to me that although she was raised in a wonderful home, with parents who loved God, she didn't feel like she knew God personally. She, her husband, and children attend church regularly, but still something was missing, and she didn't know what it was. I explained to her that this was simply God's way of gently beckoning to her because He wants to know His daughter.

When God created us with this "God Spot," His plan was to live there with us. He didn't want to force us to love Him, so He gave us the gift of free will. God wants us to *want* to love Him, and He wants us to choose to spend time with Him. He is a true gentlemen. I love our Heavenly Father's gentle words to us in Revelation 3:20, "*Behold, I stand at the door and knock; if any man (or woman) hear my voice, and open the door, I will come in to him, and will sup with him, and he with me.*" He's waiting to be invited into our lives, and the minute we ask Him in, He will fill that void with Himself. At that very moment, He will fill the void deep inside.

Something else beautiful happens when we ask our Heavenly Father, our Creator, to assume His place in our hearts. Romans 8:10,14–17 confirms that when we invite God to dwell in our lives, He adopts us as His girls. "*But if Christ is in you, your body is dead because of sin, yet your spirit is alive because of righteousness. And the Spirit of Him who raised Jesus from the dead is living in you, He who raised Christ from the dead will also give life to your mortal bodies through His Spirit, who lives in you. Those who are lead by the Spirit of God are sons of God. For you did not receive the spirit that makes you a slave again to fear, but you received the Spirit of son–ship. (daughter–ship) And by Him we cry, Abba, Father. The Spirit Himself testifies with our spirit that we are God's children. (God's girls.) Now if we are children, then we are heirs—heirs of*

God and co–heirs with Christ, if indeed we share in his sufferings in order that we may also share in His glory."

You might be wondering...if God created us His children why would He have to adopt us as children? That's a really good question. When sin entered the world through the free will of Adam and Eve, all of man–kind was separated from God. That's why He sent Jesus to die on the cross to cover our sins.

The Blood Jesus' shed on the cross serves as a telephone line to God. Jesus paid the price, (paid the phone bill with His very own Blood) and gave us a direct line to our Heavenly Father. This phone line is one that we can choose to use at any time to invite Him into our hearts. After we make the call and personally invite our Christ into our lives, the void in our heart is filled with the very Spirit of God, and this is the beginning of a woman's spiritual journey with a Holy God.

What part of a house is constructed first? The foundation, of course. It would be true to say that the foundation of a house is truly the most important part of the house considering it supports the entire structure.

The same is true of a woman. Her spiritual wellness should come first, before all else. Henry Blackeby states this so clearly in Experiencing God when he says, "Intimacy with God is the single most important factor in my life."

The Bible is very clear about how His girls should prioritize their lives. God should be first, then our husband, then our family, then God's church. This doesn't mean that God is to be one of several priorities or just one area of my life. God is to be the sole priority of my life, and the other items, including family, are to come under Christ. Just like a "spiritual umbrella."

Philippians 4:13 says, that *"I can do ALL things THROUGH Christ who strengthens me."* One day, I was pondering this scripture and the words ALL and THROUGH jumped out at me. Instead of hearing, 'God will give me strength to do all things,' I heard ALL of the things in my life should be done THROUGH Christ; everything in my life should take place in Christ.' My relationship with Christ must be my life, and everything else is conducted through Him.

I love how Paul expresses his priority, his purpose for living in Philippians 1:21. *"For to me to live is Christ, and to die is gain."* Christ was life itself to Paul. Is He that to you and me? Is there anything in your life that is taking God's place? First place? If so, you can change that right now. Just ask God to take first place in your life, and surrender your husband, your children, and everything in your life. What better hands to place those you love. They will be safe and sound in the hands of God.

They'll be much safer in His hands than yours, and doesn't that make perfect sense.

Think about an umbrella for a minute. The condition of everything under it depends on the quality and condition of the umbrella itself. If it's kept in great condition...all is dry and well underneath. However, if the umbrella hasn't been cared for and maintained properly, everything will be damaged by the weather. This is another reason for making our spiritual umbrella first priority in our lives.

God created us for a love relationship with Him. If you cannot describe your relationship with God by saying that you love Him with all your being, then just ask your Heavenly Father to hold your hand and to bring you into that kind of relationship with Him.

He's our Abba Father. That means He is our Daddy, and we are His little girls. God spoke these words to the Israelites in Deuteronomy 6:4–5, *"Hear, O Israel; The Lord our God, the Lord is one. Love the Lord your God with all your heart and with all your soul, and with all your mind. This is the first and greatest commandment."*

Everything in our lives does depend on the quality of our love relationship with our God. If that is not right, nothing in our lives will be right. In Matthew, Jesus tells us, *"Do not worry, saying, What shall we eat? Or What shall we wear? For the pagans run after all these things, and your Heavenly Father knows that you need them. But seek first His kingdom and His righteousness, and all these things will be given to you as well."*

A love relationship with God is more important than any other single factor in your life. This is our sole purpose in life. God wants to be invited into our lives to enjoy sweet fellowship with His girls.

For most of my adult life I have prayed, "Dear Lord, have your perfect will in MY LIFE." I have always focused on my life, and God leading me in it. While going through the Experiencing God workbook study with a friend, I began to see that this life is not about me and my life, rather, it's all about GOD! I was created for the sole purpose of knowing God, so my focus should be on GOD, not me and my life.

There's such a fine line between living a God centered life and living a self–centered life. We live in a very "me" centered society. Because we are created flesh (human) and live in this physical world, our human tendency is to focus on "me"...and just fit God in where He seems to fit best.

Very good activities can contribute to a self–centered lifestyle if our motives are not pure. Things like church work, school volunteer work, and charity work are all good in nature, but they can add to a self–centered focus if your motive is to gain credit for you. Even things like, exercising and eating healthy can easily move from maintaining a healthy body to becoming obsessed with dieting and exercise. It's very easy to get off balance and begin doing these things for selfish reasons instead of purely to glorify God. It is a very fine line, and our motives must be checked every single day.

I invited Christ into my heart and life years ago, but for most of my life I lived a very self–centered life. I thought I was living a fairly God–centered life because I was a good Christian girl. As God began to teach me about the difference between living a self–centered life and living a God–centered life, He used an example of a car.

Picture yourself driving a car through life that your Heavenly Father gave to you when He created you. This car represents the gift of life that God has given to each of us. We all get a car just because we're His girls. I'm picturing a two door little red sports car. When you invite God to come into your life, it's like you invite Him to get into your car. When you asked God to join you in your car, who was driving? You were, of course, because you were the only one in your car until God joined you.

After I invited God into my car, I stayed in the drivers seat, and continued to drive. I would drive for most of the time, until I was in trouble and in need of God's help. Then, I would beg for Him to take the wheel, and rescue me from my dilemma. Sometimes, I think I even reduced Him to riding in the trunk because I didn't want His help driving.

God is a very polite passenger. He will never be a back–seat driver like some of us tend to be. He will only drive our car when invited by us.

God began to show me that His perfect plan for me involved my asking Him to sit in the driver's seat of my car. Yes, my life should be so God–centered that it's as though He is driving my car. He leads and directs me through every day. I strive to look to Him before I make a move. God wants our lives to be so much about Him, so God–centered, that it is as if we have given Him full control of our car (our life). Looking back over my life, I can't believe that for so many years I put my life in my own hands when I could have been so safe riding while God drove. I've had some near death accidents in my life because I was behind the wheel. I don't want to take chances anymore; I want Him to drive my car…every day. Who is in the driver's seat of your car?

When we ask God to drive our car, we're asking Him for more than to simply lead us through life. We're dedicating our entire existence to Him, which is what we were created for; His pleasure. In a sense, we are saying, "Thanks for this beautiful car, Lord. You gave it to me just because you love me, and you want me to enjoy it with you. I want everything I do with it to glorify you, so please drive it through me."

How does God drive our car of life? He can only drive it through us. When we ask Him to fill us with His Holy Spirit, we become more like Christ. As God begins to molds us, He begins to give us the characteristics of His son, Jesus. He can only do this when we ask Him to empty us out, and fill us with Him.

Consider yourself behind the steering wheel of your little red sports car of life. You are an empty suit of working clothes that the Holy Spirit wears. Ponder this thought for a moment. God drives our cars through us. While our physical bodies sit behind the wheel, God working through us does the steering when we totally surrender everything in our lives to Him. Our physical bodies live our lives, but God working through us leads us. This is how God works in our world.

He works in us and through us. This is how we become the temple of God. My daily prayer has become, "Dear Lord, empty Susan out of me today. Empty me out, and fill me up with Your Holy Spirit. May all I do and say this day reflect You. I give you this day. I look forward to walking with You, and allowing you to love others through me."

Today, I enjoyed a brief, but so inspiring, telephone conversation with my sister–by–marriage. She was telling me about a conversation that she and her daughter shared while driving in the car.

Her daughter was expressing her concern for a particular issue she was facing in her life. In her gifted way, my sister–by–marriage so beautifully illustrated that God wants us to rest in knowing that He is in control of every situation in our lives. She reminded her daughter of the many days and nights the two of them had spent together driving to and from soccer practices and games. She would drive, and my neice would rest, knowing that she was safe with her mother behind the wheel.

She explained that just as she drives their station wagon, God will drive for us through every life situation. Just as she trusts her mother to drive their car, God wants us to trust Him to drive. Let's let Him drive…our little red sports cars.

I truly do want to be clay in God's hand. Sometimes, I picture myself as Gumby. You remember the little clay characters 'gumby and pokey,' don't you? My sisters and I watched them every Sunday morning before leaving for Sunday School. I feel like Gumby, sometimes, and I behave like gumby sometimes, too.

Gumby would begin every episode in the form of a glob of clay. He would then be quickly formed into his cute little green self. Without fail, he would venture off, finding himself in a jam. He would always end up tumbling and crashing, and returning to that distorted glob of clay. I call this the 'Gumby Syndrome,' in which many of us live our lives.

Every Gumby episode contains the same pattern. God gives us a new day, a fresh start, and what do we do? We run off into our day without consulting Him, and we crash. If Gumby would have just taken his time, and allowed his creator to lead Him through his weekly adventures, he would have had fewer injuries. This is just like us. When we venture out on our own, without God's guidance, we often begin to experience the affects of the world. I have said, "Good–bye, to Gumby" forever. I don't want to follow in his footsteps, anymore.

In Jeremiah 18:6, God says, *"Like clay in the hand of the potter, so are you in my hand, O house of Israel."* He is the potter, and we are the clay. If I will just stay in His hand, He'll mold me and make me more like Christ.

Consider the life of play dough. We all love play dough. (Except when we find it dried into the carpet.) When it stays in the warm tiny hand of a five year old, it remains warm and pliable, and when it is kept in it's sealed container, it also stays soft and moldable. It's only when the play dough is not in a warm hand or in it's container, that it begins to harden.

It's amazing how play dough can transform into a beautiful piece of artwork when it remains in the hands of it's little creators. However, when it leaves its little potter's hands, the harmless little pieces of play dough can dry up and become sharp glasslike objects that we accidentally step on in the middle of the night. Don't you just love it when that happens?

After play dough has been left out of it's container, it is possible to soften it up again.

You simply seal it up in it's container with warm water, and after allowing it to remain there for a time, it will return to it's softer, more moldable state. Do you get it?

We are the hard play dough, the hand of God is the container, and the Holy Spirit is the warm water. All we need to do is to remain with God, without jumping out of His loving potter's hands. Just stay there, and just live there. The molding process is much less painful when I am already in a soft state. We must abide with Him daily as He has intended for us to do. Only then will we remain soft and moldable for Him.

I remember one day, I was in a huge hurry, as I jumped onto an elevator at work. I had just been listening to the song, 'The Potter's Hand,' while in my car, so it was still on my mind. In my hurry, I began to sing, "I am the potter, you are the clay…da…da….da…da…" Do you notice what is wrong with the words I sang?

In my rush, I made myself the potter, and God the clay. This spoke volumes to me about my tendency to run my own life. The tendency we all have is to misuse our freewill. I thanked God for this little reminder. It's so easy to forget that we are the clay, and we need to remain with the potter. Lord, help me to remember this important truth.

John 15:1–7 says:
"I AM the true vine, and my Father is the husbandman. Every branch in me that beareth no fruit He taketh away; and every branch that beareth fruit, He purgeth it that it may bring forth more fruit. Now ye are clean through the word which I have spoken unto you. Abide in me, and I in you. As the branch cannot bear fruit of itself, except it abide in the vine; no more can ye, except ye abide in me. I am the vine, ye are the branches; He that abideth in me, and I in him, the same bringeth forth much fruit; for without me ye can do nothing. If a man abide not in me, he is cast forth as a branch, and is withered; and men gather them and cast them into the fire, and they are burned. If ye abide in me, and my words abide in you, ye shall ask what ye will, and it shall be done unto you."

I remember reading this passage close to midnight one evening. I'd read it many times over the years, but this time was different. It was as though I could hear God saying over and over. "Susan, I AM the vine. You are not the vine. I AM the vine. You, my dear, are only a branch." I began to hear the power in this truth like never before. You, Oh Lord, are the vine. I am not the vine. You are the vine, and I am only a branch. The vine still exists without the branch, but the branch cannot exist without the vine. You are everything. I am only a branch. You are life itself; the life source. I, a branch, exist if I abide in you, the vine.

John 1:1–3 reminds us of this fact. "*In the beginning was the Word, and the Word was with God, and the Word was God.*" In the beginning was God. God has always been. This whole existence is completely about God.

Life is about the vine, not the branch. The branch only exists *for* and *because of* the vine. The vine provides everything the branch needs to flourish in life. Wow! If I abide in God, He will provide me with everything I need to live life full and free. He is in control. I just need to abide in Him.

I have four raspberry red, heart shaped boxes each with it's own lid. The four heart boxes are four different sizes. I use them to reinforce the principle of 'abiding in Christ.' I begin by removing all of the lids and separating all the boxes from each other.

First, I take the largest heart box, which represents God, the Father. Then, I take the second to largest heart box, which represents Christ, and I place it into the largest box. I do this because Jesus abides in the Father.

I, then, take the third heart, which represents you and I, (God's girls) and I place it into the second heart. I do this because Jesus tells us to 'abide in Him.'

Last, I take the smallest of the four heart boxes, which represents Christ, and I place it into the others. I do this because John 15:4, tells us that if we will abide in Christ, He will abide in us. Wow! Can you see how protected we are when we live sandwiched in this order; God the Father, Christ, Us, and Christ.

Jesus says, "*I abide in the Father; if you abide in me, then I will abide in you.*" Finally, I place the lids on each box, and 'Ta! Da!', we are safe and sound abiding in the safety of God's shelter. Storms of life will come and go, but they can not overtake me. I may get bruised while in the boxes, but never consumed.

Why would I ever, in a million years, choose NOT to abide in this safe, safe place? Why would I ever venture out and face the world all by myself? It's simple. I forget that I'm the branch, and I need the vine to live. Lord, help me to remember that I must abide in you, the vine, to live. Because *"I choose to dwell in the shelter of the Most High God, I can rest in the shadow of His Almighty protection."* (author's translation of Psalm 91:1)

You and I can abide with Christ daily. We do this two ways. One is to simply acknowledge His presence throughout the course of everyday. Abide with Him every minute of the day. Talk with Him in your car, at work, while grocery shopping. He's always with us, we just need to be conscious of His presence.

The second way in which we can abide in Christ is described in Matthew 6:6, *"But when you pray, go away by yourself, all alone, and shut the door behind you and pray to your Father secretly, and your Father, who knows your secrets, will reward you."* We are to set aside time that we will be alone with God.

I usually begin my quiet time with God by reading a daily devotional that contains scripture from the Bible, or just the Bible itself. It's amazing how God speaks to me through my daily devotional books and scriptures. After my devotional time, I just begin to thank Him and praise Him, not for just His blessings on me, but simply because He deserves my praise. I thank Him for being such a wonderful Father, and Holy God.

The book of Psalms has some beautiful chapters of praise that David sang to the Lord as He spent time alone with God. Sometimes I read a chapter aloud, as a prayer of praise to God. Then, I just spend time talking with God. I love beginning my prayer time with God with the Lord's Prayer.

Prayer is not something to be intimidated by or fearful of. Prayer is simply conversation between a daughter and a Heavenly Father. It's an intimate time in which we draw close and sit upon our Heavenly Father's lap. We rest our heads onto His chest, and He wraps His loving arms around us. Hmmm. If we stay with Him long enough, He will whisper wonderful things into our ears, guiding us with His gentle, wise words.

Our relationship with our Heavenly Father is the foundation of our very existence. Everything in our lives will be influenced by the condition of our relationship with God. Our spirit was designed to be connected to His Spirit.

Our spirit is like a lamp. It's only when it remains plugged into the light source that the power flows into the lamp. The lamp lights up, and spreads it's light to those around it. To experience a life full and free, we must invite Christ to take His place in the 'God Spot' of our lives. When we do this, He will move in and take up residence in us. The void that we once felt, will no longer exist, because God's Holy Spirit will breathe new life into our spirits every day, as we invite Him to drive our *little red sports cars*.

Intimacy with Christ is the single most important factor in my life.
—Henry Blackaby

— 6 —

Heads Up, Girls!

Through wisdom a house is built, and by understanding it is established; and by knowledge shall the chambers be filled with all precious and pleasant riches. A wise man is strong, yea, a man (woman) of knowledge increases strength.
Proverbs 24:3–5

Wisdom and knowledge lead to understanding. As a woman gains wisdom and knowledge, she's empowered with the gift of understanding. When she has a better understanding of her God, herself, others, and life's issues, her entire world will change for better.

With increased understanding a woman's perspective changes. We are no longer bound by or limited to the perspectives in which we have lived life to this point in time. Many times we are freed from the blinders that we often acquire through the various cultures in which we are raised. Knowledge is imperative to living the victorious life that God has intended for His girls to live. We learn this in Hosea 4:6 when God says, "*My people will be destroyed for lack of knowledge;*" These powerful words serve as a warning from God Almighty, Himself, to His girls.

There is an abundance of avenues which we can utilize for learning and expanding our knowledge base. Kent Nerburn addresses education and learning in his book Simple Truths. He says, "Formal schooling is one way of gaining education, and it should not be underestimated. School, if it is good, imparts knowledge and a context for understanding the world around us."

In today's society, we can take advantage of the many formal educational opportunities which exist in most communities to further increase our knowledge base despite our age. From college courses and internet courses to home study course with video and cassette lectures, the sky is the limit in our high tech information oriented world in which we live.

Nerburn distinguishes between knowledge and wisdom when he says, "Still, formal education will not inform your spirit and make you full. So, along with knowledge, you must seek wisdom. Knowledge is words, wisdom is silent." A great musician was once asked which was greater, knowledge or wisdom, and he replied, "Without knowledge, I could not play the violin. Without wisdom, I could not play the music."

Information is everywhere from the internet to the endless number of books that are being published daily. There are so many wonderful books for women, containing valuable, life altering information on millions of topics that are extremely important to women, as they strive to live their best life.

Many of us have stacks of books in our homes waiting to be read. I have learned to be very wise when buying books, so I only buy a book when I really feel drawn to it. I've asked God to direct me to the books that will impact my life the greatest; thus, helping me to make the most of my reading time.

Because we are an information based society, it is very important for us to remember what the most important source of knowledge is. It's our manufacturer's manual, of course. The knowledge base for all created beings must come from the Inspired Word of God, as it is our most valuable source for increasing our wisdom, knowledge and understanding.

The Bible is our main source of nourishment and all other modes of information are to be considered supplemental. Consider the physical body for a moment. Physicians and Registered Dieticians tell us that food should be our main source of nutrition, and vitamins should be used to supplement our daily food intake. This is the same approach we should take when feeding our minds, and my reason for focusing the contents of this chapter on the knowledge we gain from God through His Word.

The Bible is the only book which contains words from God Himself written for His creation. It contains words of love and encouragement, but it also includes words of caution, warning, and specific instructions concerning how to successfully live this life.

In Paul's second letter to his friend Timothy, he explains the purpose and process in which the Bible was written. Timothy 3:16 says, "*All scripture is inspired by God and profitable for teaching, for reproof, for correction, and for training in righteousness, that the man* (woman) *of God may be complete, equipped for every good work.*"

In 2 Peter 1:20–21, Peter explains, "*No prophesy recorded in the Scripture was ever thought up by the prophet himself. It was the Holy Spirit within these godly men who gave them true messages from God.*" God spoke to the prophets through His Holy Spirit to write the Bible.

The Word of God is described to be "as sharp as a two–edged sword." This is powerful knowledge; because it's God imparting His wisdom and knowledge to His girls.

The knowledge and understanding of God Himself, which we gain through spending time with Him and time studying His Word, is the channel God uses to grant us all good things in life. Throughout the Bible, we are told that we receive all things *through the knowledge of God.* Peter says, "Grace and peace be yours in abundance *through the knowledge of God* and of Jesus our Lord." He also says, "His divine power has given us everything we need for life and godliness *through our knowledge of Him* who called us by His own glory and goodness."

How can we seek knowledge? Proverbs 2:1–12 answers this question for us:

"MY SON (daughter), if you accept my words and store up my commands within you, turning your ear to wisdom and applying your heart to understanding, and if you call out for insight and cry aloud for understanding, and if you look for it as for silver and search for it as for hidden treasure, then you will understand the fear of the Lord and find the knowledge of God.
For the Lord gives wisdom, and from His mouth come knowledge and understanding. He holds victory in store for the upright, He is a shield to those whose walk is blameless, for He guards the course of the just and protects the way of His faithful ones. Then you will understand what is right and just and fair—every good path. For wisdom will enter your heart, and knowledge will be pleasant to your soul. Discretion will protect you, and understanding will guard you. Wisdom will save you from the ways of wicked men."

As we read God's Word, we can obtain book knowledge of God, but the key to gaining the knowledge and wisdom that brings eternal life is found only when we begin to know the Author of the Book Himself. *Knowledge of God* is not the same as *Knowing God*, although they both involve the Word of God. While knowledge of God can be acquired by studying the Bible, knowing God intimately results when a girl loves God and desires to actually *know* the God of the Bible.

Paul addresses this is 1 Corinthians 8:1–3, "*We know that we all possess knowledge. Knowledge puffs up, but love builds up. The man who thinks he knows something does not yet know as he ought to know. But the man* (woman) *who loves God is known by God.*"

In the early years of his life, Paul's incredible knowledge of the law of God puffed his head up, enlarging his own ego. However, years later after discovering love for God, the knowledge he had acquired in his brain spoke understanding and wisdom of God to his heart.

John 6:39–40 says, "*You diligently study the Scriptures because you think that by them you possess eternal life. These are the Scriptures that testify about me, yet you refuse to come to me to have life.*" We should not study the Word of God just to increase knowledge, but for the purpose of increasing our love for the Heavenly Author!

Success in every area of our lives is ours when we treasure God's words and direct our hearts and minds toward His knowledge and wisdom. This is not only exciting news, but it's information that can change a girls life forever. The knowledge that comes from God, brings wisdom, so it is much different than the knowledge that comes from just learning facts.

God's wisdom is so penetrating and all consuming when described so eloquently in James 3:17–18, "*But the wisdom that comes from heaven is first of all pure and full of quiet gentleness. Then, it is peace–loving and courteous. It allows discussion and is willing to yield to others; it is full of mercy and good deeds. Those who are peacemakers will plant seeds of peace and reap a harvest of goodness.*" What a loaded passage. I find myself drawn to pray this passage often. I ask God to work this heavenly wisdom in me.

Recently I heard someone say, "There is a strength in quietness." As I pondered this statement, I agreed. I thought of some of the people who I consider to be mentors in my life, and how I admire the way they demonstrate this trait. In the above passage, God is telling us that quietness is a sign of His divine wisdom.

This strikes a humorous cord inside of me, as I think of certain individuals who are very knowledgeable; and want to tell world just how smart they are. We all know someone who fills this bill. Dear Lord, please grant me your wisdom and knowledge, and keep me from this self–exalting display of knowledge.

I want to focus on some very important knowledge that God gives to us shortly after creating the first woman, Eve. This piece of information will impact the very life of every woman and her family. I want to preface the warning from God to His girls, by reviewing the choice God sets before every woman every day. Let's look at Deuteronomy 30:19–20:

"This day I call heaven and earth as witnesses against you that I have set before you life and death, blessings and curses. Now choose life, so that you and your children may live and that you may love the Lord your God, listen to His voice, and hold fast to Him. For the Lord is your life, and He will give you many years in the land He swore to give to your fathers, Abraham, Isaac and Jacob."

Every day, God sets before you and me a choice between a blessing and a curse. In this scripture, you'll notice that when a woman chooses the blessing, she is ultimately choosing life. If she chooses the curse, then she is ultimately choosing death.

This life and death affects the spirit and body of a women; the spiritual and physical dimension. The spirit is immediately affected by the choice, and the physical is eventually affected by the choice. When a woman chooses the blessing, her spirit immediately receives new life directly from the breath of God. If she chooses the curse, her spirit weakens, and will ultimately die, due to her choice to move away from God.

We choose the blessing or the curse by the way we choose to live each day. Everyday, we are choosing life or death, in our spirits and our bodies, whether we realize it or not. With every day comes change. With every day comes opportunity. The way we live our lives today makes us who we are tomorrow. What may seem like a small, insignificant decision may, in the spirit realm, mean life or death to your spirit.

The decision to read the Word of God or to spend a moment with God in prayer is a perfect example of woman clearly choosing life and blessing. Our daily activities reflect this important, life altering choice God sets before us each day. God wants to enlighten us of this fact, so we will choose wisely.

God's desire for us, His girls, is that we will choose life, so we will choose the blessings He has waiting for both us and our children. If we choose the blessing, God will grant life to us, and to our children. If we choose the curse, we are choosing death for ourselves, and our children. If we choose to obey God's Word, we are choosing the blessing. However, if we choose to live by our own knowledge instead of relying on God's Word, we are choosing curse for ourselves, and our children.

I want to go back to Genesis, and take a look at how Eve's choices impacted her life…and ultimately ours. She was God's very first daughter. Imagine the honor of being God's first created girl. She truly was God's girl. My first thought is, Gee what a lucky girl. However, my second thought is, *What an awesome responsibility*. She was God's first created woman. Her first born girl responsibilities and pressures make mine look minuscule.

In Genesis 2:15–17 God spoke His truth to Eve; or did He? I am, of course, not questioning the truth of God's words. What I am questioning is to whom God spoke this instruction of truth. It sounds like God gave this instruction to **Adam**, the designated 'spiritual leader' of the God's first family. Let's read it.

"And the Lord God commanded ***the man****, "You are free to eat from any tree in the garden; but you must not eat from the tree of the knowledge of good and evil, for when you eat of it you will surly die." The Lord God said, "It is not good for the man to be alone. I will make a helper suitable for him."*

I find this point to be very interesting, considering the numerous times, women and men, tend to blame Eve for the fall of mankind. She seems to always get the bad rap for being the first human to make the first choice on earth to disobey God.

In the above verses, could it possibly be that God is telling Adam to stay away from the tree of life. Eve hasn't even been created yet. This leads me to wonder how Adam might have relayed this message from God to his wife. Just a thought. Maybe if Adam had relayed the importance of obeying God's command to stay away from this tree in a more serious manor, maybe Eve would have made a better choice.

Could this be an example to us, how important the man is in a home. How important His spiritual leadership is to the life of his wife and their family. Just a thought to ponder, as we look at this choice that Eve made.

Adam must have relayed God's message to Eve concerning the tree of life, sometime after God created her, but before Satan lied to her. God told Adam, then Adam told Eve, to stay away from the tree of life. With this command, came a choice. A choice to obey God or disobey God. The gift of free will that God gave to his creation gave them this gift of choice.

Genesis 3:2–6 describes the day that Eve's choices brought a curse and spiritual death upon herself and her children. (This include us, girls.)

"The woman said to the serpent, "We may eat fruit from the trees in the garden, but God did say, 'You must not eat fruit from the tree that is in the middle of the garden, and you must not touch it, or you will die.'" "You will not surely die," the serpent said to the woman. "For God knows that when you eat of it your eyes will be opened, and you will be like God, knowing good and evil." When the woman saw that the fruit of the tree was good for food and pleasing to the eye, and also desirable for gaining wisdom, she took some and ate it. She also gave some to her husband, who was with her, and he at it."

Eve's first mistake was choosing to enter into a conversation with Satan. After Satan concocted this lie, he convincingly presented it to this beautiful created daughter of God. He fabricated a lie that really resembled the truth. He wanted it to fool her, so he knew it had to really look like the truth; and so he did just that.

Unfortunately, God's girl, Eve, fell into the trap that Satan set for her. As I studied this temptation plot against Eve, I asked myself the question, Why did Satan choose to tempt Eve instead of Adam? I believe that Satan knew that if he could get the woman in the family to fall, he would get the entire family. This would support the truth that the woman has such a powerful influence in the lives of those in her home.

I love the way T.D. Jakes explains 'why Satan sought Eve out to tempt her', in his book, Woman, Thou Art Loosed! He explains that Satan knows that women are God's chosen door to life. He says, "Women are the only legal entry into the earth realm. If it is to be born, it is going to be born of a woman."

Never before reading Jakes' book did I think about the act of giving birth in this way. I love it, though. New life only enters into this world one way; and that one way is through the body of a women. Wow! That's powerful. Jakes' goes on to say, "We each were chosen by God from the foundations of eternity, but in order to get us from eternity into time, God has only one method—that we be born of a woman."

God is so serious about this law of His creation that when He got ready to pour Himself into human flesh and live on this earth, He didn't violate His own method but rather, was born of a woman. It is this fact that puts women on the devil's hit list. The enemy is opposed to life. He deals in sickness, destruction, denial, devastation, thievery, and death. The enemy knows that if he is going to be successful, he must conquer the legal entryway to life. Woman, guard your doors and lock them. Slam your fence gates shut and chain them tight. Be very careful what you let come through you…what you let affect you…what you let influence you…and be careful what spirit you let loose in your mind….in your emotion…in your family."

This is a very serious warning which contains pertinent information for you and me concerning our own protection. It's like a 'Heads Up, Girls' warning. If this is new information for you, the fact that Satan is real and at work in our world, don't be alarmed.

It's a normal tendency to fear the unknown, especially when the unknown involves evil. For this very reason, God wants us to have knowledge of Satan. When we gain knowledge of him, we are empowered against him. God is not the author of fear. Satan is. He lives for the opportunity to magnify fear in our lives. Be courageous, my sister, in your knowledge. Not courageous because of your own strength, but courageous because of your Heavenly Father's strength.

Remember, you are God's girl. You are God's girl, and God has intended for you to receive all the knowledge that He has placed in His Word. If you believe that His Word is just that...His Word, then, trust Him. You have nothing to lose, and everything to gain. Trust Him to walk with you, and reveal His wisdom to you.

As you read the Bible, ask God to reveal the wisdom which it contains. I promise you, He will. As God imparts His wisdom and knowledge upon you, you will be empowered to live a better life; to make choices that involve life and blessings instead of death and curses.

When Eve chose to disobey her Heavenly Father, she was choosing death, and a curse for herself and her children; whether she realized it or not. In the third chapter of Genesis, we see Eve's choice to disobey God brought curses and spiritual death to her children, and all of mankind.

As a result of Eve's choice that day, all of mankind was separated from God by sin. Years past, and God sent Jesus, His only Son, to bear the sins of the world; our sins, you and I. Jesus literally took our place on the cross. He allowed His Blood to be shed instead of ours.

Someone had to pay this price for sinning against a Holy God, so God sent His only Son to die in our place. It's only by the Blood of Jesus, that we can once again be united to a Holy God; our Heavenly Father. Nothing we could possibly do in our lifetime could ever unite us with God.

The Bible tells us that it is only through the Blood of Jesus that we are given the opportunity to become adopted into God's family. When we ask God to forgive us of our sins, and invite Him into our hearts and lives, He forgives us and makes His home in us. That's why I love thinking of myself as God's girl.

The knowledge that God makes available to us in Genesis 3:14–15 is imperative for living a victorious life on this earth.

"So the Lord God said to the serpent, "Because *you have done this, 'Cursed are you above all the livestock and all the wild animals! You will crawl on your belly and you will eat dust all the days of your life. And* ***I will put enmity between you and the woman, and between your offspring and hers; he will crush your head and you will strike his heel.'***

When I read these two verses, I just about jumped out of my skin with excitement. Do you get it? Do you get God's warning to His girls? He's telling us in plain and simple words, "Hey, Girls. Heads Up! I'm going to clue you into to a truth that will serve as a reminder to 'be alert' and 'be on guard' all the days of your life. Satan is going to be your enemy and the enemy of your children for all your life. Be on guard because he will always be trying to strike your heel and the heel's of your children." After God gives us the 'heads up,' he reminds us that we, and our children, will have the power to crush the very head of Satan. Now, that's worth shouting about! I love that part! Yeah!!!!!!!!!! Let's all sing together, 'We've got the power...da...da... da...da...da....'

Okay. God has issued us a 'heads up' warning that we are to be aware that Satan's goal on earth is to bring us down. He's angry because of God's girl, Eve, he was cursed by God. Throughout the Bible, God also reminds us of our enmity with Satan, as we see how Satan attacked God's people in pathetic attempts to get them to disobey God. He wants us to believe that we don't need God. He wants death for us. God gives us this 'heads up' warning so that we will not be caught off guard.

This knowledge that Satan is 'after us' can cause fear to rise up in a girl. Well, don't you dare allow that to happen.

We serve God Almighty, my dear. When God told Satan that the woman and her children would crush his head, he meant what he said. God gave his girls the power to 'crush Satan to smithereens.' Yeah!!! Pardon me, while I shout with excitement, one more time!!! "You are going down, Satan. In the Name of Jesus, you are going down. Praise God!!"

Not only does God give us the 'Heads Up, Girls' to warn us about Satan's attacks on our lives, but God gives us the power over our enemy, the devil. In Revelations 12:11, He tells us exactly how we will overcome Satan. "*And they overcame him by the Blood of the Lamb, and by the Word of their testimony.*" We will overcome Satan by *asking God to cover our families with the Blood Jesus*, and by *praying the Word of God* for our families. We have no reason to fear evil, if we use the wisdom and knowledge which God has so generously given to us in His Word.

There is divine, supernatural power in the precious Blood of Jesus. This is exactly why the Blood of Jesus will protect us from Satan. Where the Blood of Jesus is, Satan cannot go. If you've never studied the protection of the Blood of Christ, you'll want to do this ASAP. Get a translation of the Bible that you understand, and also a Bible Commentary. Look up and read every scripture you can find on the Blood of Jesus.

You may want to read Billye Brim's book, The Blood and the Glory. It's a study on the Blood of Jesus, and it's full of powerful insights from the Bible. The knowledge of the Blood of Jesus will prove to be very important information to you and your family.

You can actually pray the Blood of Jesus around your home to protect you; and God will honor that prayer. It's powerful stuff, no doubt. Buckle up, girls...and go for it. Go after the knowledge and wisdom God has for you. Don't be afraid; this is God stuff. Your very life, and the lives of your family depend on it. You have nothing to lose when your counting on God, but everything in life to gain. Trust Him.

God has designed for us a spiritual armor to wear while walking through life. I understand that the thought of armor may sound a bit violent to some of you, but it is what God chose for us to wear. It's not fanatical. It's a God thing, and He instructs His girls to wear it everyday to ensure victorious living.

In Ephesians chapter six, Paul instructs the believers in Ephesus to *"be strong in the Lord and in His mighty power. Put on the full armor of God so that you can take your stand against the devil's schemes. For our struggle is not against flesh and blood, but against the rulers, against the authorities, against the powers of this dark world and against the spiritual forces of evil in the heavenly realms."*

God instructs us to wear the shoes of peace, the belt of truth, the breastplate of righteousness, the shield of faith, the sword of the spirit, and the helmet of salvation. This is a powerful suit of spiritual armor.

If we choose to overlook this protective suit of spiritual armor, we are choosing to disobey God. He has designed this unique protective suit for us, that will protect us from every arrow that the enemy will throw our way. Why, in the world, would we choose to refuse God's armor for any reason.

Let's think of it in terms of physical war. If there was a war in our country, and every single person had to be exposed to the actual fighting, what would you do to protect yourself?

Let's say, the government had designed special suits of armor that would completely protect you from every type of attack, including anthrax infection…would you say, "No thanks, it's too scary for me and my family. We don't believe God likes violence, so we'll just take our chances, and face the attacks without any protection."

I don't think so. Some women have shared with me that they have viewed the armor of God described in the Bible in this manor since childhood, but recently have come to appreciate the powerful gift they've found the armor of God to be in the lives of their families.

My oldest son was only three years old when he and I made a little 'Armor of God' sign to help him learn to pieces of God's armor. After I listed the six pieces of armor, L.B. cut out various pictures of articles of clothing from a magazine and glued them by each piece of armor they represented.

He carefully selected each picture beginning with a pair of sneakers to represent the shoes of peace. He chose a brown belt for the belt of truth, a jacket for the breastplate of righteousness, a ball glove for the shield of faith, a ball bat for the sword of the spirit and a baseball hat for the helmet of salvation.

We taped his little sign to the inside of our front door where we would stop as a family and pretend we were putting on our armor every morning. My son Blake learned to put on the armor of God the same way, and we still put on the armor as a family, as a reminder of the power that we have over Satan in our lives when we put on the character of Jesus by reading His Word and praying every day.

My thoughts go directly back to the Words of God found in Hosea 4:6, as He warns His people of the high price they will pay if they reject His knowledge. He says that, "*they will be destroyed by their lack of knowledge.*" Girls, let's obey our Heavenly Father, and take advantage of every nugget of knowledge and wisdom He will grant us through His Word, and the power of His Holy Spirit in us.

The only way that we can put on the armor is to stay in the Word of God, meditate on it daily. We must "*love the Lord with all your heart and with all your soul and with all your strength. These commandments that I give you today are to be upon your hearts. Impress them on your children. Talk about them when you sit at home and when you get up. Tie them as symbols on your hands and bind them on your foreheads. Write them on the doorframes of your houses and on your gates,*" Deuteronomy 6:5–9.

Not only did my parents teach my sisters and me to wear the armor of God as little girls, but they also prayed the promises of protection from the Bible for us. My mother has always prayed Psalms 91 for me, and because of her lifelong example, I now pray this powerful chapter of promises for my family too.

When my son Blake was only four years old, he and I were playing in our backyard one spring afternoon. I stepped into the house for a moment to use the restroom, which was in clear view of our back yard, when I heard my little guy urgently calling to me as he ran into the house. He was yelling, "Mom, there is a cobra in the back yard. There is a cobra in the back yard. Come quickly!"

Smiling at him, I patted his back and assured him that mommy would take care of the cobra, which I assumed was a harmless little black snake. As Blake and I walked into the back yard, I asked him to describe to me where he saw the snake. Using hand gestures, Blake described the snake as being over four feet in length and three inches in diameter.

He told me that he was on the swing when the cobra slithered and stopped directly under him, raising his head like he was going to bite Blake. At that point, Blake said he jumped off of the swing right over the snake's head, and ran to me in the house.

As I listened carefully to Blake, I still couldn't fathom a snake by that description wondering into our back yard, rearing it's head so close to my little guy.

As Blake and I scanned the backyard, there was no cobra to be found, until I saw out of the corner of my eye what looked like a deflated bicycle tire...a big deflated bicycle tire, and it was draped across our sand box. The longer I studied it, and the closer I got to it, I realized to surprise that it was indeed a four foot snake that was about three inches in diameter, and not a deflated bicycle tire.

I ran into my neighbor's front yard, where he was mowing his lawn, and I called to him asking him to come quickly and help us. After an extended struggle with an assortment of weapons, my nice neighbor, George, won the victory over the cobra in our back yard.

After killing the snake, we did have it identified as a poisonous water moccasin.

As I was sharing this story with my mother over the phone, she said, "Susie, this is a perfect example of God honoring our prayers from Psalms 91." Then, I realized exactly what scripture she was referring to...Psalms 91:11–14, "*For He will command His angels concerning you to guard you in all your ways; they will lift you up in their hands, so that you will not strike your foot against a stone. You will tread upon the lion and the cobra; you will trample the great lion and the serpent. 'Because he loves me,' says the Lord, 'I will rescue him; I will protect him, for he acknowledges my name.'*"

I knew at that very moment that God had honored my prayers, while keeping His promise to give his angels charge over us to keep us safe even in the presence of a cobra. Praise God! His Word is powerful, and when prayed by a woman for her loved ones becomes protection granted by a Holy God. The power of praying the Word of God is right at our fingertips, just waiting to be opened and explored.

I want to close this chapter with an excerpt from the Book of Proverbs. Throughout the Book of Proverbs, God gives us the gifts of His wisdom, His knowledge, His understanding, His discernment, and His Divine direction. He makes these priceless gifts available for all of His girls. Those who choose to read them will be empowered by God, to live a life, full and free, the way He planned for His girls to live.

In Proverbs 31:10–31, we find a beautiful example what a virtuous women resembles after a lifetime of God's working in her life. God didn't include this description of the Proverbs 31 woman in the Bible to intimidate His girls, making us feel as though we are failures if we fail achieve this standard of virtue, rather, he meant for it to be a beautiful example of what He wants to do in us if we will simply invite Him into our lives.

God's purpose for this passage is to encourage us, His girls, to allow Him to grow us and develop us into virtuous women. It isn't an instantaneous process, but when we give God permission to mold us according to His perfect plan, we will emerge as a woman who has the characteristics described in Proverbs 31.

I want to encourage you, before you read this beautiful passage, ask God to reveal to you the areas in which He wants you to grow. Be sensitive to His leading. He loves you, and wants the very best for you. He wants *His* best for you. As I began to ask God to help me apply this passage to my life, I translated it into my own words.

A Woman After God's Own Heart

A woman of this character is rare in our society.
This godly woman takes a firm Biblical stand on life issues...
and does not allow the world to influence her to compromise.
Her desire is to please God; not people. She's God's girl.
She doesn't measure her worth by the world's standards.
She is worth more than the rarest of rubies.

Her husband trusts her with his life.
He is confident in her in every way.
He considers himself to be blessed to be married to her.
She completes him in all ways.
She prays for her husband.
And he considers her a precious gift from God...
Not lacking in value in any area. Not perfect, but balanced.

She only brings good to her husband in all she says and does.
She is eager to work with her hands to care for her family,
helping them create healthy, balanced eating habits.
She provides nutritious foods for her family.
I'm sure this would include chocolate on occasion.

She is a good steward of her money. She makes wise financial decisions.
She is not a spend thrift. She is a wise shopper.
This means that she probably knows what a gallon of milk costs.
She is energetic in her work. She is a hard worker.
She is passionate about her work. She is motivated in her work.

Maybe she prays for her family as she cleans up after them... while scrubbing their toilets, for instance.

She rises early in the morning to prepare for her day.
Sometimes, she sleeps late.
She provides for those who help her...her servant girls.
I wonder if this means that God will send us lots of servant girls...a nanny, my very own personal chef, a full–time housekeeper maybe?
I won't hold my breath; but I won't limit God either.

She takes proper care of her physical body. She lives a physically active lifestyle that enables her to be conditioned to complete all of her tasks with ease.
She's not obsessed with her physical body. She has a healthy body image.
She is committed to the work that the Lord has called her to do. Because of her dedication to her God–given assignments, she works into the evening to complete her work.

She doesn't doubt that the Lord will supply all of her family's needs.
She demonstrates a strong faith in God and doesn't allow worry to consume her.
She is a giving, caring woman. She is sensitive to the needs of others.
Her daily activities demonstrate her kindness and concern for those around her.
When God places something on her heart, she acts immediately in obedience to Him.

She can sew items for her family and home.
Sewing buttons on a shirt, I'm sure would be considered sewing.
She makes her house a home by being creative.
Her loving personal touch makes her home a warm, safe haven for her family.
The atmosphere of her home is peaceful, even in the midst of family activity.
Her home reflects her love for her God and her family.

Guests are always welcome in her home.
She is not controlled by perfectionism and it's behaviors.

Her home is clean enough to be healthy, and dirty enough to be happy.
She is a tasteful dresser. The way she dresses never brings disgrace to God; instead, it exemplifies Christ.
She is strong in the Lord. She is not a wimpy, whiny woman, who needs to be treated like a china doll.
She is a seasoned woman of God. Her husband is not afraid to share details of life with her in fear that she might be too fragile to hear it.
She is a strong women, in spite of her life circumstances.

She doesn't fear the aging process. She is actually joyful in growing older.
She can even laugh as she grows older because she values the wisdom that a comes with age.
She is not lazy. She doesn't procrastinate or waste valuable time.
She makes wise use of the hours God has entrusted to her. She redeems her time wisely.

Her words are wise. They are words of kindness that lift up and heal.
They are words of Biblical, godly instruction.
She is very careful in her speech; never speaking ungodly words.
She doesn't gossip or vent even to her husband or her closest friends.
Her words bring health, encouragement and growth to those that hear them.
Her words draw others closer to Christ.
Her words and actions never bring disgrace to God's name.
She is not a complainer.
She always strives to look for the positive in life's situations.

She is an efficient family manager.
She manages her home in an organized manor.
She has a healthy balance between work and home.
She views her God–given responsibility to care for her husband and children seriously.
She understands the powerful influence she has in the lives of her family members.
Christ is her priority in life, followed by her love for her husband, then, her love for her children.
Because of her godly example and godly mothering, her children are proud that she is their mother. Yes, even the teenagers.

They tell others how wonderful and Christ–like she is.
Her children's friends love to visit.

Many women in the world may be viewed as noble, she is more valuable than all…because of her obedience to her God; because she fears Him and honors Him all the days of her life.
Reward her godliness and let her Christ–like example bring her God's favor and the admiration of other women.
Let her be respected and honored among all the people in her city.

God loves us so much that He has given us the gifts of His knowledge, His wisdom and His understanding. He's wrapped them in the most beautiful floral wrapping paper; and on top, He has placed the most beautiful rose of the palest of pink in all of His garden, delicately tied with a sheer white bow. All we have to do, is unwrap His gifts of love. When we do, our lives will never be the same. By His knowledge and wisdom, will we gain His perspective and better understand all of life's issues.

As we draw knowledge and wisdom from His Heavenly well, we will hear Him saying, "Heads Up, Girls" steering us safely through life. I can almost hear the Lord saying, "My precious girls, I love you. Hold on to My wisdom, and she will protect you; love her, and she will watch over you." With grateful hearts, His girls reply back to God with the words His heart yearns to hear, "Dear Precious Lord, We love you, too." Lord.

"You are special. God made you. His undeserved love makes you somebody!"

—Alma Kern, You Are Special

— 7 —

I Will Trust You!

I will say of the Lord, He is my refuge and my fortress; my God; in Him will I trust.
Psalm 91:2

Trust in the Lord with all your heart and lean not on your own understanding; in all your ways acknowledge him, and he will make your paths straight.
Proverbs 3:5–6

"*Do not let your hearts be troubled. Trust in God; trust also in Me.*"
John 14:1

Emotional wellness also involves developing healthy stress management skills. Life on earth involves stress, thus dealing with the stresses of daily life is a fact of life. Job + family + finances + deadlines + relationships + illness + car trouble + negative co–workers + household appliance trouble + bad drivers + spilled hot coffee = *stresssssssssssssss*.

The choices we make each day can decrease the amount of stress in our lives; however, it is virtually impossible to completely remove stress from our lives as long as we live in this world with other human beings. God uses struggles and storms to stretch and strengthen us. Learning to trust Him is the key to developing healthy stress management skills.

Stress is neutral. It's the way we choose to react to stressful situations that determines if the stress becomes negative or positive. If I choose to respond to stress in a positive way, I will become a better, more positive person.

On the other hand, when I choose to respond negatively too stress, I become a more bitter, more negative person. A positive response to stress will increase my emotional strength, whereas, a negative response will weaken my emotional state.

Consider the physical stress of a hand weight as an example of the importance of our reaction to emotional stress. Pretend you have a five pound hand weight in your hand. The five or ten pound weight represents the stress being applied to the bicep muscle when doing a bicep curl.

If you control the weight while performing a slow, controlled bicep curl, then the stress applied to the muscle during the exercise will have a positive affect on the muscle. The muscle will become stronger as a direct result of controlling the movement while using the weight.

If the exercise is performed in an uncontrolled manor, the stress of the weight would most likely have a negative affect on the body, increasing your risk for injury. Whether you're dealing with physical stress, or emotional stress, our response, to a large degree, determines it's affect on your life.

You may not always be able to alter your circumstances to minimize stress in your life, but you do have control when it comes to choosing your reaction to stress. Secure a plan of action to implement immediately when you know that you may face a particular stressful situation repeatedly. Don't react; just act. Proverbs 27:12 says:

A sensible man (woman) watches for problems ahead and prepares to meet them. The simpleton never looks, and suffers the consequences.

Consider this example. During the winter months, the population in my town greatly increases; thus, traffic on the main streets is greatly increased. I have two choices. Either I can choose an alternate route to use during these months, or I can change my attitude.

Choosing to change my attitude means I will need to view this time in the car as an opportunity to relax, rather than an inconvenience. I must expect the traffic, and pre–plan for this additional time in the car. I will need to allow for more driving time, and pack cassettes, CD's, books, and any other items that may help me make the most of this additional time in my car.

Before you act, ask yourself three questions. Will this matter in one year? Will it matter in ten years? Will this matter in 10,000 years? Very few things will matter in one year. Fewer things will matter in 10 years. Only one thing will matter in 10,000 years, and that's where you spend eternity. When we put things into a healthy perspective, it's much easier to recognize what's not worth sweating.

I used to become upset over petty things like forgetting my earrings, discovering a run in my pantyhose, or spilling my coffee in the car. These little things could ruin my mood and sometimes put a damper on my entire day. Now, looking back, I think, "How silly of me to allow something so little to steal a whole day from my life.

Becoming a mother has greatly impacted my stress management skills. These days, when I leave the house, I'm just thankful to be fully dressed and to have my car keys in my hand.

A couple of Sundays ago, a friend noticed a hole in my pantyhose and brought it to my attention. I calmly positioned the hole towards the inside of my leg and didn't spend another minute worrying about it! I am making progress in my quest to stop sweating the small stuff in my life. I have learned that a hole in my pantyhose won't matter at all if I choose to minimize it's importance.

I am a fan of Richard Carlson's "Don't Sweat the Small Stuff" books. 'Don't sweat the small stuff' is easy to say, but it takes a lot of commitment, concentrated effort, and discipline to really live it.

Perhaps Paul was referring to 'small stuff' when he wrote Philippians 4:4–7, "*Rejoice in the Lord always; again I will say, rejoice. Let all men know your forbearance. The Lord is at hand. Have no anxiety about anything, but in everything by prayer and supplication with thanksgiving let your requests be made known to God. And the peace of God, which passes all understanding, will keep your hearts and your minds in Christ Jesus.*"

This scripture doesn't mean that we won't experience fear and anxiety in our lives; it simply tells us that we are not to accept fear and worry as a way of life.

Trust and worry are two things that are utterly incompatible even more so than oil and water. When you have placed your life, your body, mind, spirit and soul in the Divine hands of the Almighty God, and you continue to spend hours on anxious thoughts and worrisome questionings about a certain matter, can you really call it trust?

When a believer really trusts anything, she ceases to worry about the thing she has entrusted to God. And when she worries, it is plainly and simply that she does not trust God for the matter.

When we test ourselves by this rule, we will find painful but clarified truth of how little real trust in God there is in the lives of so many of us God's girls. We've all experienced moments when fear attempts to overtake us, and this is the exact moment that we are to roll the fearful worrisome thought over into God's hands and refuse to wear the heavy coat of fear and worry with which Satan wants to burden us.

According to Billy Graham, "Anxiety is the natural result when our hopes are centered on anything short of God and His will for us." The key to trusting God is to stay centered on Christ so that when fear comes knocking at our door, we will, by the supernatural power of God, look right through it and see God holding our entire existence in His hands. Praise His Holy Name!

Matthew 14:28–29 says, "*And Peter answered Him and said, 'Lord, if it be thou, bid me come unto thee on the water. And He said, 'Come.'" When Peter first stepped out of the boat and onto the water, he didn't look at the storm, but he fixed his eyes upon Jesus.*

Suddenly, when he looked away from the Lord, he glanced at the waves beating about him and he began to sink. He found himself sinking and in danger of drowning; not because he left the boat not because he was in the storm, but because he took his eyes off of the Lord.

The moment Peter took his eyes off of Christ, he was overcome by doubt and fear. Peter may have been distracted by the sounds of his fellow believers calling to him in disbelief and fear from the boat. Can you imagine a fellow believer distracting you from focusing on God? It happens.

Can you recall a time when you allowed yourself to focus your attention and energies on the storm of a situation, or people around you, instead of God? I sure can. We must not focus on the storms around us; which may be people, illness, personalities, circumstances, attitudes, opinions, etc. Our eyes must be focused on Christ.

When the storms are raging about us, when things seem darkest, we can choose either to focus on the waves of our circumstances and sink or we can choose to focus on God and trust Him to help us rise above the waves and walk victoriously. He has the power to quiet the storms of our hearts, bringing calmness, quiet, peace, and rest.

Several years ago, I had a dream. I was sitting at a small square table across from Jesus. My right hand was gently resting in the palm of His right hand. It was a warm, smooth hand. I could feel the power of God all around me and flowing through me. His presence completely engulfed me.

The very air around me was saturated with His pure and potent sweetness, quietness, gentleness and loving–kindness towards me. There was a crowd of people standing around us watching, much like an arm wrestling match. In the middle of this table sat a sharp round saw–type machine. The saw was moving very fast, and it was easy to see that it would hurt very much if my skin touched the blade.

The Lord looked at me and calmly and lovingly said, "Trust Me. Let Me hold your hand and just trust Me, My daughter." I was a little nervous because that machine looked like it could cause some very painful damage, but the Lord's hand seemed to sooth me, and my fear simply faded away.

I heard His voice again say, "Do not be afraid. Trust me." After flinching once or twice, I focused my eyes only on my Lord's precious eyes.

As everyone watched in disbelief, my hand touched the sharp wheel and to their surprise, I felt nothing. There was no blood or even the tiniest of cuts. This was a true miracle.

When I woke up, I knew immediately what I was to learn from this dream. God just wanted to remind me that if I focus on Him, He will hold my hand and walk me safely through every circumstance life will bring. This is His promise to each of us. We're His girls, remember. Almighty God can and will defy all the laws of man. He will make full proof of His Divine Power and defy the natural with His supernatural power in our lives, if we will only trust Him!

We are warned numerous times in the Bible to keep our eyes focused directly on Christ.

Joshua 1:7–8 says
Be strong and very courageous. Be careful to obey all the law my servant Moses gave you; ***do not turn from it to the right or to the left,*** *that you may be successful wherever you go. Do not let this Book of the Law depart from your mouth; meditate on it day and night, so that you may be careful to do everything in it. Then you will be prosperous and successful."*

Deuteronomy 5:32–33 says: *"So be careful to do what the Lord your God has commanded you;* ***do not turn aside to the right or to the left.*** *Walk in all the way that the Lord your God has commanded you, so that you may live and prosper and prolong your days in the land that you will possess.*

Psalms 28:11 says:
The Lord will give strength unto His people; the Lord will bless His people with peace.

The Lord allows the storms of life so that we may learn necessary lessons and so that He may give us opportunities to be brought into a closer walk with Him. Sometimes our disobedience of Him may lead us into a storm.

He has promised us an unlimited supply of strength, equal to our needs. It comes from waiting upon the Lord. "*They that wait upon the Lord shall renew their strength. They will soar on wings like eagles; they will run and not grow weary, they will walk and not be faint.*"

As a storm approaches, the eagle is the only bird that will not seek shelter. She faces the storm with her wings spread allowing the wind to carry her higher. In the same way the strength of the Lord enables us to bear the pressures of the storms in our lives carrying us to higher spiritual heights. The peace of God keeps the disturbing elements of the outer storm from penetrating our inner being.

There are many situations and circumstances in this life that we will never understand. We may never understand why bad things happen to good people; or why bad things happen to God's people.

The scripture that brings insight to this fact is found in Isaiah 55:8–9, "*For my thoughts are not your thoughts, neither are your ways my ways, sayeth the Lord. For as the heavens are higher than the earth, so are my ways higher than the earth, so are my ways higher than your ways, and my thoughts than your thoughts.*"

There are many things in our lifetime that we will never understand. That is why God is God, and we are not. We must learn to rest in the assurance that He will keep His promise to "work everything for the good for us because we love Him and live for Him," Romans 8:28.

I am learning to 'trust Him' in the midst of every situation of life. God commands us repeatedly not to fear or worry, but to trust in Him. There is freedom from fear and worry when we truly trust God!

The following story exemplifies the power in trusting God to work everything in our lives out for our good, even when we don't understand them:

Two Traveling Angels

Two traveling angels stopped to spend the night in the home of a wealthy family.

The family was rude, and refused to let the angels stay in the mansion's guest room.

Instead, the angels were given a small space in the cold basement.

As they made their bed on the hard floor, the older angel saw a hole in the wall and repaired it.

When the younger angel asked why, the older angel replied, "Things aren't always what they seem."

The next night the pair came to rest at the house of a very poor, but very hospitable farmer and his wife.

After sharing what little food the couple had, they let the angels sleep in their bed so they could have a good night's rest.

When the sun came up the next morning, the angels found the farmer and his wife in tears. Their only cow, whose milk had been their sole income, lay dead in the field. The younger angel was infuriated. He asked the older angel, "How could you have let this happen? The first man had everything, yet you helped him!" he shouted. "The second family had little, but was willing to share everything, and you let their cow die."

"Things aren't always what they seem," the older angel replied.

"When we stayed in the basement of the mansion, I noticed there was gold stored in that hole in the wall.

As the owner was so obsessed with wealth, and unwilling share his good fortune, I sealed the wall so she wouldn't find it.

Then last night, as we slept in the farmers bed, the Angel of Death came for his wife.

I gave him the cow instead. So you see, things aren't always what they seem."

Sometimes that is exactly what happens when it seems that things don't turn out the way they should. If you will just have faith and trust in God, you will find that every outcome is always to your advantage.

You might not know it until some time later...

—*Anonymous*

My family and I had spent spring break this past year at Marco Island. During the week, I felt drawn to study the book of Job, and I must share with you the powerful insights that God poured into me that week concerning His all encompassing power in our lives.

In Job 1:8–12, we hear God commending His faithful servant, Job, then Satan basically asks God to permit him to pass through the hedge of protection God had placed around Job. I love the fact that Satan can actually see the hedge of protection that we have asked God to place around our families and our homes.

Satan arrogantly declares to God that Job would curse his God if he lost all of his possessions. And what was God's response? He believed so completely in the strong, unwavering faith of His servant that He did permit Satan to test Job. But here's the good part. He placed a Divine limitation on Satan by telling him that he was not to touch Job, only his possessions.

After Satan killed all of Job's family and destroyed all of his possessions, Job remained faithful. He trusted His God, in spite of the great loss he had suffered. In Job 1:22 it says, *"In all this, Job did not sin by charging God with wrongdoing."* So many times when hard times hit, people blame God right away. Satan loves to hear God's people cursing their God for something that Satan did himself.

Satan went back to God and asked if he could attack Job's physical body. He told God that Job would surely curse God if his physical health were taken away.

Once again, God believed in Job's faith in Him. God gave the devil permission to attack Job's body, with the limitation of sparing his life. After all of the awful attacks Satan brought upon Job, Job stood firm. Job never cursed His God.

In short, God had to authorize and actually give Satan permission to enter into the hedge of protection to attack Job; the hedge of protection which God Himself had placed around His servant Job.

We probably all know how the story of Job ends. God revealed Himself to Job in a new way and restored Job ten fold. God turned what Satan meant for bad into good for Job, and He promises to do the same thing for us, if we will only 'Trust Him in ALL things.'

As I pondered the life of Job, God began to give me a better understanding of the hedge of protection He places around us, our families, and our belongings. Not only does He place the hedge, but more importantly, He controls the opening of the hedge. In a sense, God is the divine gate keeper of our lives.

God is not only protecting me with the hedge, but He grows me by opening the hedge and permitting Satan to enter into my life and test me by using whatever pathetic little tactics he can muster up.

When we realize that God actually opens the hedge that is meant to protect us from harm, and allows the enemy to walk right through it to attack us in some way, it can make the hairs stand up on our skin, but only for a brief moment until God imparts His wisdom and understanding to us concerning this awesome principle of hedge regulation.

What Satan sees as an opportunity to harm us or separate us from God, God uses as an opportunity to strengthen, grow and empower us. Yes! I love that! God, in His wisdom and supernatural power, transforms what Satan means to harm us into a beautiful instrument that strengthens, grows and empowers us to be the girls, His girls, that He has predestined us to be. Praise God! Thank You, Jesus!!

This is a perfect example of God's promise to us to work all things in our lives for the good. This is exactly what He does when He permits the enemy to pass through our hedges and into our lives.

God not only controls Satan's activity in our lives by placing a limitation on what he can do while he's in there, but God only issues him a temporary/short stay pass, that is unless by our own actions we have opened the hedge, allowing Satan to enter into our lives.

God holds the Divine key to the hedge He builds around us, but since it's a gift, He also gives us a key to open the hedge from the inside. The choices we make in life will either reinforce the hedge and invite the power of God in our lives, or create openings in the hedge for the enemy to enter into our lives. Daily choices to follow God's instruction manual for our lives, or our own plan will determine how we reinforce the hedge from the inside. Now, that's something to ponder.

One evening during our stay at the beach that week, as my ten year old son L.B. and I were playing catch, I began to share with him about my new understanding of Job and the hedge of protection.

We discussed how his recent broken arm was a perfect example of how I believe God had permitted the enemy to enter our lives and bring harm, but the really cool part was that God limited him to just a broken arm. God never brings harm to us, but He does have to give His permission for everything that enters into our lives.

L.B. seemed to understand right away since we, as a rule, approach the 'not so good' things that come into our lives by simply trusting that God will work them for our good even if we never see the good. God's so much bigger and wiser than we are, so we just trust Him.

Something else that God revealed to me while I was studying Job was the fact that although Job never cursed God, he did grumble a bit and questioned God. He spoke words that were not necessary to be spoken.

If Job did this, how much easier will it be for us to do it. Job was God's faithful servant. As I read about all of the horrible attacks on Job's family, his possessions, and his own life, I asked God to help me to learn to just say "I trust you" and nothing more. No matter what enters into my life, I want to focus on my God and simply say, "I will trust You, O Lord."

Sometimes I picture myself like a little girl who doesn't want to hear what someone is saying to her, so she covers her ears and closes her eyes and begins to sing very loudly, "La, lala, lala, lala, I can't hear you" in an attempt to drowned out the words that are being spoken to her.

When my son Blake was four years old, I bought him Karyn Henley's cassette entitled, Down By The Station, God Made Me To Do What's Right! On the tape, my favorite song is called "No, No, No."

Karyn talks about how Satan really wants us to make choices that will lead us further away from God and His plan for us, and that we just need to scream in his ears, making it perfectly clear that we are aware of his attempts to trick us and that we are going to follow Jesus, no matter what.

The chorus goes something like this, "No, No, No! In Jesus Name, No! I'm gonna follow Jesus, so NO, NO, NO!!!" This is exactly what I picture myself singing when I cover my ears and declare my trust in God. When I feel a wave of fear or a thought of worry coming my way, I just cover my spiritual ears and sing, "No, No, No! In Jesus Name, No! I'm gonna trust in Jesus, so No, No, No!!!

I must admit, as I tried to sympathize with Job, I did hope God would keep those awful attacks that Job endured out of my hedge and off of my body.

I had this strange feeling that Satan would be wanting to make his slimy self known to me following this powerful insight into God's Almighty Hand controlling the hedge that protects me, because I've learned that he most often attacks after God has revealed Himself to us in a newer way.

After I came home from the beach, I noticed I had a rash. The rash quickly became so severe that I was itching uncontrollably, as it spread to most of my body except my face. You can only imagine my expression, when the First Care Emergency Unit doctor described my condition as, 'tiny little worms under your skin.'

In disbelief, I said," You have got to be kidding me. I have worms wiggling under my skin." He assured me that, yes, I did have swimmers itch, and it is caused by little worm–like mites under the skin. They fill up and fester, and then they will scab up and go away.

As I sat there on that hospital table, waiting for the doctor to return with more information concerning my condition, I knew that the meaning of this worms–under–the–skin issue was much more than simply a physical skin problem.

In my heart, I knew that it was no coincidence that God had led me to these new truths found in the book of Job, and then permitted me to wake up with this festering skin problem described as worms under my skin. No, He didn't cause the skin problem, but He did have to give Satan permission to enter my hedge of protection to curse me with it.

As I was inspecting the bubbling red skin all over my body, realizing that it was not on my face, I knew that this was a divine limitation on Satan's activity while in the hedge of my life. Yes. God permitted Satan to enter into my hedge and inflict this skin condition, keeping it from my face, all the while knowing what a powerful impact this would have on my life, to be inflicted with a similar skin condition that I just studied in Job. And it did.

I could hardly wait to get home to grab my Bible, and turn to the book of Job. I just knew that Job had worms under his skin. Sure enough, in the seventh chapter, verse five, it said, "*My body is clothed with worms and scabs, my skin is broken and festering.*"

"Yes!" I thought, "I have a condition that's similar to what Job endured." As crazy and absurd as it may sound, I was so excited to share in this same curse. I knew that my God was in control. I knew that He was going to work good things from 'worms under my skin.'

I imagined hearing God warn Satan, "You may infect the skin on her entire body with this same wormy rash that you put on Job, but you may not touch her face or her organs." What a wonderful thought. Actually, I found it to be kind of humorous to a point.

Just in case you're wondering, many good things did come from my experience with what I now refer to as, 'the worms of Job' experience. God is faithful. After gaining a better understanding of God's power and wisdom to open and close the hedge of protection, I have a renewed respect for God and a healthy fear of Him. I trust God to work everything for my good.

I'm learning to look for the blessing of God's divine limitation on the enemy in every situation in life, instead of the curse, attack, or undesirable issue itself.

When L.B. broke his arm playing football, my first response was, "You've got to be kidding me! We leave for vacation tomorrow morning." My second response was to thank God that it wasn't his collar bone or neck.

Recently, my friend, Sally, spilled her coffee on her white cotton t–shirt just as we were arriving at Cypress Gardens for an all–day field trip. When I saw her, her shirt was all wet from where she washed the coffee out in the restroom. I hugged her and said, "The stains came out. That's a great thing."

A couple of days later, I saw Sally in the school parking lot. She jumped out of her van and waved for me to come over. She pointed to the coffee that she had just spilled all over her van seat and floor. I smiled, then hugged her and said, "Thank God it went in the floor and not on you."

God promises us that we will find a blessing and limitation in every situation. I have found that the more I am tuned in to God, the quicker I see the blessings in the situations in my life. Learn to look for the blessing and limitation in every circumstance.

The only true way to stop sweating the small stuff and the big stuff is to truly understand who controls ALL of the stuff of life.

On my bathroom wall, I have a print of a young girl with long blonde hair. She's swinging care–free in a wooden swing. The wooden swing is attached to two ropes. The two ropes are held in the hands of this little girl's great big God. This is how I see myself when I trust God.

The scripture at the bottom of this print is Proverbs 3:5–6, "*Trust in the Lord with all your heart and lean not on your own understanding; in all your ways acknowledge Him, and He will make your paths straight.*"

We can find strength and comfort in knowing that nothing can take place in our lives unless God personally authorizes it. In the midst of every storm, every circumstance, focus on God and boldly declare, "I WILL TRUST YOU, LORD! No matter what happens, I WILL TRUST YOU, LORD!!!"

Wherever we are today, we are there, not by chance, but by choice. God's choice! Trust in Him!

—*Millie Stamm, author*

— 8 —

He Will Make A Way

I waited patiently for the Lord; and He inclined to me, and heard my cry. He also brought me up out of a horrible pit, out of the miry clay, and set my feet upon a rock, and established my steps. He has put a new song in my mouth—praise to our God; many will see it and fear, and will trust in the Lord.
Psalm 40:1–3

We are pressed on every side by troubles, but not crushed and broken. We are perplexed because we don't give up and quit. God never abandons us. We get knocked down, but He helps us up and to keep going.
2 Corinthians 4:7–10

He restores my soul; He leads me in the paths of righteousness for His name's sake.
Psalm 23:3

Emotional wellness is a desire that all women share. As reports of depression and anxiety among women have escalated over the past ten years, more women are seeking help from psychologist and psychiatrists than ever before. There are many factors that have contributed to the rise of depression and anxiety in women.

As we listen to the media, our hearts my become fearful due to the state of the affairs of our world. Women worry about business, finances, world conditions, families, health, marriage, and the uncertainty of the future, while sometimes being predisposed to depression and anxiety. Many women never share their experiences with depression and anxiety; therefore, they never receive the help they need to overcome it.

Depression and anxiety are real. Whether you have been diagnosed with clinical depression or anxiety disorder or experience fear and worry on a daily basis, your quest for emotional and mental health should always begin by seeking God's guidance through prayer and His Word.

I am not discounting the help that we can receive by meeting with a Christian counselor or therapist because God has called men and women to serve Him by helping others deal with depression, anxiety and other emotional and mental disorders. I'm simply stating that before we act upon any crisis that arises into our lives, we should obey God by go directly to God in prayer and to His Word.

During this past year, my son, L.B., developed a fear of being hit and possibly killed by a fast pitched baseball. This fear was consuming our little nine year old to the point that he would actually 'freak out' at the thought of his upcoming games, while refusing to get in the batter's box during some of his games.

This meant that his team would have to take an automatic out, which was not a good thing. L.B. would have major 'melt downs' crying and crying, declaring, "I hate baseball, and I want to quit." You must understand that L.B. loves baseball, and this fear that had taken residence in him was literally stealing his love for the game. This fear soon began to overshadow ever waking hour of his days even affecting his school work.

Following L.B.'s most severe 'melt down' episode, my husband and I were determined to do whatever it took to help our son overcome this fear. Several people advised us to get him to a therapist as soon as possible to be treated for his anxiety problem; however, as Brad and I began to pray and consider our game plan for L.B.'s treatment, I felt certain that we were not to go directly into therapy. I just knew that we were to wait on God and not rush off in a panic to seek out a counselor just to find a solution.

I sensed a seriousness in relation to the importance of handling this crisis the right way; God's way, and I felt like we would be putting the cart before the horse, if we had bi–passed the Word of God and gone directly to a therapist. I knew in my heart of hearts that we were to go to God's Word first, and then, God would lead us to a Christian therapist if that was the tool He would use to help L.B. win this battle over fear.

In Galatians 1:15–17, Paul describes how following his eye–opening encounter with God, which led to his conversion, he *"did not consult any man, nor did he go up to Jerusalem to see those apostles before he was, but he went immediately into Arabia..."* Paul recognized that at this moment he was to be alone with God and seek Him only, and later would be the appropriate time to go to Jerusalem to speak with the other apostles.

When her child is experiencing pain, a parent will resort to just about anything to help him. As Brad and I discussed our options, he said, "Sue, if L.B. had a brain tumor wouldn't we take him to see a doctor right away."

My natural response was, "The first thing I would do would be to drop to my knees and literally *"pour out my heart like water before the Lord...for the life of my son,"* as we are instructed to do in Lamentations

2:19. Seeking direction from Word of God would be my next step, followed by seeking godly counsel, as the Bible advises Christians to do.

There's a big difference in seeking the counsel of one or two individuals that God places on your heart, and talking with everyone you come into contact with about your problem. Too many opinions can often lead to confusion, and the Bible tells us that Satan is the author of confusion.

After a time in prayer and reading the Word, I would focus all of my energies on being still while waiting for God to lead me down the best path to treat L.B.'s physical condition, trusting Him to direct us to the physicians that would help our son."

I think of Anita Corrine Donihue, co–author of the devotional, A Gentle Spirit, who asked God to lead her to people who could help her deal with her depression. She prayed:

> I realize I need Your help more than ever.
> Life is too tough for me to handle.
> Lead me to people who can help.
> Open my mind to ways for me to overcome this terrible depression. I know You watch over me and will help me through this.

Anita began her search for help and recovery by seeking God, trusting in Him alone to direct her on the path to recovery, leading her to those individuals who He would use to help her recover from her depression.

After asking God for guidance, Brad and I enlisted our closest friends and family into the prayer team for L.B.'s victory over this fear. As I began to pray about L.B.'s fear, I realized that God was using this situation to teach us how we were to approach every issue that would arise in our family. This revelation was exciting to me because I knew God was going to take this issue, and multiply the good that would come from it. I began to thank Him, in advance, for His direction and for L.B.'s healing.

God led me to the following three scriptures to pray for L.B.

> *"L.B. can do all things through Christ who strengthens him."*
> Philippians 4:13

> *"Fear not, L.B., for I am with you; be not dismayed; for I am thy God; I will strengthen you; yes, I will help you; yes, I will uphold you with the right hand of my righteousness."*
> Isaiah 41:10

"I will give My angels charge over you, L.B., to keep you safe in all your ways."
Psalm 91:11

"L.B. don't worry about anything; instead, pray about everything; tell God your needs and don't forget to thank Him for His answers. If you do this, L.B., you will experience God's peace, which is far more wonderful than the human mind can understand. His peace will keep your thoughts and your hearts quiet and at rest as you trust in Christ Jesus."
Philippians 4:6–7

I'll never forget the first time L.B. read Isaiah 41:10 written with his name in it, hanging on his bedroom door. His peaceful smile spoke volumes to my heart, and I could feel him saying, "Thanks, Mom, for reminding me that God loves me, and He will protect me." They still hang in his bedroom, and I know they continue to bring him comfort because he has told me so.

We did take L.B. to see a counselor, who deals with fears such as L.B.'s, and the visit seemed to serve as a time for L.B. to simply relax and talk openly with another person about his fear. Although we didn't note any great impact from this visit, I do believe it was a part of L.B.'s healing process.

Later that same week, while jogging with my close friend, Karen, she shared with me that she watched her brothers go through similar fears concerning baseball. She encouraged, "Sue, you and Brad are doing a great job as godly parents, and I know you two, your boys, and the Lord will team up and get through this together; victoriously. You need to get a teenage baseball player to pitch some fast balls to L.B. over and over and over until L.B. faces his fear, and feels confident behind the plate again."

Her words were so simple, but so enlightening. I believe God used her anointed words to guide me to the next step in this process.

I immediately knew that I was to call Brett Trudeau, the thirteen year old son of a close friend of mine, who was known for his fast pitch balls. Brad, Brett and L.B. spent over two hours together at the baseball field that day. Brett pitched fast balls to L.B., and shared a similar baseball fear that he had to deal with when he was 8 years old.

This helped put L.B. on his way to overcoming this fear as he became more confident and less fearful with each game he played. This battle in his mind was being aggressively fought and soon to be won. To God Be All The Glory For The Things He Hath Done!!!!

L.B. continues to tap home plate in the form of the cross when stepping into the batter's box, which serves as a reminder that His God is able to handle everything that may come his way in life, while promising to *"work everything for the good for him because he loves Him and lives for Him."* This experience, which as an opportunity for our family to establish our game plan for handling issues that arise throughout the course of life; **PRAY** to God, **READ** the Word, **WAIT** to hear for direction from God, and **WALK** one step at a time as God leads.

This is the exact procedure that Brad and I followed two years later when L.B. broke his wrist while playing football in the backyard, so now we know the Biblical procedure which we are to follow when responding to any unexpected issue or obstacle in life whether it be emotional, mental or physical.

Several years ago, I began to wake up in the middle of the night with night sweats. I knew my hormones were changing, but I never expected the bouts of night anxiety that I was going to face.

During this time, I would allow my mind to run wild. I would replay everything that I had said or done during the day before, and just scrutinize myself. I'd feel like such a bad person. If I had raised my voice to my son, I'd feel like I had failed as a mother.

If my family didn't like the dinner I had prepared, I had failed them as the family nutritionist. I was in turmoil in my mind. I would think of every area of my life in which I was failing my family or my God, and beg Him to help me do better. Needless to say, these sleepless nights were awful.

During a four month period, I spent three out of seven nights each week, awake torturing myself for not doing better the day before. I began to dread going to bed each night in fear of another sleepless night full of my own self–inflicted interrogations.

Brad began to tell me that I was just too hard on myself. "Well, of course," I thought, "He never takes anything serious enough, and he never spends enough time regretting things he has wrongfully said or done." I know my reaction to Brad's advice sounds harsh. Let me explain.

Brad is the third born of three boys, and I am the first born of three girls. We couldn't be farther apart in birth order or personality types. I am the typical first born, and my dear, sweet Brad is the typical third born. I'm the serious, mature one, and he is Mr. Fun, with not a care in the world. I have to admit, many times, I considered his light–hearted, carefree approach to life, as immature and irresponsible.

We've always had this little joke between us concerning our birth order differences. He would ask me to "Lighten Up, Francis." (You know the old saying that Jackie Gleeson used to say to his wife.) My reply to this request would always be, "I'll lighten up, If You'll Grow Up." The truth of the matter was, God was going to use me to help Brad tighten up a little; and, as hard as it was for me to conceive, God was going to use Brad to help me lighten up, a lot.

During this period in my life, I began to admire my husband for his carefree attitude. The more I knew him, the more God began to show me the freedom in which Brad existed. Freedom from his own condemnation.

When Brad would make a 'bad call' or say something he shouldn't have said, he'd simply admit his mistake, ask forgiveness, accept forgiveness, and move on. It took me a long time to understand that Brad wasn't oblivious to his mistakes, he just would deal with them, and let them go.

God is so good. He knew that my high intensity first child traits would take more than just one 'third child' to help me learn to chill out. Believe it or not, my very best friend is a third child too. She and Brad are so similar in nature, but of course, I'm not as critical of Becky. Why is that? She's my girl friend, not my husband. Isn't that interesting?

Looking back, I now see how God began to use these two people in my life. Slowly and gently, He began to show me that there was freedom in letting go of guilt. I didn't need to punish myself over and over and over. He wasn't, so why should I?

My early morning anxiety attacks had been going on for about four months. One morning, I awoke as usual, at about 4:00 am. When my eyes opened instead of laying there, tossing and turning, I decided to get up. I could feel the fear of the hours of anxiety coming, but this time would be different.

As I walked through our home, I began to pray. I began to thank God for His many blessings in my life. My prayer of thanksgiving turned into praise. Guess what happens when we praise God. The Bible says that "*God inhabits the praises of His people*." God moved into my living room that morning, and began to make sense of my anxiety.

I remembered that God was in control of everything in my life. He had to authorize everything before it could enter into my life. If He did authorize these anxiety attacks, then, He promises to make them work for my good. "Yes!" I thought, "Yes! That's just what He's going to do. My God is going to work good in my life from this series of sleepless nights. As I began to praise God, for reminding me of this powerful truth, I began to fell a surge of strength and courage deep within my spirit.

God never brings bad things into our lives, but He does allow Satan to test us. He allowed Satan to test his faithful servant Job; and He worked it all for Job's good. He will do the same for us.

God is the author of all good, and Satan is the author of all bad. Hello, Susan. How could I have allowed my mind to run away with all of these condemning thoughts for all of these nights, and not recognize the work of the enemy in my life.

Realizing the author of these anxiety attacks, I remembered Revelation 12:11 and proclaimed in out loud. "*They will overcome Satan by the Blood of the Lamb, and by the Word of their testimony.*" I took authority over Satan with my words. I boldly said, "I bind you Satan in the name of Jesus Christ. I bind you in my life and in my mind. I apply the Blood of Jesus over my mind and my thoughts. You have no power where the Blood of Jesus has been applied. Flee this place in the name of Jesus."

That night I gained victory over the anxiety of my mind. Brad was right in encouraging me to 'ease up on myself.' I realized how I had allowed my own thoughts to torment me and then the enemy found an open door to my mind. He jumped on it and added to the turmoil and confusion. "No more!" I declared, "No more!"

That morning the dark cloud lifted and my 4:00 anxiety attacks, that I dreaded so much, turned into precious opportunities to spend quiet time, intimate time with my Heavenly Father.

From that day until now, when I awake in the early morning hours, the very first thing I do is say hello to my Lord. I begin to thank Him and praise Him for His many blessings on my life. I thank Him for loving me enough to wake me up and spend time with Him. I ask Him, "what wonderful things do you want to show me this day, my Lord?"

Since that cloud lifted, these early morning anxiety attacks have become precious moments spent with God. I call them my "dates with God." God has begun to use these 4:00 a.m. dates, to impart His wisdom on his daughter.

I remember when my sister–in–law first shared with me that her husband would schedule dates with each of their daughters. I thought this was the neatest idea. What a perfect way for a father to show his daughter that she is special to him. This is exactly what God has done for me. He has scheduled special 'date times' for us to spend time together.

He has revealed many things to me during these early morning moments with Him. He gives me very specific instructions that have impacted my life and the lives of my family for good. Whatever He asks me to do during these times, I have learned to obey quickly. One early December morning, several days after giving me our "prayer X" assignment, God drew me to my computer to type this Christmas message to send to our family and friends.

> *Dear Friends and Family:*
> *God has blessed our family with a wonderful year. As our Christmas gift to you, we'd like to share our new family tradition that will take us into the year 2000. Friends of ours told us that they stand together in their kitchen each morning and pray together. Brad and I decided that this would be a wonderful...and powerful way for our family to begin each day together. We could think of no better way to regroup and unite as a family and...thank our God for the gift of a brand new day...and ask Him to order our steps, our words, our choices and even our attitudes throughout the day. We believed this would reinforce, to our sons, that we are a team...and Christ is the center, most important part of our home; and that they can walk through their day knowing that their God has given His angels charge over them to keep them in all their ways and that they have nothing to fear; that they really can do all things through Christ who strengthens them. We always end by verbally putting on the Armor of God from Ephesians 6:17–18. Wow! What a powerful, victorious way to begin each new day! We've placed an "X" with bright blue tape in the center of our kitchen floor to serve as a daily reminder...to stop, gather together, join hands and pray before running out to start the day. Our little prayer "X" has served as a reminder to pray together each morning, as well as, a witnessing tool of the power of prayer. Very few people enter our home without inquiring about the blue "X" taped in the center of the kitchen floor. You may want to consider placing an "X" in your home...then pass this note on to a friend...and encourage them to do the same. As we celebrate the most important birthday of all, Our Lord Jesus Christ, The Messiah...we pray that He will make Himself known to you in a new way during this new year, 2000.*
>
> *Celebrating His Birth Together,*
> *The Dantzler Family,*
> *Brad, Susan, L.B., and Blake*

I doubt you'll see this prayer "X" idea featured in the next issue of "Martha Stewart Living." Nonetheless, it's the best addition we've ever made to our home.

During another early morning date, He gave me the idea to hang a dry erase board in our kitchen to use as a 'prayer board.' I was to write the names of family and friends who we would remember in prayer each day. I got up right away, moved the unused dry erase board from L.B.'s bedroom to the kitchen wall. By 6:00 a.m., the Dantzler family had a 'prayer board' hanging in the kitchen. Now, when we have guests in our home, it's not unusual for them to ask to be placed on our prayer board. What a joy and an honor for God to want to spend time with me. I look forward to these early morning moments with God. Psalm 16:7 describes my early morning dates with God. "*I will bless the Lord who counsels me; He gives me wisdom in the night. He tells me what to do.*"

In 1997, my friend Kathryn was diagnosed with Rheumatoid Arthritis at the very young age of forty–three. At this time in her life, she was a single girl in her senior year of college just about to complete her internship as a teacher at local high school.

The pain she had been experiencing had spread throughout her body, becoming so severe that she couldn't even hold a pen and write. After months of suppressing her feelings and denying her pain because of the many responsibilities to the people in her life who depended on her, she realized she couldn't overlook her critical state any longer.

After her primary care physician diagnosed her with Rheumatoid Arthritis, he prescribed a special diet that he believed would help decrease the pain she was experiencing and help her deal with her physical condition. This diet was without question the most radical diet that Kathryn had ever considered.

Depriving herself of the foods she so enjoyed began to draw her into what seemed to be a depressed state. After experiencing these extended bouts of depression, Kathryn decided she would research her condition herself. After researching, she decided that she could not stick to this unrealistic diet regimen which denied her of all of her favorite foods, but would take the route of medication instead.

Kathryn began to take many different types of drugs in an attempt to relieve her pain, but her pain seemed worsen in spite of the drugs.

Since her diagnoses, she had begun to spend a lot of time fasting, praying and reading her Bible. She was committed to do all she knew to do in a situation like hers. She would read Christian books and listen to Christian worship music in an attempt to lift her spirit and draw her closer to God, but to her dismay, the more she tried to seek God, the further she felt from Him.

In February of 2000, Kathryn attended the Deeper Life Crusade presented at her church. The anointed words of evangelist Kip Laxson became God's chosen instrument which opened Kathryn's spiritual eyes to the fact that although she had always been committed to serving God in music and church ministry, she had simply been going through the motions. She realized that she had been serving God and overlooked the beautiful fact that she could really know Him deep within her soul in a personal way.

Kathryn describes her renewal by saying, "After this revival, my heart and ears were opened, and I began to actually soak in the truth that I had been reading in the Bible." In her spirit she was strengthened, and she knew that no matter how bad the pain became her God would walk with her leading her each step of the way. She began to learn to trust Him with her very life.

After praying again about her physical condition, Kathryn knew that she needed to return to the physician who had recommended the radical diet, and commit to implement it into her lifestyle. It was evident that this physician had a strong belief in God. He presented the diet in such a way that Kathryn truly believed that God was going to use this diet as a vehicle that would help her on her road to health.

As her body began to adjust to the drastic changes in her eating habits, the pain quickly grew worse, affecting every aspect of my life, once again. She describes this time as follows. "Some days I surrendered to the darkness of pain and other days I fought the dark and lonely depression that I knew in my heart Satan had brought to my life. I'd lose entire days doing nothing with my life to glorify God, feeling as though I had allowed Satan to steel my days from me.

If I could have mustered up the strength to drag myself outside of my apartment and scream at the top of my lungs, I would have felt so much better. Then, there were the days that I wanted to just roll myself up in a cocoon, and hide away from the world in a quiet corner."

During her depression she relied heavily on the scriptures found in the book of Psalms. She could relate to the dark places that David seemed to go, and found comfort in his journey with God. Psalms 143:7–10 was a passage she read most often. *"Come quickly, Lord, and answer me, for my depression deepens; don't turn away from me or I shall die. Let me see your kindness to me in the morning, for I am trusting you. Show me where to walk for my prayer is sincere. Save me from my enemies, O Lord, I run to you to hide me. Help me to do your will, for you are my God. Lead me in good paths, for your Spirit is good."*

She became more frustrated because she couldn't do the activities that were important to her. Kathryn, who was now teaching school, often found herself paralyzed with excruciating pain, alone in her apartment unable to even get out of bed.

Over the course of the next summer months, the pain intensified, spreading throughout her body, but she never failed to trust God for her health.

I've always enjoyed listening to Kathryn's angelic voice as she so beautifully interpreted words into music that always spoke encouragement to my heart. She enjoyed singing with three other women in a Christian group known as Arise.

This particular summer they were scheduled to travel to South Carolina to record their first CD. Because her husband was having to help dress her every morning due to her pain, she knew that she couldn't possibly make the trip. Although singing had always been a part of Kathryn's life, she felt God cautioning her to step back, slow down, and stay home. She obeyed God, and resigned from the group. She knew God was taking care of her, and she had peace and trusted Him to work even this situation for good for her.

Kathryn knew God had given her a passion for teaching, so she began to ask Him to clearly show her if she should return to school in August or take a year off. Following her time of prayer, she felt lead to select an internist specialist from her insurance booklet, and was promptly given an appointment with him. Without any delay, He referred her to a highly recommended specialist, who was able to see her right away. God's hand prints were all over His little girls life. Kathryn realized that God had truly led her here, and she felt at peace about taking the medication the specialist prescribed for her.

Amazingly, this medication began to cause her pain to subside, slowly diminishing. Kathryn did return to school that August., and she is convinced that God uses both doctors and drugs as His instruments to bring healing and wholeness to His girls.

With excitement in her voice, Kathryn explained to me that God has taught her to trust Him first in all situations. She realizes that if she places 'getting to know Him' first in her life, everything else will fall into place.

A favorite passage that has brought Kathryn comfort during her dark days of depression caused by her chronic pain is *Romans 5:3–5, "We rejoice in our sufferings, knowing that suffering produces endurance, and endurance produces character, and character produces hope, and hope does not disappoint us, because God's love has been poured into our hearts through the Holy Spirit which has been given to us."*

She explains to me that God was trying to build character in her and it was a very painful process. She realizes that He isn't finished with that process yet because Rheumatoid Arthritis is not curable. "But," she says with conviction, "He can heal me however He chooses to heal me...in body, mind and spirit, and I will trust Him. I wouldn't trade the last four years journey, not one day, for the reward God has given me in knowing Him and His perfect plan for my life is a precious, irreplaceable treasure."

These days Kathryn describes her quiet time with her Heavenly Father much like a little girl would talk about her time with her earthly Daddy. Kathryn shares, "God's love is like the best hug in the whole world. Being in His presence is like crawling into His lap, as I almost feel Him stroking my hair just loving me like I am His little girl. He's so much a Father, who knows my bruises and freckles, and He is so God, knowing the details of every single person on earth."

Over the past several years, God has used the music of Christian recording artist, Kathy Tracoli, to minister and speak to my very soul, encouraging me and growing me stronger in my relationship with my Heavenly Father.

I first heard Kathy Tracoli sing at a Billy Graham crusade at the Tampa Stadium several years ago. Her song *He Will Make A Way For Me* reminds us that our God is able to make a way for His girls in every situation of life. My God use the anointed words of this song to encourage you as it did me.

I know that you're discouraged but you're not alone
There is absolutely no situation out of His control
One door my close Another will open
Jesus is healer of all that is broken

He Will Make A Way
Kathy Tracoli, (Corner of Eden CD)

God is in complete control of every aspect of our lives. As we crawl up into His great big lap, sharing our unbearable pain and giving Him our broken dreams, He will bring His peace and deliver His girls from the darkest of days. We can trust Him because He promises that He Will Make A Way for His girls!

"The same sun that hardens clay, melts wax..."
There is no change or variation in the sun itself.
It's just the way the clay or wax responds.

Trials and suffering will harden some just like breakable clay,
baking in bitterness and resentment.
The same circumstances can melt others,
teaching them patience and endurance.

—Joni Eareckson Tada, His Hidden Strength

— 9 —

Café Mocha with Whipped Cream, Please!

Everything is permissible for me—but not everything is beneficial. Everything is permissible for me—but I will not be mastered by anything. 1 Corinthians 6:12

The good man eats to live, while the evil man lives to eat. Proverbs 13:25

So whether you eat or drink or whatever you do, do it all for the glory of God. 1 Corinthians 10:31

God created His girls with amazingly complex physical bodies designed with many intricate systems working together to support and sustain the body by healing and repairing themselves. From the beginning of creation, good health was without a doubt part of God's perfect plan for us. It was never intended to bind us or preoccupy our thoughts by becoming the primary focus in our lives.

In 3 John 2, John THE ELDER opens his letter to Gaius saying, *"Beloved, I wish above all that things that thou mayest prosper and be in health, even as thy soul prospereth. For I rejoiced greatly, when the brethren came and testified of the truth that is in thee, even as thou walkest in the truth. I have no greater joy than to hear that my children walk in truth." (KJ)*

John is commending Gaius for walking in the truth of God, acknowledging that the prospering state of his soul is what brings the greatest joy in life, and because his soul is prospering, John wishes that Gaius' health will also prosper.

Eating a balance of healthy foods which meet our individual nutritional and emotional needs is the key to good health. We should strive to live in a way that will actually promote the healing, repair and function processes of the body, rather than hinder them.

In this chapter, we will be addressing the nutritional component of the physical dimension of a woman as it applies to an apparently healthy individual. Women who have been diagnosed with disease or other medical problems may have additional issues that should be addressed by their physician and registered dietician when developing a healthy eating plan.

After centuries of viewing nutrition mainly as a part of therapy for illness and disease, rather than an integral part of a normal or healthy individual's lifestyle, research has helped us to realize that we can greatly impact our already healthy state by deliberately choosing to eat foods that have been proven to have positive health effects on the body.

Although, not new, this news is encouraging. Many people in our society have gone to the opposite extreme, allowing themselves to become obsessed with dieting. Neither of these extremes were part of God's original plan for His girls concerning food.

In the beginning, God placed man and woman in the most beautiful garden in all the world, and said to them in *Genesis 1:29, "Behold, I have given you every plant yielding seed which is upon the face of all the earth, and every tree with seed in its fruit; you shall have them for food."* I can only imagine the breathtaking beauty of this Garden that was created by God for Adam and Eve, which was filled with all of the beautiful endless varieties of plants, trees, and all species of animals.

In this passage, God instructs Adam and Eve concerning the purpose for the plants and trees He created when He said, "*you shall have them for food.*" The Webster's New Collegiate Dictionary defines the word food as 'material consisting essentially of protein, carbohydrate, and fat used in the body of an organism to sustain growth, repair, and vital processes and to furnish energy.'

God's purpose for food in our lives is for enjoyment and functional purposes of the body rather than appearance purposes. Just as with every beautiful, perfect creation God gave to us for our good, Satan has perverted, distorted and infected them to lead us into a state of addiction, obsession and bondage, instead of a life filled with freedom, enjoyment and abundance, which God intended for His girls.

It is crucial that we remember that Satan's only purpose on this earth is to separate us from God, keeping us from enjoying the freedom God intended for His girls. He will do this by distorting our perspective of the things God created for our good, and detouring us to a place where we become imbalanced, preoccupied, controlled and even obsessed by things like food.

We find many passages in the Bible that caution us to not be controlled by anything on this earth, except the Holy Spirit who lives in us when it says in Proverbs 13:25,*"The good man eats to live, while the evil man lives to eat."*

In Corinthians 6:12–13, Paul addressed this issue of allowing habits to control us when he wrote, *"I can do anything I want to if Christ has not said no, but some of these things aren't good for me. Even if I am allowed to do them, I'll refuse to if I think they might get such a grip on me that I can't easily stop when I want to. For instance, take the matter of eating. God has given us an appetite for food and stomachs to digest it. But that doesn't mean we should eat more than we need. Don't think of eating as important, because some day God will do away with both stomachs and food." (LB)*

We should eat food to nourish our bodies and to enjoy life with family and friends, never permitting it to preoccupy our thoughts but keep our focus on God.

I don't want to give Satan more credit than he deserves, but at the same time I want to enlighten God's girls to the fact that he and his imps do exist and are working in our lives to trap us in any way they possibly can. I picture Satan and his workers as puny and rotting squid or octopus with slimy, stinky, clingy tentacles constantly flying around us attempting to trip us, tangle us and bind us up any way they can.

The really great news is that when we are bathing ourselves in the Word of God every day, talking with God continually, binding Satan in the name of Jesus, and living our days in the very presence of God, we have nothing to fear because God will direct us, exposing the potential traps along the way.

Keeping our focus on God directly affects every area of our lives, helping us to live, functioning in the balanced manor which God has planned for His girls.

In her book, Hidden Treasures: Abundant Life In The Riches Of Proverbs, Gloria Copeland teaches women to, "Deposit an abundance of God's Word in your heart today. Find time to hear the Word, meditate on the Word and talk the Word. For God's Words will also keep our thinking straight. And they will keep us strong and aggressive to walk in the wisdom of God in every area of life."

In John 1:1, we learn that the Word of God is God Himself, so when we spend time reading the Word of God, the Holy Spirit of God draws close to us revealing the wisdom of God from it's pages, placing it directly into our hearts, and then helping us apply it to all areas of our lives. When we spend time reading God's Word, we are spending time with God Himself.

Truly, "Intimacy with Christ is the single most important factor in your life," as author Henry Blackeby reminds us in Experiencing God. As we cultivate our relationship with Christ, we grow closer to Him, and it is impossible for us to remain the same while in the presence of Holy God. The light of God shines brighter into our lives as we move closer to God, exposing habits that need to be changed or removed so that the life can better reflect Christ.

Over and over in the Word of God scripture reinforces this truth that is the very key God gave His girls to open the door to living a life of freedom from bondage to food, drink, and anything that might tend to bind and control you. In Matthew 6:33 this key is described with the words, "*Seek ye first the Kingdom of God, and His righteousness; and all these things shall be added unto you.*" In Psalms 37:4, David so eloquently describes the key to a life of freedom in Christ as, "*Delight yourself in the Lord, and He will give you the desires of your heart.*"

I have read, quoted and sung these scriptures since I was a little girl, but it's only been recently that God has begun to reveal to me the supernatural power that moves in our lives to 'add all these things to us, as we seek "God first above all other things."

For so many years I truly believed I was seeking God first, but I was actually attempting to balance the areas of my life and solve problems, while seeking God's advice and help concerning all my life issues.

No where in the Bible does God refer to Himself as a consultant, so maybe it's not such a good idea for me to treat Him like one. He is God Almighty, who desires our 100% full attention. He wants us to set aside everything in our lives, and truly seek His face. He wants us to seek Him because we want to know Him more intimately, not just because we need His help.

Many times He will use (never cause) problematic nutritional issues that arise in our lives to bring us to Him in hopes that we will realize that we don't just want to seek Him for advice, but we love Him so much that we truly want to spend time with Him, getting to know the very heart of our Heavenly Father.

If we begin to spend more time alone with God, the light of His presence changes us, magnifying God's love, while diminishing the problems that had consumed us. We can very easily become overwhelmed when we look at weight–loss and food addiction struggles instead of keeping our focus on God.

If we ignore God's gentle call to be with Him, we will become consumed by the troublesome issues of life, permitting problems to occupy our attention instead of God. When this happens we can easily become frustrated and overwhelmed by the struggles in our lives, such as out–of–control eating habits, failure to lose unwanted weight and to eat balanced meals.

Recently, God moved in my life in a supernatural way to teach me the awesomeness of a God who loves His girls in such a way that He would take complete care of their nutritional needs, if they would only seek His face.

I must begin my story by informing you that for most of my adult life I have considered myself to be an extremely dedicated coffee connoisseur, drinking two large (okay, extra, extra large) coffee mugs of very strong black coffee every morning, and sometimes enjoying a cup of flavored coffee in the afternoon during the fall and winter seasons.

During the past five years, my seemingly harmless coffee drinking hobby has become ritualistic in nature to the point that I humorously refer to the kitchen cabinet that holds and protects my coffee maker, grinder, carafe, and fresh Starbuck's coffee beans as my coffee shrine. Many nights before going to bed I would find myself anticipating my first fresh cup of Starbuck's that I would enjoy the next morning.

I enjoyed the entire coffee experience beginning with carefully removing my deluxe Krups coffee maker from its protected place in the famous cabinet. Then I would wipe any residue remaining from the prior days coffee beans from my grinder and carefully open my Starbuck's House Blend coffee beans from their air tight container pouring the precise amount of them meticulously into the prepared grinder. I would press my grinder for exactly fifteen seconds, indulging in the aroma of freshly ground coffee beans, and carefully transfer the freshly ground beans to the mesh coffee filter, which I would line with a paper filter to increase the purity of the coffee, straining every last ground from the brew.

Comforted inside as I heard the brewing sounds of my first cup of coffee beginning to brew, which was music to my ears, as I selected the perfect cup for the morning's coffee, depending on the season of the year or the mood for the day.

Of course, in the spring I tend to choose cups adorned with flowers, in the summer, I chose bright plaids or daisies, in the fall I choose my pumpkins, and at Christmas time I pull out my treasured Christmas cups.

Many times when I was thinking of a special friend, I'll select a cup that reminded me of her, and celebrated her while enjoying my morning coffee. Selecting the cup was definitely the best part of this entire ritual for me.

When it comes to coffee, the cup is a huge part of the ritual for me, drinking from a puny little Styrofoam cup just doesn't interest me. What can I say, I enjoy pretty coffee cups.

I must also confess that when I went on vacation I packed a special tote that I've designated as my coffee travel bag which contained my entire arsenal.

When I would visit my parents in Ohio, I would pack my Starbuck's House Blend coffee beans and grinder in my suit case. During my stay, my Mother would brew my Dad's coffee before I would get out of bed, and I'd grind my own beans and brew my own coffee. My Dad always joked about my coffee being as thick as mud and way out of his league, while I would comment that his coffee looked like dirty water. We'd have fun with our coffee differences.

Can you imagine going away for a family Thanksgiving weekend at the hunting camp and attempting to explain to my new Mother–in–law that I brought my own coffee supplies, so she didn't need to bother making coffee for me.

Although she responded so graciously, I probably would have wondered what kind of coffee crazed, kooky girl had my son had married. Who takes their coffee tote on vacation with them? I guess I would have been the perfect woman to buy a license tag holder that says, "Have coffee, will travel!"

Now, looking back, I chuckle at myself, realizing that I had allowed a routine cup of coffee to snowball into a ritual that resembled the preparation of Holy Eucharist, rather than a simple morning cup of java.

I had begun to notice that the caffeine in the coffee I was drinking would affect me in ways that were different from earlier years. Caffeine is a stimulant that enabled me to enjoy mental clarity, mood elevation, and increased work productivity after drinking a cup or two of my special brew.

I'd always drink my coffee before jogging in the morning followed by my banana and glass of water because of the mental boost it would give me during my thirty to forty minute run.

Because I am well aware of the pros and cons of caffeine consumption, I considered myself to be an informed coffee drinker, knowing that I was drinking it in moderation as my body could handle it. I would always try and drink an additional 8 ounces of water to make–up for each cup of coffee I drink, taking into consideration that caffeine is a diuretic.

I would only drink coffee in the afternoons during the holiday season, which for me started as soon as Barnie's Coffee Store began to stock their Pumpkin Spice coffee beans. After enjoying Pumpkin Spice coffee each September and October afternoon, I would move on to bigger and better blends for the holidays. If you're a coffee drinker, I bet you know where I'm headed here. You guessed it. The ultimate Barnies' Christmas coffee beans, Santa's White Christmas. They smell like cookies, they look like miniature cookies covered in powdered sugar, and the coffee tastes like fresh Christmas cookies. If I would have donated blood during the month of December in years past, it probably would have smelled and looked like Santa's White Christmas.

Five years ago, when I begun to ask God to "point out anything in my life that makes Him sad, and help me to change it," I began to notice that when I drank coffee prior to a speaking engagement, Bible study group, or any setting where I was to interact, the caffeine had a negative affect on me physically, mentally and emotionally.

My nervous system would be affected, as I would tremble while speaking and participating. Many times I would become more talkative than usual, speaking words and exhibiting attitudes that I would regret the next day. While caffeine stimulated my brain, it definitely decreased my abilities to handle stressful situations appropriately, especially where my husband and children we concerned.

Although it took me quite a while to come to the conclusion that I should not drink caffeine in the afternoon's, finally after unnecessarily losing my temper and raising my voice in an unacceptable manor towards my boys, I accepted what was very clear to me, caffeine didn't make me a better Mom. In fact, it provoked me to be a grouchier Mom responding to my boys with little love, and more harshness than necessary.

When I would pick up my boys from school and greet my husband for dinner, I noticed the tone of my voice was sharper and my replies were curt, while under the influence of caffeine. These three guys own my heart and God knew that if He allowed me to see how caffeine in my day was affecting the way I loved and cared for them that I would get the point, realizing the seriousness of this habit that needed to be addressed. Finally, I did get God's point.

Yes, I am hard headed and strong–willed because it ways only after many sleepless nights spent regretting the less–than–loving words I had spoken and the harshness in the tone of my voice to the ones I love the most, that I began to accept the fact that drinking coffee had become more than an occasional indulgence, but a bad habit that I had allowed to impact my life in a negative way.

Night after night, I would cry before God asking for His forgiveness and help, while kneeling before Him embarrassed and ashamed of my behavior that resulted from my failure to obey Him once again concerning my coffee drinking habit. Finally, I began to limit my afternoon coffee consumption to an occasional indulgence, while continuing my intense morning coffee ritual.

During this past year as I have felt the presence of God's Holy Spirit drawing me to spend time with Him, I have begun to shift my entire life focus from the various factors in my life to God Himself.

I believe God has been gently tugging at my heart, calling my spirit to Himself, as He does to all of His Girls. The circumstances in my life reinforce this fact, convincing me that my spiritual food is the most important factor in my life because it connects me to my Heavenly Father.

In recent months, I have been walking with God in a place I've never been before with a confidence that HE IS EVERYTHING to me, not just a compartment that I open on Sundays. HE has truly become like the air that I breathe. He's everywhere I am, and He makes Himself known to my spirit in ways that are private and personal between Him and me.

Not to long ago, after kissing my guys goodnight I prepared to meet God for awhile. As I was sitting in my favorite chair enjoying a cup of Sweet Dreams tea, I opened my Bible and began to chat with my Lord. I felt His sweet presence move in close to me, in the quietness of that moment, bringing the warmth of His peace and the gentleness that accompanies His tender love for me.

After the extremely hectic day I had managed to live through, I asked God to clear my mind and calm my spirit, so I could receive the wisdom He wanted to reveal to me during this quiet time together.

I looked down at my Bible which I had unintentionally opened to Psalms 91 and noticed a scripture that I had written in the margin. It said, "*Deliverance from everything*!" Psalms 34:19. As I looked at this reference, I wondered why I wrote this particular scripture on this particular page because it didn't seem to correspond with any other scripture on the page.

Then, I smiled, and said, "Oh, I get it Lord. You had me write that there a time ago for such a time as this." As tears began to roll down my face, I quietly thanked God for caring enough to orchestrate the details of my life in such a beautiful loving way.

I can't exactly describe to you what happened next except for the fact that I felt the peaceful presence of the Holy God melt something inside of me. God seemingly whispered to my spirit that I don't need to be preoccupied with the habit of my morning coffee ritual anymore. I knew at that moment that God was honoring my request to "empty me of all the empty things that I hold onto and fill my heart with HIM."

The chain, which I had never really perceived as a chain, had been supernaturally removed by a Heavenly Father, who cares so much about every detail in His little girls' lives. I knew in my spirit that this was not about me vowing to never drink coffee again, rather it was a supernatural cutting of a chain that had become a hindrance in my life. I know if I want to enjoy a cup of coffee from time to time, I may do so without it becoming a controlling factor in my life, but I also know I won't be fanatically brewing coffee on a daily basis anymore in the Dantzler home. The chain that had began to control me is gone! Hallelujah! Thank you, Lord!

The next morning was Sunday and to my surprise, my desire for my morning coffee ritual was gone, taking with it my strong desire for that first strong cup of morning coffee. My morning cup of coffee wasn't an issue any more.

I shared my experience with my husband, and he was shocked finding it hard to believe that I was not going to be making coffee every morning. Understanding the magnitude of this change in me, he knew immediately that God had indeed moved in my life, releasing me from the needless ritual that had taken a controlling roll in my life.

I am beginning to understand what "*Seek ye first the kingdom of God*" really means. It's all about focusing our energies on God. If we truly begin to "*delight ourselves in Him*", He will take care of every area of our lives, including what we eat and drink! Wow! Now that's a key to abundantly free living!

God cares about every detail in His girls lives, and that includes what we put into their physical bodies. He created us, one by one, making each of His girls unique in design, and for this reason we require specific nutritional needs that will vary from woman to woman. What works for me, may not work for you; and that's okay. You may not be delivered from your bad habit overnight like I was, but you can be delivered.

Along with the physical design of our bodies, our life circumstances and lifestyles each need to be considered when developing the healthy eating plan that is best for us. While we know there are no two women on earth who are 100% biologically and physiologically the same, we do have some factors in our lives that are common.

Frustration and confusion are commonalities that many women share in their pursuit and desire to eat in a healthier manner. Diet, health and nutrition shelves are jammed packed in bookstores, and there really are some great author's out there who have written books which do provide women with sound nutritional information that can be helpful as you seek to develop a program that best suits your individual needs.

We live in an age where nutritional information is everywhere, providing the general public with the latest research studies and it's positive or negative affect on our lives. While simply standing in the grocery store checkout line, we can read endless headlines of new information about common foods and drinks, along with exotic potions and remedies that have been found to enhance some area of human life when consumed in various quantities.

Bookstore shelves are loaded with thousands of nutritional books promising lasting results. Over the years, many women have shared with me the frustration and confusion they have felt while trying to make sense of the research presented in one book when the book next to it says the exact opposite.

One woman described her visit to a local bookstore as this, "I picture myself standing in front of those shelves lined with diet plan, after diet plan, becoming sleepier, and sleepier, and dizzier and dizzier, and then the shelves seemed to grow miles taller right before my eyes, slowly surrounding me, blurring my vision of any single book, and in the end serving no purpose other than to reinforce the fact that I have no idea which of these programs or diets is best for me."

Should we increase our protein while decreasing our carbohydrates, increase our carbohydrates while decreasing our protein, should we eat fruit only in the morning, anytime, or not at all, should we eat proteins and carbohydrates at the same time or always at different times, should we eat for our blood type, our body type, or our ring size? Who's right and who's wrong? Whose research should we believe?

Over the years, I've watched diet plans come and go. Some making a real difference in the lives of some women. Quick fix diets don't work, rather healthy eating for life works! Registered Dietician Pamela M. Smith refers to quick fix diets in her book, *Eat Well, Live Well*, as a throat lozenge for a strep throat infection.

She says that "the lozenges soothe the pain and even make the redness go away! But treating only the symptoms allows the infection to run rampant and get worse. As soon as you go off the throat lozenges, the strep infection rears its ugly head. It's the same with dieting; the weight comes back after going off the diet."

Weight is never the problem or main issue; it's only a symptom. The problem is that somewhere along the way, we have distorted our eating patterns and perspective about food. We often forget that food is to nourish the body by meeting it's nutritional needs, not emotional needs.

This is where we need to remind ourselves that our main focus in life is not how we look on the outside, it's who we are in Christ on the inside.

As our focus is locked firmly on Christ, when we're tempted to worry and fret over our physical appearance, we can respond confidently, knowing that our God is aware of our emotional and physical needs. He will not only reveal to us the issues in our lives that need to be addressed, but He will also take our hands and walk with us, helping us to make the changes that are necessary.

I have a basic knowledge of the nutritional needs of a healthy woman of my age, and I eat a healthy diet most of the time, indulging on occasion. I am also basically satisfied with the way I eat on a daily basis. Having a foundational understanding of basic nutrition is in the best place to begin your journey to finding what foods work best for you.

Pamela M. Smith, as I mentioned earlier, has written what I consider to be the most simplistic and easy to understand approach to healthy eating, which contains basic nutritional information, life application examples, and healthy recipes.

In her book, *Eat Well, Live Well*, Ms. Smith demonstrates her God given gift as she so beautifully simplifies the sometimes complex and complicated facts of basic nutrition, transforming them into bite size pieces of healthy eating guidelines that seem so easy to apply to life.

I encourage you to read her book and find vital information about making choices that can help you stay healthier and feel better. Her book will be a great help as you begin your journey to discover what to eat, when to eat and how much to eat for peak stamina and performance for you. Learning to listen to what our bodies are telling us by the way they respond to various foods can give us valuable insight. Only then will it be possible to for us begin to find out what types of foods we should consume to better enhance the function of our individual bodies. This is simply done by trial and error.

Over a period of time, by carefully observing how my body responds to particular foods, I have been able to make some intelligent, informed decisions regarding what foods I should eat and when I should eat them. Who better than myself would know how I feel physically, as well as, emotionally, intellectually, socially and spiritually, in relationship to the foods I'm eating.

Simply by listening to my body, I have come to understand and accept the fact that I am very sensitive to sugar, particularly refined sugar; especially when I eat it on an empty stomach in the afternoon. I've been aware that a sensitivity to sugar runs in my family so this was no surprise to me. I can remember my Mother buying one of those twelve packs of single Reese Cups, and she'd have to write each of our names on the them to ensure that one of us three sisters wouldn't get carried away and gobble them all at one time. What I wasn't aware of back then was the secret fact that my Mother bought her own special chocolate which she kept in a safe place far, far away from the hands of little people.

Over the years, my sisters and I compare stories and we have found that we each love chocolate and sweets very much. We bake brownies or chocolate chip cookies for everybody and every occasion.

Whether our reasoning is 'It's Monday and I love my family, so I think I'll bake some chocolate chip cookies,' or 'the neighbors just came home from vacation, so I'll bake them some cookies,' my sisters and I just love to bake delicious desserts. We do enjoy giving them as gifts of love, but, if the truth be known, sometimes, we are primarily motivated by a selfish desire of the flesh to eat cookie dough.

My sister usually has her own personal stash of gourmet chocolate chip cookies hidden away in her own personal little safe place in her kitchen, unknown to her husband and two sons.

My sister Leslie and I will joke with each other saying, "Oh, I better bake some cookies today, I think somebody in my neighborhood needs them…or maybe I need to bake some for the teachers at school."

We laugh and laugh, but we know deep down inside of us that sugar is an issue that each of us must address in our own lives in our own ways.

For me, as I began to ask God to show me the things in my life that needed to be removed, He began to reveal to me the affects that my sugar addiction was having on my family. Just like with coffee, I would speak to my sons with unnecessary harshness that was a result of my sugar induced mood swings, and this fact brought me to my knees once again, asking God to intervene in my life, helping me to gain control over my sugar addiction.

That evening after praying I felt lead to open my "The Spirit–Filled Woman" devotional book, and to my surprise, the title of the devotional for that particular day was "Contemplating Candy." I could hardly believe my eyes. Right away, I began to thank God for once again reminding me that He was aware of the tiniest details and issues in my life.

I woke the next day feeling like I had a new lease on life, confident in the fact that though my intense desire for sugar might exist for the rest of my life, it was possible for me to gain better control in this area.

Years ago, I began to pray Psalms 139:23–24 as *"Search me, O God, and know my heart; test my thoughts. Point out anything you find in me that makes you sad, and lead me along the path of everlasting life."* my personal request to God.

As this prayer has become a regular part of my daily prayer life, I've prayed it in regards to the food and drink I put into my physical body. God has been truly faithful in revealing to me which eating habits need to stay and which need to go. He directs me so gently, by allowing me to see for myself over a prolonged period of time how certain foods and beverages directly affect my physical body and also how I deal with stress, process thoughts, interact in relationship situations, and respond to my Heavenly Father.

For some women including myself, eating certain types of foods at particular times in the day can affect their emotional state, many times decreasing the ability to successfully deal with the stresses of every day life. We need to become more aware of how our bodies are responding the foods at particular times of the day. Trying different foods at different times throughout the day will help you learn which foods work best for your body at what time. Certain foods may make you sleepy, while some make you cranky.

I have realized that I function better when I eat a banana and cottage cheese for breakfast, rather than a bowl of cereal. Cereal's not bad, but I know that it isn't a wise choice for me at breakfast time.

As you work within the basic food groups in the Food Guide Pyramid to provide your body with a balance of nutrients, a simple system of trial and error will help you decide what and when to eat.

Prior to beginning any nutritional program, I encourage you to seek the advice of your Heavenly Father, asking Him to reveal to you anything, food or otherwise, that has become binding in your life.

Then, pour out your heart to Him, begging that He draw you closer to His side, placing a hunger and thirst inside of you to know Him in a more intimate way.

As you commit to making your relationship with Him priority over all else in our lives, even family, He will honor that obedience and He will "add all these things unto us." Placing God before our families means giving GOD HIMSELF first place in our personal lives by making quiet time alone with Him priority.

We must remember the important truth that our commitment and participation in regards to the organized church we are associated with is not the same as intimate time along with God, and can never replace a personal relationship with Him. We know this because the Bible tells us that a personal, intimate relationship with God should be the most important factor in our lives, followed by our relationship with our husband and then our children. Matthew 6:33 says, "*Seek ye first the kingdom of God, and all these things shall be added unto you.*"

God desires to walk so close to His girls that He can feel our breath on His face. He loves us so much that He carefully designed each of our bodies, taking special care in assigning them specifically to each of His girls. Because our bodies are a gift from our Heavenly Father, we should take seriously our responsibility to supply them with the healthiest of nutrition on a daily basis.

As we trust Him, He will direct us to the vehicles He wants us to use to gain the information we will need to provide nourishment to our bodies. Whether it is a sensible nutrition book, a physician, a Registered Dietician, a lifestyle counselor, or a Christian counselor, He will direct our paths if we 'trust Him with all of our hearts and lean not to our own understanding.

Our bodies are designed to run much like a car, with the natural need for fuel and maintenance to function properly. They are both greatly affected by the quality and quantity of the fuel we choose to place inside of them.

During my high school years, I drove my parents' 1973 Chevy Impala, which was black with a cream colored vinyl top. It seemed like a big tank to me, as I drove it around the snowy streets of our little town in Ohio.

My Dad never used the cheapest gasoline in his cars because he knew how the quality of fuel one put in a car would eventually effect the performance and life of the car. I, on the other hand, would buy the cheapest gasoline possible. I simply saw no need to waste my hard earned wages on fuel that disappeared into the gas tank when it could be spent on new clothes.

You must understand that I was on a much smaller budget than my father, with a humble income derived from giving baton lessons, babysitting, and working part–time during the summer at McDonald's.

Not only did my dad buy high quality fuel for his vehicles, he would always fill the cars up with gas when we would go into town. I remember the old Bonded gas station that Dad would pull into as we entered town. It was a tiny little gas station painted red, white, and blue with a two mechanics garage and a small business office where the gas station attendant would go to ring up their sales after pumping our gas.

Those were the days when, even on the snowiest of nights with below freezing temperatures, a friendly gas station attendant would greet you at your car window with a friendly, "Good evening, Ma'am. What can I get for you?" Unlike my dad, who would always respond with a jovial "fill her up with the high–test, Joe," I would smile and say, "Just $5.00, please…of regular."

One snowy winter evening as I was driving through town I spotted the freshly fallen powder–like snow covering the empty parking lot that belonged to the Shelby Autocall Company. It was as though the snow was calling me to play in it, saying, "Come on, spin some donuts. Have some fun for once." Oh, my. Could I? Should I? This was something I had never done before because remember, I was the 'safety–before–fun' kind of girl.

After surveying the parking lot for cars and potential risks, I determined that this would be a perfect opportunity for me to try my skills at making snow donuts, so I proceeded to drive to the middle of the parking lot.

I stopped the big black Impala, rolled my window down a bit to enjoy the cool fresh winter air and the snow flakes flying through the car, and then, I did it. I turned the wheel as far as it would go to the right, and I hit the gas pedal.

As the car began to go into a gentle, almost graceful, spin, I began to actually relax into the moment, and enjoy this rare moment of attempting to be a risk taker.

I continued to spin all over the parking lot for thirty minutes (okay, maybe more like ten minutes), not noticing that my gas gauge had dropped below the little red empty line, and the old Impala's engine had taken on a rasping sound.

After noticing that the car was making a weird sound, I immediately looked at the gas gauge and realized that not only did the engine sound funky, but I was very close to running out of gas. I knew if I could just get the car to the gas station around the corner I could buy $4.00 worth of their cheapest gasoline, and then, I'd just have to pray that there was nothing wrong with the engine.

Several weeks had passed, and for some reason, my dad and I were talking about the car (not my idea, I'm sure), and he asked me what kind of gasoline I usually put in the car. When I told him that I always ask for the cheapest gasoline, he grimaced in dismay, and began to explain to me how damaging the lower grades of fuel can be on a vehicle making it more likely to have mechanical problems prematurely, and eventually shorten the expected life of the vehicle.

My Dad knew a great deal about the mechanics of vehicles, considering he had been employed at General Motors for years, so I knew that what he had said was indeed accurate.

Out of respect for my dad, I made a commitment to myself to stop buying the lowest grade of gasoline, in an attempt to take better care of the car he had so graciously permitted me to drive. As for me and my ultra–safe, donut spinning adventure, I (little miss safety queen) had some safe fun, and embraced a brief moment of feeling wild and free without harming myself, the car or anyone else.

Just as my earthly father entrusted me with his black Impala to use during my high school years, my Heavenly Father has entrusted me with this physical body to use during the part of my life that I'll be spending on earth. Just as I realized the impact that the quality fuel that I chose to put into my dad's car directly effected the car's performance and ultimately it's length of life, each of us must reach a point where we realize the same is true with our physical bodies.

Our bodies do not belong to us, but are simply on loan to us by God, to use during our visit to earth. God reminds us of this very important fact in 1 Corinthians 6:19–20, *"Haven't you yet learned that your body is the home of the Holy Spirit God gave you, and that He lives within you? Your own body does not belong to you. For God has bought you with a great price. So use every part of your body to give glory back to God, because He owns it." (LB)* When I am reminded that it is my responsibility to choose healthy fuel for my body, I find it much easier to commit to a balanced eating plan.

It's when I forget that my body isn't really mine (which I tend to do sometimes) that I abuse it by choosing to overeat on the lower quality fuel foods, such as coffee, chocolate, cookie dough, bread, junk food, fast food and soda. Realizing this Biblical truth can actually spare us from the paying the painful price that abusing our bodies demands.

Whether your physical self–abuse has been overindulging on foods that are not healthy or denying your body the nutrients it needs, both will take a toll on the body, eventually effecting it's performance, appearance and life. The absence of healthy eating habits can be just as dangerous and damaging as the presence of unhealthy habits.

I'll never forget the evening I walked passed my lonely little vitamin packet which had been laying on the kitchen counter for at least a week. As I glanced at my vitamins (with no intention of swallowing them), it was as though I heard a calm, deep voice ask me, "And just who might you think your are…to deny the body I've loaned to you…these needed nutrients."

Needless to say, I immediately swallowed those vitamins, and have done so every evening since that day.

I recall the prayer that my father always would pray for the blessing over our food at meal time. He would pray, "Dear Lord, Bless this food and make it nourishment to our bodies." As I contemplate saying this prayer before placing anything into my body, whether it be food or drink, I think I might think twice before eating that fourth big scoop of cookie dough or second piece of Italian Coconut Cream Cake. What about you? Would the servings and selections you aim for your mouth cause you to hesitate to pray this prayer?

Think about it for a moment. In your personal life, what foods or beverages might cause you to hesitate in saying this prayer. It might be a good idea to say this little prayer, asking the Lord to reveal to you some items that you would be better off without.

Our bodies, like cars, are not invincible to the effects of low quality fuel; some simply take abuse longer and better than others. It's never too late to begin to give better care to the body that God has chosen for you, committing to make healthier food choices.

There are two extremes when it comes to eating. Picture a horizontal line with the healthy extreme on the far right and the unhealthy extreme on the far left.

The unhealthy extreme example would be someone who eats junk food, no nutritional value foods, fast foods, high sugar foods, too much food, or not enough nourishment on a regular basis.

The healthy extreme example would be those individuals who never eat refined or processed foods, sugar, caffeine, white flour, alcohol, or meat. They always eat balanced meals, never indulging on rich desserts like chocolate chip cheesecake or a movie theater popcorn, and they may be vegetarians. They eat mostly raw, fresh foods as opposed to cooked, frozen, boxed or canned foods.

At the middle of the line, you'll find a realistic approach to healthy eating, which is 'Eating Healthy Most Of The Time, And Indulging On Occasion." This simply means exactly what it says, we will eat healthy most of time, (maybe during the work week) and not feel guilty about enjoying an indulgence or two on the weekends. This is controlled moderation in it's truest form.

For example, if you're eating very healthy, balanced meals during the week, you won't feel guilty eating pizza on Friday night when you have family pizza night. A mint chocolate chip ice cream cone with your son, daughter, or grandchild on a Saturday afternoon won't seem like a big, bad sin when you're eating healthy most of the time.

If you placed yourself on this 'eating line' based on the foods you eat on a regular basis, where would you be? Instead of feeling pressure to eat the way some else eats, decide where you are and where you want to go, and be confident in your food choices.

Because God created food for our nourishment, let's focus on giving ourselves the precious gift of nutritious foods, instead of denying ourselves. Changing our perspective in this way will enable us to shift the focus of our eating from denying ourselves of the foods low in nutritional value to nourishing our bodies with the foods loaded with nutrients.

This is exactly what Paul is instructing us to do in Philippians 4:8, when he says, "*Finally, bothers (sisters), whatever is true, whatever is noble, whatever is right, whatever is pure, whatever is lovely, whatever is admirable—if anything is excellent or praiseworthy—think about such things.*" Think about what is healthy and nourishing for us to eat, refusing to all unhealthy foods to consume your thoughts.

For most women, a realistic guide to follow when setting goals would be to commit to make one change at a time. Begin by writing down the foods and beverages you consume on an average day, and comparing it to the Food Guide Pyramid.

Next, make a list of the servings of healthy foods you will need to add to your meals to provide yourself with a balanced eating plan. As you choose to add one nutritious food at a time, you will probably find that eventually you will want to subtract the foods with lower nutritional value.

As you begin to add foods full of nourishing nutrients, while subtracting the less nutritious foods, you're body will respond in positive ways, helping you to realize how much control you can have over your energy level, stress management, health and well–being.

Here's a good example. You have become aware of the fact that you are not giving your body the recommended eight 8–ounces of water that it's needs per day, so you want to increase your water intake. Realizing that you will need to decrease the amount of soda, coffee and tea you're drinking to make room for the water you plan to add, you begin to plan your strategy.

After praying about this first goal, for the first week you might decide to drink a glass of water in the morning and in the evening, continuing to drink your four sodas during the day. For the second week, you might substitute 8–ounces of water for one of your sodas, reminding yourself that the water is a gift to yourself. Then, each week thereafter add 8–ounces of water and subtract a soda until you are drinking eight 8–ounces of water and only one or zero sodas per day.

Making relationship with God your primary focus in life, growing discipline and self–control in you, empowering you to eat healthy during the week, while enjoying the guilt–free freedom to indulge in any foods on the weekend. It's the intimate relationship that will start you on your journey and on God's intended path for you to find freedom from the bondage of food.

Then in Proverbs 4:20–23 we're advised, *"My son (daughter), pay attention to what I say; listen closely to my words. Do not let them out of your sight, keep them within your heart; for they are life to those who find them and health to a man's(woman's) whole body. Above all else, guard your heart for it is the wellspring of life."*

God's life plan for His girls is so simple, yet we make it so complicated. If we give cultivating an intimate relationship with our Heavenly Father priority in our lives, in return, He promises to help us address and settle every issue in every area of our lives.

On that closing note, since today happens to be a Saturday, I think I'll call a friend, and meet her at the coffee house downtown, and enjoy sweet conversation and order a hot cup of tea…or a Café' Mocha…with Whipped Cream!

Since habits become power, make them work for you and not against you.

—E. Stanley Jones

— 10 —

Fitness Unlimited

"Haven't you yet learned that your body is the home of the Holy Spirit God gave you, and that He lives within you? Your own body does not belong to you. For God has bought you with a great price. So use every part of your body to give glory back to God, because He owns it." 1 Corinthians 6:19–20

She girdeth her loins with strength, and strengtheneth her arms. She sets about her work vigorously; her arms are strong for her tasks; she is energetic and strong. Proverbs 31:17

The physical dimension of a woman's life consists of two primary physical self–care components; physical activity and healthy eating. In this chapter, we will be addressing the physical activity component of caring for your physical body in an apparently healthy state. This means that most of the exercise information included in this chapter will be specific to women without a diagnosed medical condition or disease. Women with diagnosed medical conditions may have additional issues that should be addressed when considering physical activity.

Stop right there…I know you may be tempted to skip this chapter because you have just realized where I am headed…to a place that is a disguise for exercise, but don't abandon ship just yet. Stick around, and allow me to share with you what God has been teaching me about the physical health of His girls. I believe you'll find it enlightening, and maybe a bit liberating, unbinding, and emancipating, too.

Consider this chapter simply 'food for thought' that may shed some light on the self–care of the physical body God has entrusted to you. There isn't a fitness program or exercise workout in this chapter, so relax and sit back, and read on with relief.

God is helping me to better understand His perspective concerning the care of His girls' physical bodies, and guess what; we've been way off base on this subject for decades. God isn't as interested in *what* we do for exercise, but *why* we do it.

Our society, in general, has become obsessed with the quest for a younger, stronger, leaner looking body, and this is greatly credited to the film makers and advertisers of our time. As we discuss in the "You Go, Girl" chapter on self–esteem, for years advertisers have been fabricating perfection in hopes of selling their products to the American public through sex appeal.

Because our society over–emphasizes the physical dimension, by obsessing over it, many women tend to run to the opposite extreme, and completely ignore the importance of physical fitness, giving themselves a pat on the 'spiritual back' for obeying the Word of God by focusing on their spiritual health, instead of their physical health.

I've always subscribed to the 'better safe than sorry" motto so, I can't say I blame them. The truth, however, is that neither extreme is God's perfect plan for His girls physical self–care.

Isaiah 55:8–9 says, *"God's ways are not our ways; and God's thoughts are not our thoughts. As the heavens are higher than the earth, so are my ways higher that your ways, and my thoughts than your thoughts."* Just when we think we've figured out God's will in our lives and His way concerning a detail in our lives, He surprises us with His awesomeness, and brings clarification to areas in our lives that we never expected.

When this happens, it's just a gentle, but clear reminder to us, His girls, that it's only as God changes us to be more like His Son, will we begin to better understand His ways and His thoughts concerning the details of our lives. While we're on earth we will never completely understand a Holy Omnipotent God.

In 1 Timothy, Paul instructs Timothy to teach the people at Ephesus, who were athletic in nature and followed the calling of the Stoic ideal person to give their spiritual fitness training priority over their physical fitness training.

In 1 Timothy 4:8 Paul says, *"Spend your time and energy in the exercise of keeping spiritually fit. Bodily exercise is all right, but spiritual exercise is much more important and is a tonic for all you do. So exercise yourself spiritually and practice being a better Christian, because that will help you not only now in this life, but in the next life too."*

This was a new teaching for the Ephesians, as it may actually be for many women in our own society, who have been drawn into the calling of the ideal woman with the perfectly sculpted body. The obsession of the physical body is not something new to our society, it's been the tendency of women for a long, long time.

If you think about it, in the natural, physical realm, it makes perfect sense to focus on the part of ourselves that we can visibly see; the outside.

Every morning when we wake–up, what part of ourselves do we see in the mirror? It's usually not our spirit, but our physical bodies, right?

I can't remember the last time I looked into the mirror and said, "Wow, you've got a great spirit going here, girl." Many times I see skin that's thinning, fat that has mysteriously appeared over night, and signs of aging that are screaming, "Yikes, you need to workout, girl!"

We see billboards and advertisements with perfect bodies, and it's understandable why we would compare ourselves to these standards when we look into our mirrors. This makes it easier to understand why many women can be easily blinded and end up focusing their time and energies on refining their physical health, instead of their spiritual health.

When a woman has a viable relationship with her Heavenly Father, one that is fresh every day, it is easier for her to more fully recognize the important role of her spiritual workout, over and above her physical workout.

Spending time with God is much like looking into God's mirror. When we look into God's mirror on a daily basis we are more apt to have His perspective when we look into our bathroom mirrors.

Because of the pressure that the media places on women through their standard of perfection, it is imperative that women spend time looking into God's mirror to gain His perspective on our lives, both the physical and the spiritual.

In our physically minded society, it's very easy for a woman to become obsessed with her physical body. After working in the fitness field for many years, I have watched as some women first begin to acknowledge the importance of living a healthier lifestyle, and many times, after they see how exercising can change the way they look, they go over board.

Their lives seem to revolve around their workouts, and the way they look begins to overshadow every area of their lives. Often times they begin to go to extremes to look younger and thinner, spending thousands of dollars on plastic surgeries. Plastic surgery can have a healthy impact on a life, but can become dangerous when abused in an obsessed, uncontrolled manner. Sadly, I've watched this natural progression lead some women into a life of perfection obsession, distorted self–image, regrettable affairs, family break–ups, and life destruction.

When a woman continually places more emphasis on her physical workout than her spiritual workout, this can throw open the door of her soul, allowing Satan to enter in and begin his methodized plan to slowly lure her away from God.

I feel so compelled to encourage you concerning this danger of placing too much emphasis on your physical workout, especially after reading what Paul wrote in Hebrews 3:13, "*Speak to each other about these things every day while there is still time, so that none of you will become hardened against God, being blinded by the glamour of sin.*" (LB) We're all God's Girls, in this life together for the purpose of encouraging one another along the way.

Remember, the 'heads up, girls' warning that God gave us in Genesis when He explained that all the days of our life on earth, Satan's sole purpose would be to 'take us down?' Why? He knows that if He can lure a woman away from God, beginning to gradually disconnect her from Him, he will eventually destroy her relationship with God; and the odds are in his favor, that he will destroy her family, as well.

This is exactly what happened in God's first family, when Eve was lured by Satan to disobey God. Eve sinned and her sin lead her husband into sin. Heads up, Girls! The enemy will use anything he can to lure us away from focusing on God, and this includes our natural tendency to want to look good.

On the other hand, instead of putting physical health above spiritual health, some Christian women tend to fault in the opposite direction, ignoring the value and importance of physical health.

Some women use 1 Timothy 4:8 as their reason for being unfit, inactive and neglecting their responsibility to care appropriately for their physical bodies, ignoring the reality that God designed the human body for regular physical activity.

Paul prescribes a balanced approach to health in 1 Corinthians 6:19–20, saying, "*...your body is the temple of the Holy Spirit which is in you...glorify God in your body, and in your spirit.*" If the health of the body was not important to God, Paul would have just referred to the spirit, but he explains that it's not just the spirit, but both body and spirit are to glorify our Lord!

In 3 John 1:2, we're also reminded of the importance of putting our spiritual workout before our physical workout, when John writes, "*I am praying that all is well with you and that your body is as healthy as I know your soul is.*" John knew that his friend Gaius was spiritually fit, so he prayed that he would be physically fit too.

As we work daily towards better balance in life, we will constantly be faced with decisions that involve choosing one activity over another. It is our responsibility to give our spiritual workout priority over our physical workout.

For many years, I would take a thirty or forty minute jog early in the morning, and then spend about the same amount of time reading my devotions and praying. Some days I only have time to do one or the other, my devotions or my run, so I must choose.

I admit that I haven't always chosen wisely. There have been days when I allowed myself to shift my priority from my spiritual workout to my physical, and I always paid the price. Throughout those days, I could feel the void that came with the lack of my quiet time with God.

Now, my own rule is to have my devotions before I workout. This way, my focus is already on my Heavenly Father, and it's easy to go right into a beautiful time with the Lord, as He and I jog through my neighborhood together.

Most mornings, after chugging a glass of orange juice, I read a passage from one of my favorite daily devotionals, Experiencing God, My Utmost For His Highest, Be Still and Know, or He Is Real.

While getting dressed to run, I drink a large glass of water and eat a banana, slightly green and very firm if it's a 'good banana day.' As I anxiously head for the quiet neighborhood street in front of our home, I stretch my arms over my head, close my eyes, and slowly inhale the fresh air of the new day. I look up into the sky at the newly risen sun and I greet my Heavenly Father with a smile, and a "Good Morning, Lord."

As I begin to jog along the street, I thank God for the gift of the new day; the gift of the sun, the clear blue Florida sky, my healthy body and strong legs that enable me to run one more day alone with Him.

As we place our spiritual workout first, and begin to work towards a healthier body, let's vow to hold one another accountable so that we do not shift from our spiritual focus to a physical focus. Having a close friend to keep you in check is as important as your workout itself.

My friend Becky and I have vowed to always hold each other accountable, especially in this area of physical health. When one of us gets a little carried away with focusing on our physical bodies, we simply remind each other of what's the most important in this life, our relationship with Christ.

We continue to help each other balance life, so we won't make the awful mistake of sacrificing our spiritual health for our physical health, and in the end be lured away and destroyed by the enemy.

Something that God has used to helped me cultivate a healthy perspective on the importance of staying physically fit, Paul addresses in 1 Corinthians 6:19–20, when he reminds us that our bodies are the home(the temple) of the Holy Spirit of God. Then he even goes a step further telling us that our bodies are not even our own because God bought them with a price, so we are to glorify God by the way we care for our bodies.

Paul clearly explains that our responsibility to provide the highest quality of care for the bodies is for the purpose of glorifying God and not ourselves. We glorify God's beautiful creation, our physical bodies, as we care for them and provide a healthy home for our spirits. Knowing this truth, helps me to approach my physical workout in the healthy manor in which God intended for His girls.

God is not as concerned with *what* we do for exercise, but *why* we exercise. He wants us to care for our physical bodies for the purpose of glorifying Him and not ourselves.

There's a fine line that separates glorifying God with your body and glorifying self, but a healthy perspective concerning the physical care of the Holy Spirit's temple can be adopted through the power of God who lives in each of us.

When it comes right down to it, the specifics of a woman's physical self–care plan are highly personal. We even might have had the tendency to think 'it's my body, my life, and my business how I care for my body.' Well, this may be an acceptable point of view for God's girls who haven't yet realized that even their physical bodies belong to God, however, for you and I, God's girls who are aware of God's instructions, we are held accountable by them.

In Roman 12:1, Paul says, *"Present your bodies a living sacrifice, holy, acceptable unto God, which is your reasonable service."* It's very clear that it is our responsibility to provide the highest quality of care for the body God gave us to use while living on earth.

Living a physically active lifestyle is a part of God's perfect wellness plan for His girls, and it takes commitment and discipline. Some women seem to have more natural self–discipline that others, but self–discipline is actually a learned skill that each of us can acquire.

Discipline is a matter of the mind, which begins by deciding 'this will be done', and 'it will be done at this particular time' and 'this particular way.' The toughest part comes next when you must put legs on your commitments; this is where the rubber meets the road.

If you have been unsuccessful in making lifestyle changes to incorporate exercise into your daily life, understand that you aren't alone, and don't you dare be discouraged if you feel like you lack discipline in this specific area of your life. Most people have at least one area in their lives where they lack a bit of self–discipline and this just happens to be yours.

Throughout the Bible, God often instructs us concerning the important role that self–discipline and self–control play in our lives. God has promised to help us in our quest to acquire these traits. God wants His girls to live our lives with energy and strength for our journey, and He is faithful in all things.

When the prefix 'self' is place before the word discipline, it can be misleading, implying that discipline can be acquired entirely through the efforts of a woman without God 's divine intervention. Although God does expect us to make conscious choices that will work discipline into our lives, He wants to divinely work His discipline into our lives.

In Galatians 5:22–23, Paul teaches us that *"when the Holy Spirit controls our lives, He will produce self–control"* in us. As we spend intimate time alone with God, He pours more of Himself into us by working the fruit of His Spirit into the fiber of us.

It's during our spiritual workout, which takes place when we spend time reading the Word of God and talking with God, that God reveals His truths concerning discipline, self–control and other principles which He has established for us to live by.

The effectiveness of our spiritual workout is immeasurable because it is during this workout that the Holy Spirit will impress upon us important changes that we need to make improvements in all areas of our lives.

He may impress upon your heart to set your alarm clock for 45 minutes earlier and go for a brisk walk before starting your day; He may reveal to you that you are abusing sugar or carbohydrates or soda; He may convict you of sleeping in too long each day, taking unnecessary naps or not making good use of your time during the day. It's during my time with the Lord that

He brings to my attention the habits that need to change to grow me to a higher level of living. In Proverbs 16:3, we are told to *"Commit your ways unto the Lord, and thy thoughts will be established."*

This trip towards improved self–discipline requires initiative on our part to act upon our commitments; and God will be right beside us all the way. God's promises that if we make a commitment and step out in faith initiating action, He will respond to our actions by working in us the very thing that we have committed to change. God is telling us that our actions do speak louder than our words; even to a Holy God.

As the Nike ads say, "JUST DO IT!" Get up and do something! Any activity on a regular basis will be a beginning of your new and improved 'temple maintenance' program, giving better care to your physical body, which is a home for the Holy Spirit of God.

About eight months after recovering from the birth of my second son, an unbelievably large episiotomy, and an excruciating painful eye injury, all taking place during the week following my delivery, I began to realize that I needed to become disciplined again to exercise on a regular basis if I truly wanted to feel better mentally and physically.

I had reached the point where I was desperate to lose the extra weight I'd gained during my pregnancy (over 60 lbs.) and feel better for me. I already knew that, for me, this meant jogging thirty minutes, five days a week.

I called my close friend, and proclaimed, "I'm ready to do it." Because I had two young sons and Becky's four sons were practically grown, she agreed to drive twenty minutes to my house Monday through Friday at seven a.m. What a gift she gave to me every day she drove over to run with me.

Whether it was chilly, foggy, wet or muggy, we met, and we ran. I was determined to stick with it.

I'll never forget the morning Becky showed up in her favorite pair of long sleeved, baggy, severely stretched out pajamas. She had just crawled out of bed, determined to support me, she climbed into her car and drove to my house for our run. I could hardly make it through the first mile because I was laughing so hard at her running in her pajamas.

During our thirty minute runs, I not only benefited physically, but also spiritually, emotionally, intellectually, and of course, socially, because our conversations were so healthy and well rounded. Because our friendship was centered around Christ, so did our conversations.

When our hearts and motives are pure, God acknowledges this by multiplying the benefits we gain from being with one another. I love it when God does this. It's much like multiplying the fish and the bread to feed the five thousand, but on a much more personal level.

As a direct result of my thirty minute five days a week runs with Becky, God honored my commitment to become healthier physically.

I remember the disappointment, panic and even fear, that rushed through me one morning when Becky called at 6:30 am. to tell me she was ill. I was reluctant, actually a bit fearful, to jog alone because years prior I had been chased a huge Rottweiler dog. Another time I was chased by two very muscular albino pit bull dogs, and on a third occasion I was chased by a strange man, so running alone was not something I looked forward to doing.

I hung up the phone, continued to put on my running shoes, and began to pray. My prayer was the simple prayer, a plea of a needy little girl to her great big God. That morning I asked God to be my running partner, and I walked out the front door believing that He would do just what He promised in Isaiah 41:10. *"Fear thou not; for I am with thee; be not dismayed; for I am thy God; I will strengthen thee; yea, I will help thee; yea, I will uphold thee with the right hand of my righteousness."*

I began reciting the words to the famous veggie tales song that goes something like, " God is bigger than the boogie man; He's bigger than Godzilla and the monsters on TV. My God's bigger than the boogie man, and He's big enough to care for me." Yea, I thought. My God is bigger than the boogie man, and He's bigger than anything that could threaten me on my run.

As I ran my regular route that morning, I enjoyed an enriching chat with the Lord. I thanked Him for my wonderful husband, my two precious sons, my extended family members, my friends, and my church. I spent the entire thirty minutes thanking Him and praising Him not only for all the blessings He had bestowed upon me and my family, but simply for Who He was; God Almighty, my Creator, worthy of all my honor and praise.

I vowed that morning, as I still must do every morning, to continue my early morning runs, with or without a friend because I had to do it for me.

I remember pouring my heart out to God that morning committing to run alone if necessary, while asking Him to help me become disciplined in my physical workout once again; and He did just that. Within a matter of weeks, my thirty minute run had become routine again, and I was feeling more disciplined and healthier mentally, spiritually and physically. Praise be to God who is faithful to empower us in all areas of our lives, and thank God for friends who care.

Susan Cantwell recently wrote a book entitled, *Mind Over Matter...Personal Choices For A Lifetime Of Fitness*, which acknowledges the fact that for many women the problem isn't lack of discipline or motivation, but lack of planning.

Ms. Cantwell explains that "people feel discouraged when they try to start exercising and eat properly, only to revert to their former bad habits. Most of us who fail to reach our goals and stay there permanently fail because the most crucial step on the road to implementing healthy change is the one we most often overlook." She believes the key step is the pre–planning or preparation phase, and she teaches that it is the foundation on which success is built.

I agree with Ms. Cantwell, that with many women who are unsuccessful in their attempts to become more physically fit, the problem may be the lack of planning. It's just so easy to skip the planning process and make impulse purchases of new books featuring the latest healthy fitness plans, or pieces of exercise equipment from the home shopping network, and be hopeful that we've finally found the answer we've been waiting for...our key to a lifetime of healthier living.

Let's face it, there are hundreds of programs designed to help us become more healthy, and while some are more credible than others, the best method for each of us is the one we can stick to for a lifetime.

What may work for your best friend, co–worker, or neighbor may not be the program best suited for you, so be careful when selecting a form of physical activity.

Physical activity is defined as any movement of the body or substantial parts of the body produced by muscles and resulting in energy expenditure. Any physical activity(movement of the body) whose purpose is to improve some dimension of a woman's wellness is referred to exercise. Could the word exercise actually be defined in such a simple non–threatening, painless way? Exercise shouldn't be something we dread, quite the contrary, it should be something we enjoy or at least tolerate and something we are actually thankful we can do.

Sitting in a hotel room in Keystone, Colorado, I was moved to tears while watching a television interview of a teenaged boy who had been born with no legs. As I admired this boys courage and dedication, God gently reminded me that afternoon that my healthy body with two healthy strong legs was not only a blessing, but also a privilege which I had never thanked God for making possible.

From that day forward, whenever I began to dread my workout or my run, I travel back in my mind and visit that brave young man, and immediately I begin to thank God for the blessing of healthy legs and the privilege to move them.

I encourage you to read the awesome testimonies of people who do not have the physical use of their bodies, as you do, and you will find a renewed sense of gratefulness for the privilege to move your healthy body.

Recently, a refreshing advertisement for New Balance running shoes for women caught my attention, as it emphasized the true meaning of exercise; to improve a women's wellness, by simply making her better. The advertisement read,

You can run to become a better runner
Or you can run to become a better mother,
Or a better doctor, Or a better teacher, Or a better friend.
You can run to become a better runner.
Or you can run to become better.

I can really identify with this ad because I'm not running to become a better runner; I'm not even a runner. I'm technically a jogger, who jogs and does a few resistance exercises for the purpose of becoming a better woman. I have found that when I am exercising on a regular basis, I feel better mentally and physically.

Because of the positive affect that exercise has on my mental state, I am a better wife, mother, and friend. I exercise because it makes be healthier inside and outside.

Several years ago my friend Karen and I decided to train together for the Disney Half Marathon which is a 13.1 mile run through Disney World in Orlando.

We found that the best time for us to run together was in the evening after our children were bathed and tucked into bed. Karen would drive to my home three nights a week since my neighborhood had better lighting than hers. We would run at 8:30, 9:00, sometimes 9:30 or 10:00, depending on our family's schedules.

I know this sounds almost insane to exercise at such a late hour, but we were determined to discipline ourselves to run together to get into better shape, and to train for this half–marathon. It was important for us to have our family's settled in each night before we left them to exercise, this way we could feel good about putting first things first.

God truly smiled on our time together. Night after night, we enjoyed wonderful conversations in which we would share what was on our hearts, the issues that our family's were facing, and how God was working in our lives on a daily basis.

After successfully finishing the half–marathon in 3:21 minutes, once again our families' schedules changed and so did our running routine. Karen went back to running at 5:30 a.m. in her neighborhood, and I would run at 7:30 a.m. in mine.

From season to season, as our families grow older, our lives and our priorities will change, and so will the nature of our physical workouts. That's simply the natural progression of life; from one season to the next our lives are constantly changing, whether we like it or not.

I encourage you to take into consideration where you are in life, your season of life, when setting goals and beginning a new exercise regimen. It's so easy to apply unnecessary pressure upon ourselves by setting unrealistic fitness goals.

Ecclesiastes 3:1 addresses the different seasons of life, *"To everything there is a season, and a time to every purpose under heaven."* Allow me to give you a personal, real life example.

Before I was married I had all the time in the world to spend on myself and my exercise program, so I worked out in a gym five to six days a week. I owned and operated a small aerobics studio, Fitness Unlimited, in which I taught two and sometimes three classes per day to keep instructor overhead down.

This was the season of my life in which I was able to basically exercise whenever, however, and wherever I chose because I didn't have a family's schedule to consider.

This was also the season in which God began to plant the desire inside of me to help myself and other women to become healthier and more balanced, working fitness into their individual lifestyles in a way that would work best for each woman in their unique life situation.

Many times women limit themselves to exercise routines that they followed when they were in an earlier season of life, which is unrealistic because ever–changing life circumstances can impact all areas of a woman's life. We tend to limit ourselves to what we've always done or what society and those around us may feel is acceptable at the time. Fully exposed, this is peer pressure at it's best, and we do not have to fall captive to it's trap.

Not only can we approach our physical fitness from an unlimited point of view, but we can also strip the traditional limits from the other areas of our lives, allowing us to become more healthy and fit in every area of our lives.

God never intended for His girls to limit fitness to the physical dimension. He desires that we live a life that is focused on spiritually fitness, first and foremost followed by a balanced approach to physical fitness, social fitness, emotional fitness and intellectual fitness.

As our lives naturally change when we pass from season to next, we must make changes in the way we approach our fitness, being sure not to limit ourselves to the routines that worked best in the earlier seasons of life. (i.e. unmarried, married with no children, married with children, etc.)

If it sounds like I'm giving you a permission slip to do anything that you feel works for best for you in the season of life you're presently in, I am. God wants to tear down the crazy boxes filled with 'what's excepted' and 'what's expected' of us when it comes to physical fitness, so consider yourselves free of the weight of guilt that comes from not measuring up to someone else's fitness program ideals.

What you decide works best for you is between you and God, and don't doubt for a minute that He isn't 100% interested in your physical health because He cares about every detail and every aspect of each of His girls' lives.

He created us and is well aware of the fact that the state of our physical health and fitness directly affects our emotional state. God's desire for His girls is to live free of bondage in all areas, including physical fitness, enabling us to live the life that He intended for us to live, focused on Him, and healthy in all areas.

Fitness Unlimited was the first seed God planted in my life that began to grow into my passion to help women experience the freedom that comes with embracing the unlimited approach to fitness.

After I was married I entered into a new season of life, married without children, in which my priorities changed. Because I wanted to spend time with Brad, I chose to workout with him, thus changing the times and nature of my workout.

As I took the big leap into the next season of my life, married with one child, wow, did my priorities change. My baby was a priority because that tiny little person depended on me for his entire existence. Needless to say my workout change drastically. My husband and I purchased a baby jogger and when I couldn't jog before Brad left for work, I'd take my baby jogging with me in a baby jogger. My time at the gym had decreased considerably because it was much more convenient for me to workout at home while the baby napped.

Then, my biggest adjustment came after my second son was born. As I described to you earlier in this chapter, I found that it was best for me to run in the morning before Brad left for work rather than attempting to take both boys with me. Although I'd seen women walking and jogging with double baby joggers, and biking with double baby carts behind them, running without my boys first thing in the morning worked best for me.

Choosing what type of workout and what time works best for you in your present season of life makes a huge difference in the success of making your workout a regular part of your daily life.

I hear women say it all the time, "I was in such great shape when I was twenty–five," or they'll say, "I only weighed 120 lbs. on my wedding day," and I want to ask them why in the world would they expect themselves to be the same today as they were years ago, when everything in your life has changed.

As we grow older our physical bodies change and that's the fact, sisters. It doesn't have to be something we dread, in fact, in Proverbs 31:25 encourages women to "*be a woman of strength and dignity; and have no fear of old age*." I know this is much easier said than done, but God does promise to work His word into our very being if we obey Him by believing and obeying His Word.

Up until the age of twenty–five our bodies naturally increase in energy and strength. But then a woman's body begins a long slide as her energy reserves and strength begin to gradually decline.

Somewhere from the mid to late thirties to the early forties, most women begin to notice drastic changes in their body as their metabolism begins to slow down, hormones begin to fluctuate, and our bodies require more physical activity in order to simply maintain our present body weight. At forty, I am presently experiencing all of these changes and I will say nothing and no one could have prepared me for such drastic, even mysterious changes in my body.

Many times in our younger years we can tend to neglect our bodies and maybe even abuse them by not eating healthy foods or exercising regularly, then, we have this "wake–up call" and it can be quite an eye opener and difficult to deal with at first.

Recent studies have shown that it is never too late for a woman to benefit from taking better care of her physical body by incorporating some form of weight bearing exercise. Weight bearing exercise promotes improved bone density, an extremely important consideration in the prevention of osteoporosis after ages 50 to 60. A great example of weight bearing exercise is walking, in which a woman bears the weight of her own body with each step.

As we address the topic of regular physical activity (exercise) in a woman's life, just remember that each of us will need to choose an activity and program that best suits us, considering our schedule and life circumstances.

Exercise is simply a form of physical activity where your muscles are moving, calories are being expended, body is growing healthier and stronger, and you are feeling better because of it.

While the purpose of this chapter is to address the importance of WHY we should exercise instead of WHAT we do for exercise, I want to briefly highlight the four basic components of a balanced exercise program for women.

Benefits of Physical Movement

Reduces .... anxiety, stress and fatigue
Enhances .... feeling of well being; release of endorphins (body, mind and spirit)
Improves..self–image
Builds ....confidence in making positive changes
Increases .... flexibility, joint mobility, and range of motion
Increases .... muscle strength and muscle definition
Increases ....bone density
Increases .... physical capacity
Increased... cardiovascular fitness
Provides ....rehabilitation benefits
Decreases... cholesterol
Decreases... hypertension
Decreases...body fat

The American Council on Exercise (ACE) makes the following statement concerning the health benefits of exercise for healthy individuals. "Regular exercise enhances a person's physiological or functional capacity and enables him or her to achieve an improved quality of life. With a heightened physiological reserve, the regular stresses and strains of life, whether physical or psychological, are taken in stride."

Prior to beginning any type of exercise program, I encourage women to first consult their physician for medical screening. After receiving a green light from your physician I recommend that you seek the guidance of a reputable fitness professional who can help you set realistic health and fitness goals, establish your fitness baseline by conducting a fitness evaluation, and design a basic program for you, which includes cardiovascular training, strength training and flexibility stretching, and demonstrate proper form and execution of specific exercises based on the amount of time you have to invest per workout. Begin by taking small steps, for example, if you're not exercising at all at the present, begin by setting aside 15 minutes for your physical workout, and simply increase as you can.

Remember, what may work for your best friend, co–worker, or neighbor may not be the program best suited for you, so be careful when selecting a form of physical activity.

Whether you have chosen to follow a specific training regimen, such as Bill Phillips' Body for Life program or a basic program consisting of fitness walking and basic strength training exercises, some guidance on proper form and execution of the prescribed exercises can reduce your risk of injury.

When considering your choices for exercise keep in mind the importance of implementing exercise into your life as a permanent lifestyle change which will continue throughout your lifetime, as apposed to a short–term, quick fix, injury inducing, killer workout.

Of course, when your desire is to increase muscle strength and decrease body fat, your program will be more intense in nature until you reach the point in which you are ready to simply maintain your present state.

When setting realistic fitness goals, one must not forget to consider your present season of life. It is imperative to the success of making fitness a lifestyle instead of simply a weight–loss or weight–gain program.

You'll save yourself much unnecessary stress, caused by the guilt of not measuring up to unrealistic expectations. Remember, with each new season of life comes new life circumstances and new reasons for exercising, thus, we need to make changes in our exercise routine based upon these pre–planning questions.

Deciding *why* you want to make exercise a part of your life, *what* type of exercise is best suited for you, *where* would be the most sensible place for you to workout, and *when* could you designate time for your workout. These are all questions that should be clearly answered prior to beginning a new fitness regimen.

There are women that know they simply need to go to a fitness center to workout, while other women realize they will only workout if they can do it right in their own homes. One is not better than the other, it's simply a matter of what works best for you. What matters the most is that you keep your exercise program as simple and convenient to perform as possible.

These days, I am not working out in a fitness center because I have found it more convenient for me to jog in my neighborhood, return to my driveway for tricep dips off the bumper of my car, standing push–ups off the side of my car, and then to the back porch for bicep curls, a few leg exercises and abdominal crunches. Short and simple works best for me in this season of life. For me the quietness of a new morning alone with God and absent of the head banging music of some fitness centers is exactly what I choose at this time in my life.

As I jog through my neighborhood, I pray for each of my neighbors, asking God to place a hedge of protection around their homes and families. I ask Him to give His angels charge over each of them to keep them safe always, especially each of the children as they play in our neighborhood.

I ask God to make Himself known to them in a new way each day, drawing us each closer to Himself. I love giving these secret gifts of prayer to my friends and neighbors while I'm out jogging through our neighborhood. It adds a new purpose to my workout increasing my motivation and discipline to keep get out there as much as I possibly can and make my prayer run. One day, as I was finishing my run, one of my neighbors was power–walking by our home. She delivered a cheerful hello, and told me that she always says a prayer for my family as she walks by our home.

What a blessing to know someone cares enough to pray for my family. A prayer is truly a gift from the heart; a priceless treasure. Thank you, Charlotte, for your many prayers for not only my family, but all the families in our neighborhood.

Even though my professional field has been health and fitness it doesn't exclude me from dreaded my workout from time to time, and I do. Isn't it amazing how we sometimes try to find some reason, any reason NOT to workout.

I don't know about you, but my girlfriends and I laugh all the time about the hilarious thought process we go through prior to our workouts. I've caught myself walking aimlessly around the house finding the weirdest things to do, things like cleaning out drawers, closets, the refrigerator just minutes before I had planned to workout. I'll even repeated walk to the front window to analyze the clouds in hopes of seeing it start to rain. Then there's always all of my basic household chores that must be done, and always seem to heighten in importance just before I am to begin my workout.

Although most times I feel absolutely great after my run, sometimes it is difficult just to get out there, but it's something we must each commit to do.

I try to workout in the morning, but some days it's impossible for me to workout in the morning, so I designate time to workout later in the day on those days. Some days it works and some days it doesn't, and guess what? It's just ok. If we exercise on a regular basis, when life calls and we have to miss a regularly scheduled walk or workout, don't sweat it.

Many times God uses life interruptions to steer us away from becoming obsessed with our physical dimension and eventually bound by a workout schedule. By doing this He also helps us to live healthier more balanced lifestyles, keeping our main focus on our spiritual workouts.

Try to lighten up a little on yourselves, and realize that it's better to squeeze your exercise in somewhere in the day, rather than just relinquish yourself to failure for not being able to follow a specific program to the very last detail.

Making healthy lifestyle changes that involve successfully incorporating exercise into your life requires a delicate balance of determination and self–discipline, complimented by a sensible flexibility towards ourselves concerning obstacles that may arise due to life circumstances.

God honors the obedience of His girls by keeping His promises to us as we obey Him. As we act in obedience and strive to provide the highest quality of care for our bodies, "which is our reasonable service," God will honor our efforts.

In Matthew 6:33, Jesus instructs us to "*seek first His kingdom and His righteousness, and all these things will be given to you as well.*" In this passage, we find a powerful truth that when applied to our lives can bring great and wonderful blessings.

God is telling us that if His girls will place Him first above all things in our lives and give our spiritual workout priority over our physical workouts, He will honor our efforts in both of these areas by supernaturally enabling us to grow in our relationship with Him as well as work regular exercise into our daily schedules.

When we have invited Christ into our hearts and lives our bodies do become an actual dwelling place for the Holy Spirit; God's very own presence abides within us. What unfathomable value that places on our physical bodies as the home or temple of the actual Spirit of God.

While we are responsible for presenting ourselves "holy, and acceptable to God," a great truth concerning our physical bodies is that our bodies are the least important thing about us and one day they will return to the dust. Our spirits will soar to the heavens to live forever in a spiritual body in the very presence of our Heavenly Father. Praise be to God, Our Father!!

I can hardly wait but until that day while we are on this earth, our bodies are a precious gift that God has given to His girls, and the quality of care we provide for it is our gift back to our God!

Since habits become power, make them work with you and not against you.
—E. Stanley Jones

— 11 —

You Go, Girl!

And God saw everything that He had made, and behold, it was very good. Genesis 1:31

I am fearfully and wonderfully made. Psalms 139:14

During the past several years, my husband and I have been blessed with the opportunity to travel into different parts of our country, as well as to other countries. One thing I've enjoyed the most about our travels is simply observing the women in different areas of our world.

Women have such unique ways of expressing themselves. Whether we are aware of it or not, we express ourselves by the way we dress, the way we speak and in the very way we carry ourselves. Many of these expressions are directly related to the culture we were exposed to as children, and the culture of the society we are presently exposed to on a daily basis.

As I observe women, I find myself celebrating their uniqueness as it differs from mine.

When I was in Italy, I celebrated the beautiful Italian women who carried themselves with much pride on the main streets of Rome, Florence and Sorrento. I celebrated their beautiful Italian features; the deepest shades of black, red, and blonde hair, dramatic eyes and eyebrows, and what seemed to be flawless olive skin.

I enjoyed listening to the women speak with strong Italian accents sometimes in English, sometimes in Italian, but always accompanied by passionate Italian hand gestures and body language.

As I inhaled the fresh air of Italy, it was as though I wanted to take in as much of the culture, style and passion of these women as I possibly could. I truly admired their individual styles, their accents and their genuine passion for life and family. Throughout Italy and all the world, there are women of different heights, shapes, sizes, skin tones and textures, personalities, life experiences and life circumstances, uniquely different while sharing commonalities at the same time.

When women celebrate their differences in culture, dress and expression, instead of competing with one another, or worse, feeling guilty for not measuring up to another's standards, we become enhanced by one another's individualities that we bring to the world wide society of women.

The key to celebrating the uniqueness of other women is to first learn to accept and celebrate our own unique qualities. When we recognize our natural beauty which comes from deep within ourselves, and become comfortable with who we are, only then will we experience true freedom to celebrate our uniqueness and the unique qualities of the women around us.

Many times it's easier for us to celebrate women of other cultures because of the drastic differences, rather than women in our own countries, towns, and neighborhoods. The more we have in common with a woman the more pressure we may tend to place on ourselves to measure up to the same standard of these women.

Have you been to South Beach in Miami, Florida or Muscle Beach in Venice, California? Maybe, you've strolled down Rodeo Drive in Beverly Hills, California. If not, I bet you've been standing in line at the supermarket, or at the magazine rack at a book store or grocery store, and noticed on the cover the youthful and flawless, thin and tanned, seemingly perfect bodies, with what the advertiser would like for you to believe is your answer for success and happiness.

Women have been bombarded for years with the outright lie that there is one way to look and live that will bring success, respect, happiness and fulfillment to their lives. This lie is continually reinforced through the media by the super–models suggesting perfection appearing on magazine covers, in advertisements and articles in magazines, in movie theaters, and on television.

Even if we choose not to expose ourselves to these things by refusing to purchase them, we are still faced with the endless billboards with the bay watch babes.

Michelle Stacey, a regular contributor to Shape magazine, wrote an article entitled, *Beauty's Empty Promises*, in which she highlights the book *Venus Envy: A History of Cosmetic Surgery* (John Hopkins University Press, 1997), written by Historian Elizabeth Haiken.

In her article, Stacey describes the *Parable of the First Impression*, one of the most powerful ideas ever presented by modern advertising, which was first articulated in the 1920's. She explains, "The Parable insisted that all of one's success depended on first impressions.

Everything from toothpaste to house paint was sold by the Parable."

In 1927, the book *Any Girl Can Be Good Looking* translated the Parable specifically for women stating:" Being good looking is no longer optional. Competition is so keen and the world moves so fast that we simply can't afford not to sell ourselves on sight. People who pass us on the street can't know that we're clever and charming unless we look it."

Stacey suggested, "If the Parable is no longer stated so boldly, maybe that's because in the last 70–odd years, we've internalized it. The challenge now is to resist the tyranny of the Parable, to step out of the beauty rat race and say enough is enough!"

Stacey concludes her article with this challenge to women, "Most of us grew up with another parable, told to us by the ultimate authority, Mom: Beauty is more than skin deep. We can choose to live by it."

I applaud the individuals and corporations who have begun to step to the forefront of the advertising and media community, by making bold statements which reinforce healthy thoughts concerning size, imperfection, natural beauty, uniqueness and individuality.

Oprah Winfrey, through her television show, her magazine and her personal struggles and victories, has encouraged and empowered women to love and accept themselves for the unique person they are.

Fashion model, Lauren Hutton, is a great example of a woman celebrating her uniqueness. Her timeless beauty and unique look has continued for decades, and is characterized by the large space she sports between her two front teeth.

I applaud her for being so comfortable with who she is and the uniqueness of her smile that she never gave in to the pressures of the perfection perverted society that she would lead us to believe that perfectly straight teeth are more desirable than a unique smile marked with spacing teeth.

It's refreshing, encouraging, and clearly evident that Lauren Hutton has become quite comfortable in her own skin, with a beauty that is uniquely hers, as she proudly addresses real life issues that women face as we grow older. Her natural inner beauty seems to jump out at us, confidently shouting, I'm comfortable being me. She is a natural beauty, but it's truly her inner beauty and self–acceptance that makes her skin side shine.

Crystal Light has a new ad that says, *'here's to taking your own advice, making friends with your laugh lines…raise a glass and enjoy life on your own terms.'* What a great way to give women permission to be comfortable with whatever age they are, and become friends with the woman they become as life progresses.

I am encouraged and excited to see corporations like J.C. Penneys, Sprint, Crystal Light, and Dockers designing advertisements which take the emphasis away from being a perfect size, age, shape, or look, and instead, emphasizes the freedom that comes from just being comfortable being yourself, whatever age, size, shape, or look that may be.

I absolutely love the new Docker's ads for their NICE PANTS. One of their advertisements shows an average family of five standing on the beach in a row holding hands. Their white t–shirts each spell one word, and they collectively say 'HAVE A NICE DAY!' At the bottom of the double paged ad, the following sentence was typed. WOULDN'T IT BE *NICE* IF SIZE DIDN'T REALLY MATTER? IF THE LABEL IN YOUR PANTS JUST SAID, "HAVE A NICE DAY?"

Most of us girls most likely have three types of pants hanging in our closets which fall into one of three categories; skinny pants, fat pants and the–ones–that–fit–me–now pants. If you don't ask which pants I'm wearing these days, I promise not to ask you either?

After being inspired by the Dockers ads, I decided to work diligently at changing my thinking concerning the size of my pants. In my effort to change my perspective from three types of pants to just 'nice pants,' I organized my clothes in my closet by color instead of by size, working my pants into their appropriate color category instead of size.

I find it very necessary to continue de–programming myself daily as I walk into my closet to select a pair of pants to wear, and I expect that I'll have to stay aware of my tendency to allow a tiny number on a little tag to influence my attitude and emotional state for even a day.

If rearranging your closet doesn't help you reprogram your thinking, I may have just the idea for you, so listen to this funny, but true story.

One day, as I was ironing a new pair of Docker pants that my husband, Brad, had just purchased for himself, I decided to check the tag inside the pants to see if he had given in and bought the 38's. (These days we're both simply trying to hold steady at the sizes we are…and not allow our weight to get out of control as we age.) The strangest thing happened. I couldn't find a tag with the size anywhere on the pants.

Just at that moment, I remembered this new NICE PANTS ad, and I thought, could they mean that they are not putting the size inside their pants anymore?

I raced to Brad's closet to check his other Dockers pants, and sure enough, there were no tags to be found in any of his new Dockers. I love it. What a great, wonderful concept. No sizes inside of your pants to encourage you to identify yourself and your self worth with a size label. Now, this is healthy progress, I thought.

Several weeks later, sitting at my computer, I pondered the interesting fact that each pair of my husbands Dockers pants were missing the size tag inside, and for some very peculiar reason a suspicious feeling came over me.

I, then called to my sweet husband, who was reading in our bedroom, and I prefaced my question by saying, “Now Brad, I’m going to ask you a question, and you don’t need to feel embarrassed or shameful when you answer. You may answer with a simple yes or no, and I promise we won’t discuss the issue any further.”

Then, I proceeded with my question and asked, “Did you by any chance, cut out all of the size tags in your Dockers pants?” After about thirty seconds of complete silence, Brad peeped out a weak, “Yes,” at which time we both broke out into hilarious uncontrolled laughter.

Well, size is a real issue that we must address and conquer, and it will continue to affect our attitudes about ourselves until we decide to do something about it. Whether you choose to reorganize your closet or cut out those haunting little size tags, I encourage you to do whatever it takes to change the way you think about the size of your clothes.

Another Dockers ad pictures an attractive, healthy looking woman in her early fifties with graying hair, dressed in black boot–cut stretch pants, an aqua long–sleeved sweater and black boots, leaning against a brick wall, eating a tootsie–pop.

The typed sentence at the bottom of the page read, ‘WOULDN’T IT BE *NICE* IF ONLY YOU COULD DECIDE YOUR AGE? NOT THE WORLD, THE MIRROR, OR THE DRIVER’S LICENSE IN YOUR *PANTS* POCKET.’ This fresh approach to advertising brought out the reality and naturalness of the aging process, and that it didn’t mean we had to dress, act or speak any certain way as we aged.

Accomplished and well–known country singer, Trisha Yearwood, who has released her tenth album, received three Grammys and numerous music–industry awards was quoted in US Weekly concerning the pressure she felt from others to change how she looked.

She shares that when she was about twenty pounds lighter than the present she wore a gorgeous dress to the Country Music Awards, which happened to be the first year she was nominated. Trisha remembers feeling excited to wear this Marilyn Monroe dress that was body–hugging, accented with great straps, and says, “I looked fabulous!”

Trisha felt like a movie star on this magical night, and then she found out the next day that someone at the record label had called her stylist, insisting that Trisha shouldn’t show her arms in her dresses. In disbelief, Trisha said, "They thought my arms were too big, and the dress wasn't flattering."

Trisha ignored that advice and resisted other efforts people made to mold her physically or professionally into an industry standard. She said, "I've gotta be who I am. I would love to be thinner, but this is who I am, and I try to look the best that I can. I am not a slave to my body, and at this point, nobody is going to say anything about it."

Trisha Yearwood wants to spread some of this confidence around by encouraging women and girls to say, 'this is what I am, and it's cool.' Preach it, sister! You Go, Girl!

Many designers and companies are using fuller figured, middle aged, women with seemingly imperfect, but beautiful features to model their clothing, instead of a size 4, 'Twiggy–like' model from the seventies.

In her most recent advertisement, Marina Rinaldi, a designer of clothing sizes 10–22, with specialty boutiques in all the major cities of the world, shows a naturally beautiful woman, whose size you cannot estimate because of the creative photography, holding a camera while wearing a classic suede jacket.

The emphasis of this ad is definitely not on the size of the model; instead, the focus is on her style. At the top left corner of the full page ad, big, bold red letters spell out, 'STYLE IS NOT A SIZE…' I love it. What a great way to reinforce in women the truth that 'who they are' is not defined by their size, whether they are a size 4, 10, 12 or 22.

Bravo, Ms. Rinaldi. Thank you, Thank you, Thank you, for caring about the health of a woman's self–image, instead of simply selling your designs at any cost. You truly have the best interest of women at the very heart of your company.

While on vacation at the Long Boat Key Club, I noticed something interesting about the behavior of women when they spent time in their swim suits around the pool and on the beach. Many of them seemed uncomfortable wearing their swim suits, no matter what style they were wearing.

Despite size, many women appeared to be constantly adjusting those little pieces of fabric known as swim suits, sometimes wrapping in a towel, a cover–up, or attempting to hid behind a raft or inter–tube.

I have a dear friend that is a very small framed girl who has always been concerned with keeping a healthy amount of weight on her body, as she wears sizes 0–2 clothes.

During the past several years, my friend became ill, and the rate in which she recovered was negatively influenced by her low body weight.

She, too, is uncomfortable wearing her swimsuit without a cover–up when in public because she is not comfortable with her tiny body.

Truth be known, most women, including myself, would prefer to swim in long shorts and a t–shirt. One of those old fashioned, one piece PE outfits that we wore in middle school would do just fine.

You remember the one piece cotton outfit with the elastic waist band that was royal blue on the bottom half with blue and white stripes on the top half. In 7th grade, although it was so incredibly comfortable, I dreaded wearing that outfit almost as much as I dreaded taking a group shower with all of those older girls that already had breasts.

Several weeks ago, while sitting on the beach at Marco Island, I was flipping through the latest issue of the Oprah magazine, I turned to a spread on beach cover–ups. The sentence at the bottom of the page read, *'How to stop worrying about your body and learn to love, love, love the beach.'*

This is exactly what all women need to do. We must become comfortable enough in our own skin; comfortable enough to enjoy family moments around the pool and at the beach, and refuse to waste these precious memory making moments being preoccupied by how we look in our swimsuits and if a body part has been unintentionally revealed. How do we do this? How do we become comfortable with the skin we are in, and continue to work toward positive change at the same time? Who says you have to wear a traditional swimsuit anyway? Why not wear shorts instead? I am thrilled with my new board shorts, and will probably never return to a traditional swimsuit again.

The good news is that we can control the way we think about ourselves, and develop a healthy body image which will greatly impact our self–esteem, and the not so good news is that the media will continue for years to come to highlight the most beautiful women with close–to–perfect bodies in our world to sell their products.

To protect ourselves from unnecessary self–judgment, we must make a point to acknowledge what we actually have in common with a woman, before comparing ourselves to her, whether it be at the mall, at a fitness center, in a magazine, at the beach, in the school pick up line, at the office, or in the supermarket or airport.

Ask yourself, these questions. Has this photograph been touched up? What do you and this woman have in common? What does she do for a career? What are her obvious priorities in life? What 'season of life' is she presently in? What culture and atmosphere was she raised in as a child and teen? What life issues, struggles and victories, has she experienced in her lifetime? What do you know *for sure* about this woman that isn't just media hype or speculation on your part?

Our answers to the above questions might help you understand the importance of acknowledging the unique differences that exist between ourselves and another women, and how ridiculous it would be to compare ourselves to them.

As we accept the fact that God created us each uniquely different from every other woman on earth, we will begin to accept ourselves and become more comfortable with who we are. Self–acceptance, (accepting ourselves), will help us to boost our own self–image, (the way we view ourselves), which will increase your self–esteem, (the amount of worth we place on ourselves.)

Dr. Phillip McGraw describes self–esteem as being 'the degree to which you assign worth to yourself.' He explains that the level of a woman's self esteem is up to her, and says, "Your self–regard may be influenced by your interaction with others and by your experiences in the world, but in the final analysis it's entirely in your hands.

For instance, if you compare yourself to others and feel that you come out on top, your level of self–esteem might be high; and if you come out at the bottom, your level of self–esteem might be low."

He clarifies, that "neither conclusion is necessarily reflective of your actual worth because that's not something determined in a contest with others." Dr. McGraw suggests that we examine the perception we have of ourselves, by listening to our self–talk. Many times when we're not feeling good about ourselves, we will have negative conversations with ourselves with many times lead to applying negative labels to ourselves.

He encourages women to, "stop the self–flagellation, criticism, whining, and pity parties and find true value as a unique human being by changing the harmful conversations and labels into positive ones."

Dr. McGraw also warns, "If you are telling yourself that you are worthless, that statement is never correct. But if your are telling yourself that you are lazy and selfish, that may or may not be true. If it is true, recognize that you must get busy and change it."

In Psalms 139:14, God is assuring us that nothing about us is worthless, quite to the contrary, we are *"fearfully and wonderfully made."* When we struggle with our self–worth, all we need to do is remember what God did for us. He loved and valued us so much that He sent His Only Son to die on the cross for us, to save us from our sins, and reunite us with Him.

For us to say or think that we, God's created girls, are worthless, would be an insult to a Holy God, who created us. God made you and I "good." We are special to Him; So special that He sacrificed His Only Son so that we might live.

God made you and me unique, and wrapped us in the skin that we're in, and He sees us as, "good," so why shouldn't we strive to do the same? Let's commit to accept ourselves, who we are in God's eyes, and no one else's, and not waste an entire lifetime uncomfortable in the skin God wrapped us in.

Not so long ago, I was speaking to the eighth graders at St. Joseph's Catholic School, concerning Healthy Eating Habits, Regular Physical Activity and Healthy Self–Image.

I wanted to help the students understand that a person cannot be defined by the outward appearance; and that the outward appearance may actually reveal very little about the heart and soul of that person.

I displayed four gifts wrapped in various styles of wrapping paper and gift bags to help me make my point. One gift was wrapped in a beautiful sky blue, twelve inch gift bag with a daisy on the bag. Another gift was wrapped in an old recycled six inch gift bag with a fishing boat on the front.

The third gift was wrapped in a sweet, tiny little two inch gift box covered with the tiniest pink and red roses and topped with a fancy gold bow. The fourth gift was wrapped in a slightly tattered, plain brown paper lunch bag with the top rolled down.

I asked the students to tell me which gift appealed to them the most. Which one would you choose? We discussed that fact that the outside wrapping had very little to do with the gift that was on the inside. All four gift wrappings could have held a beautiful gift inside, even the plain brown lunch bag. Needless to say, not one student was drawn to the plain brown lunch bag, and neither was I, for that matter, due to it's unappealing exterior.

I explained that we selected a gift based solely on the outward packaging of the gift, not knowing the content inside. We based our decision on the only part of the gift that we could see…it's outward packaging.

I helped the students understand that people are much like packages. Many times we misjudge a person based on our first impressions of their outward appearance. That is exactly what our outward appearance is, our gift wrapping.

Just as the wrapping paper covering a gift doesn't necessarily describe the gift inside, our outward appearance doesn't define the spirit of the person who lives inside of the physical body.

Our skin is simply the wrapping paper God chose to house our spirit and mind in for our short stay on earth. When we leave this earth, we will leave our physical wrapping paper behind(our bodies), and our spirits will live on into eternity without the earthly gift wrapping.

I want to share with you a writing by an anonymous author, entitled "A Woman's Look in the Mirror."

A Woman's Look in the Mirror

Age 3: *Looks at herself and sees a Queen!*

Age 8: *Looks at herself and sees herself as Cinderella/Sleeping Beauty.*

Age 15: *Looks at herself and sees herself as Cinderella/Sleeping Beauty/Cheerleader or if she is PMSing: sees Fat/Pimples/UGLY ("Mom I can't go to school looking like this!)*

Age 20: *Looks at herself and sees "too fat/too thin, too short/too tall, too straight/too curly"–but decides she's going anyway.*

Age 30: *Looks at herself and sees "too fat/too thin, too short/too tall, too straight/too curly"–but decides she doesn't have time to fix it, she's going anyway.*

Age 40: *Looks at herself and sees "too fat/too thin, too short/too tall, too straight/too curly"–but says, "At least, I'm clean" and goes anyway.*

Age 50: *Looks at herself and sees "I am" and goes wherever she wants to go.*

Age 60: *Looks at herself and reminds herself of all the people who can't even see themselves in the mirror anymore. Goes out and conquers the world.*

Age 70: *Looks at herself and sees wisdom, laughter and ability, goes out and enjoys life.*

Age 80: *Doesn't bother to look. Just puts on a purple hat and goes out to have fun with the world. (Maybe we all should grab that purple hat a little earlier in life!)*

Written by an anonymous author, The Beauty of a Woman so eloquently describes the beauty of a woman as follows. The beauty of a woman is not in the clothes she wears, the figure she carries, or the way she combs her hair.

The beauty of a woman must be seen within her eyes, because that is the doorway to her heart, the place where love resides.

The beauty of a woman is not in a facial mole. But true beauty in a woman is reflected in her soul. It is the caring that she lovingly gives, the passion that she shows, and the beauty of a woman with passing years–only grows!

As I begin each new day, I remind myself to grab that purple hat, and wear it all through the day, no matter what. I encourage you to join with me, and commit to wear your purple hat, no matter what condition your wrapping paper of life might be on any particular day, and no matter what anybody else may think.

I want to share a personal story of a friend, who has been suffering from a very low and sometimes no self–esteem. For most of her adult life, she has been searching for the perfect exercise program or diet plan to give her the thin body and physical look she desires.

Along the road to her quest for a better, more acceptable body, my friend, Kristen, has experienced the pain of constant self–criticism, harsh self–judgment of failure, and media and peer pressure to measure up to some ideal body type.

I admire her immensely for having the courage to walk through the painful process that has helped her acknowledge her low self–esteem, along with their origins and false truths, and seek out women, both personal and professional, who have helped reinforce a healthy, realistic perspective on the issues in her life.

I believe you, too, will be inspired to 'wear your purple hat everyday', instead of surrendering to outside pressures that may lead you into painful, unnecessary pursuits of the perfect, ideal body. Hopefully, you too, will stop "look'in for *help* in all the wrong places."

Kristen is a beautiful, vibrant, thirty–eight year old, Italian woman with stylish strawberry blonde hair that curls into her neck. She is a wife, a mother of three children, and a Registered Nurse, who has chosen to stay at home full–time with her children during this season of her life.

As Kristen and I sat at a local coffee bar, I asked her, "How do you feel about yourself, right now?" And this is what she said.

"I do like myself. I think I am humorous, personable, and caring. I think that society and the obsessions of other women influence the way I think about myself. They tell me that I'm not ok, but I don't feel like I'm that heavy. I'm a size 12, and that's ok with me. I feel like an average woman.

Whenever I go shopping for clothes, I look for my size, and it's always gone, while the petite racks are always full. This reaffirms to me that I'm am a normal, average sized woman. My friends encourage me to make healthier choices because they've noticed that my personality is better when I eat healthy, and I know this is true.

I'm a people pleaser, so I wouldn't dare order an entree that would be viewed as unhealthy, while dining with my girlfriends. I find that when we're at gatherings, most of the women won't go near the appetizers, while I'm dying to eat some. I usually make some kind of funny comment like, 'oh, let the fat girl in here.' I have a good sense of humor, and many times, I use it to put my self down as a way of giving myself permission to eat."

Kristen said that she doesn't want to be the 'fat girl eating' all the time, but rather the girl with the confidence and nice figure. As I sit here looking across this cozy table–for–two, I see a beautiful, funny, full of life Italian girl with many qualities that God made uniquely hers. Kristen's bubbly Italian spirit just jumps out, and draws me right into conversation with her.

"I'm Italian, and I love good food," she exclaimed. "I have wonderful memories of my Italian childhood filled with great family times always accompanied by my Mother's rich Italian recipes, which I want to prepare for my family and friends, in honor of these precious memories that are so dear to my heart."

Life is too short to give up all the foods you enjoy foods that warm the heart like the Poppy Seed Cake that Kristen's grandmother used to bake. When we eat healthy most of the time, we can enjoy these foods that bring back wonderful, cherished memories, on occasion.

As we were sitting at a cozy table for two at Richard's Coffee Shop on Central Avenue, Kristen pointed to her tummy. She said, "I think women will look at me and see this one inch roll around my waist, and not see me. They will think, 'Wow, that girl needs to lose weight,' instead of seeing the girl that lives inside this body.

Just yesterday, Kristen was in the Publix checkout line and almost grabbed the magazine with the headline, 'I lost 140 lbs.' She thought, "Why would I buy this? I'm not going to go on this crazy diet."

Most women, if they were honest, would admit to purchasing these magazines or at least being tempted to do so because they seem to be everywhere.

Our society places so much pressure on women to be thin, beautiful, rich, happy and successful. Perfection is what they portray, from People magazine to Cosmo. The truth is...being healthy is more important than being thin.

Although magazines are constantly selling women solutions for instant make–overs, lasting make–overs don't begin with a new lipstick or a better defined bicep. A true make–over that will last for your lifetime must begin inside the heart and soul of the woman. As her spirit and mind become healthier, her external self will improve as a result. Hmm. I love the fact that we change from the inside out.

How ironic that this is the exact opposite message that women get from society, and even from many of the women in their lives.

Kristen recently signed up for a 12 week weight loss program at a local gym, an experience she would not soon forget. She agreed to share this painful and degrading experience with me in hopes that other women would learn to stop "look'in for *help* in all the wrong places."

It all began when she and a couple of her friends decided to sign up for this 'boot camp' style program. When Kristen met the trainer, an unfit, fifty year old man, he greeted her with a "hi, honey." He continued to refer to her as 'honey' and 'babe' throughout the program. This made her extremely uncomfortable.

How unprofessional and inappropriate, I thought. She decided that she would put up with this...because she was desperate to succeed at losing weight. What she shared next infuriated me. He told Kristen that he would need to photograph her in a bikini. "A bikini!" she thought, "You've got to be kidding me." She hadn't worn a bikini in years, and now she not only was told to wear one, but allow a stranger to take pictures of her. Kristen thought... "If I owned a bikini, would I even be here, buddy."

Just listening to her made me want to deck this guy, and give him a piece of my mind.

As Kristen continued to share this painful experience with me, tears began to stream down her pretty face. I could see the pain in her eyes, and feel it in her words.

She arrived for her photographs in biking shorts, sports bra and a t–shirt. When it was her turn to enter the room, she felt nervous. When she entered the room, she was asked to remove her t–shirt. The male trainer remained in the room with her.

As she began to remove her shirt, she felt as though she was having an "out of body" experience. She was in a room with a middle aged, unfit man, whom she didn't even know, in clothes she wouldn't even wear in front of her husband, and he was going to photograph her.

Aaaahhhhhhggggggg!!!

Kristen's self–esteem was already so low, and there she was, feeling like she was supposed to pose for the camera like Jennifer Lopez. "Yeah, right," she thought.

Through her tears, she continues to open herself and share her painful experience with me across our cozy table for two. "There I was, standing in my spandex shorts and bra. He came up to me and began to pose my body for the pictures. He told me that I should have worn a bikini. He abruptly lifted my arms away from my body, and began to roll my biking shorts up my leg without even asking my permission.

I just stood there and allowed him to continue because I was so desperate to succeed with this program. He continued to pose me in different positions, as a girl took the pictures. Kristen became very quiet; unable to speak. I looked into her tear–filled eyes. The recollection of the assault on her person was more than she could bear. She began to describe how this man took body fat measurements with a skin fold caliper. He would grab her in numerous places all over her body to measure her body fat. Following each measurement, he would slowly rub the area, and say, "this will help prevent bruising, honey." The whole experience was degrading and humiliating.

The male trainer posted Kristen's measurements on a record sheet which he used for all of his clients. She could read the measurements of the woman who went before her. Now, everyone who followed her could view her confidential information.

This man concluded their appointment by saying to Kristen, "Honey, you're a beautiful woman, we just need to tone you up." Okay. Now I really want to deck this guy. Kristen cried all the way home from this nightmare of a consultation, and most of the evening. She felt so taken advantage of, so violated.

She did go back for her first several workouts. Her workout consisted of advanced exercises that were contraindicated for the back problems she had. The trainer said… "No pain, no gain, honey. Keep going. It won't hurt your back."

Kristen knew enough about her own body to realize that the pain she was experiencing was not healthy muscle soreness, it was damaging back pain. She didn't return to this program. Yes, she quit.

Another failed attempt to lose weight from Kristen's perspective. Is this an accurate assessment of her experience? NO WAY! Kristen is responsible for enrolling in this program. She did choose to continue on after she had already been repulsed by the trainer referring to her as "honey" and "babe."

She forced herself to endure this dreadful appointment because she wanted this program to work for her. Kristen's failure wasn't that she didn't successfully finish the program. She simply should have assessed the situation more accurately, and realized sooner, that this program and trainer was not for her.

This is 'easier said, than done.' Just a little mistake. No failure to be declared or carried by Kristen. No blame to be placed. Just the realization that this program is not for everyone, and it's certainly not for Kristen.

Let's face it. When women desperately want to lose weight, of course their emotions are involved in the decision making process, because weight is not simply a physical issue. For this is the reason so many women try programs, workouts, exercise machines, and diets that don't work because they don't suit their individual life circumstances.

Kristen had tried every weight loss program and diet plan under the sun. Low Carbs, High Carbs, No Carbs, Slim Fast. Like many women, you name it; she tried it.

She has finally found an eating plan that is working well for her. With the weight watchers, Kristen can make sensible choices, and still eat the foods she enjoys. This is a success for her, as she is making progress and gaining control over her eating, and the way she sees herself.

Kristen is more aware of the fact that she may be tempted by the passing but fleeting diets, like the famous and recently revived Hollywood Diet, and she refuses to succumb to the luring of these fad diets, and ignore their convincing statistics that promise quick results with a new lease on life.

Towards the end of our conversation that day, I looked at Kristen and smiled, as I began to share my thoughts. I told her that she was a beautiful woman; strong and delightfully humorous. I enjoyed being with Kristen that afternoon.

She is like so many of us, she has been trapped in a box of unrealistic expectations and failures that she has permitted to constrict her. I want to shout to all the women of the world and say, "It's time to tear down the boxes that somehow along the way we've allowed society, others and ourselves to use…to limit and define us.

We, as women, need to find the courage and confidence to be who we are, (which is God's girls, created 'good') and accept and love ourselves for it. It's healthy to want to change for the better, but it's important to like yourself in the process.

God wants His girls, you and me, to live free of the chains that seem to bind us, and it's not easy in a world where society creates so much unrealistic expectation for women, but it can be done. Day, after day, we must keep shaking ourselves free of these unhealthy expectations, by seeing ourselves through God's eyes.

I ask God daily to give me His perspective concerning myself, my family, my friends, and all of the issues I face daily in my life. As I pray this prayer, without ceasing, I'm finding that God is faithful in granting me His perspective on life.

He's always willing to share Himself and His perspective with His girls. We just have to move close to Him, and seek Him first, then all things will be added unto us.

Kristen sent me a refreshing e–mail yesterday. She had attended a 'get together' over the weekend. A girl friend, who considers herself to be slightly overweight, walked up to Kristen and said, "If anyone starts to take pictures, you and I will stand around this corner."

Kristen said that our conversation over coffee the day before gave her the strength to reply, "No way! Not me! I look great tonight!"

Before leaving her house, she had looked into the mirror and liked what she saw. What a satisfying sense of confidence to truly feel good about how you look and feel about yourself.

Way to go, Kristen. She's stepping out, moving closer to Her Heavenly Father, and seeking His perspective in their lives. She's finding freedom to be herself, making changes to become healthier, and learning to celebrate the gift wrapping that God chose for her to live in for this brief time on earth.

I want to encourage Kristen, and every woman in our world as they seek God's perspective of themselves and the women in their lives to learn to celebrate the uniquely beautiful women you are. I want to stand up and shout, what I can almost here our Heavenly Father shouting to us, His girls, "**YOU GO GIRLS**!"

Grace means God accepts me just as I am. He does not require or insist that I measure up to someone else' standard of performance. He loves me completely, thoroughly and perfectly. There's nothing I can do to add to or detract from that love.

—Mary Graham, The Greatest Lesson I've Learned

— 12 —

Girlfriends!

As iron sharpens iron, so one friend sharpens another.
Proverbs 27:17

God created women with the hope that they would enter into friendships with one another. Women can bring unique gifts into the lives of other women that a man cannot bring. As women, we are called to cultivate healthy relationships with other women, and by doing so fulfill God's purpose for friendship.

His purpose for friendship is to encourage, strengthen and sharpen one another, as He instructs us so beautifully in Proverbs 27:17, "*As iron sharpens iron, so one friend sharpens another.*"

The beauty of friendship, like the beauty of flowers, is difficult to describe in words. There are many kinds of friends, just as there are many different flowers and yet each has unique beauty to offer.

Friends are like flowers as they bring such beauty and fragrance into our lives. Picture a beautiful home with a landscaped lawn of only green grass, shrubs and trees. A home can be beautiful without flowers in the yard, but when beautiful colors and fragrances are added to the landscape, the beauty of the home is enhanced.

Flowers are to a home like the icing on an already yummy cake or like the cherry on the top of a hot fudge sundae or the whipped cream on the top of a cappuccino. Friends are much the same. Yes, friends are the icing–on–top of our lives. When I think about my friends, I am assured that God really does want us to enjoy the "icing–on–top" of our lives.

I find myself thanking the Lord daily for the girlfriends in my life. (and you all know who you are.) Oh, how blessed I am that God arranged for us to walk together for a season or two or three during this lifetime. God has used each of my friends to "grow me" into who I am today. How blessed we are to know the richness that comes from sharing in friendship with another woman.

Sometimes I imagine a glass vase filled with a beautiful bouquet made up of flowers selected to represent each of the special women in my life. It would be my friendship bouquet designed with unique flowers of different shapes, colors and fragrances.

A really neat way to celebrate your own friendships is to visit a florist and create our own private little celebration of the friendships that we share with the women in our lives. First, visit a florist or find a patch of wild flowers and select a flower that represents each of your closest friends. Take them all home, arrange them in your favorite vase, and place them in your special place.

As you enjoy the beauty and fragrance they add to your room, celebrate the beauty and fragrance each woman brings to your life. Allow your heart to sing praises to God for the precious women He has placed in your life, and lift them up in prayer to God as you celebrate your friendships with your friendship bouquet.

Notice how each flower adds color, shape and fragrance to the bouquet in a unique way that is very much it's own. The flowers don't compete with one another for beauty or fragrance, but simply enhance the entire bouquet. As each flower is added to the vase, the bouquet only becomes more beautiful and more fragrant.

This is so true with women and friendships, too. God designed women to complete one another, and never compete with one another. We're to be made better because of our relationships with each other.

Recently, I was enjoying dinner with five girlfriends, with whom I had been blessed to work at the Regency Wellness Center for Women. We were each sharing about where God had taken us in our lives since the recent closing of our wellness center, and as I sat listening to each woman share, I noticed each one of us emphasized the incredible ways that our lives had been positively impacted by the others around the table. God wants His girls to complete one another instead of competing with each other, and this is exactly what I've experienced in my closest friendships with women.

I have gained so much from knowing the special women whom God has so graciously placed in my life. They have encouraged me, challenged me, and held me accountable in the specific areas of my life. We've never competed with one another, but have truly made one another more complete. This is God's plan for His girls to complete one another when our paths cross from season to season.

I think of my mother, who literally poured her life into me, teaching me by example that the most important gift a mother can give her child is the gift of a consistent prayer life. She is the woman who has most impacted my life by not only investing her time and energy, but her life itself. She was my very first example of a "God's Girl," which I was blessed to know in my lifetime.

I thank God often for placing me into her safe and loving hands. Those hands that…when I was a baby, kept my little bottom smelling like Johnson's Baby Lotion; as a little girl, they gently placed a bandage on my every boo–boo; as a pre–teen, they french braided my hair day after day after day; as a teenager, they applauded me when I succeeded and held me when I cried; and now, as a woman, I am certain that those same precious hands continue to be folded in prayer for my sake. How can I ever repay you, dear Mother? I cannot repay this priceless gift which I did nothing to earn. I'll pay it forward, working the similar acts of love into the lives of my boys. I promise.

I thank God for my sisters, Jane and Leslie, who have taught me that there's only one way to love and that's unconditionally, through thick and thin. Whether we agree or disagree, we weather the storms of life side by side. Though we are different and individual, we remain united as one team, sisters forever. My sisters are blessings in my life, who bring many precious gifts to my life, uniquely their own. I am a part of each of my sisters, and they are each a part of who I am today.

My dearest friend, Becky, has influenced my life in every single area, positively impacting the way I fulfill my roles as wife, mother, friend, daughter, daughter–in–law, sister, sister–in–law, future mother–in–law, business owner, speaker and a woman who is learning that being God's girl is what life is all about.

Throughout our fourteen year friendship, God has divinely used her in my life to draw me closer to Him, while blessing our relationship in ways we'd never dreamed because it was dedicated to Him. Because of Becky, I now better understand the covenant friendship described in the Bible.

Sweet, Karen. Not only do we laugh hilariously together talking about motherhood and girl stuff, but we can talk for hours without tiring about anything and everything. Karen is a dedicated wife and mother, and she's so earnest about living her life as unto the Lord. God has used Karen in my life to make me a better wife, mother, and girlfriend. Karen makes my heart smile, not only because of her bubbly personality, but because I know she loves me as a covenant friend.

I think of Millie, my friend and mentor, who has opened my spiritual eyes to the many treasures and nuggets of wisdom that God has strategically placed in His Word for His girls benefit, and Paulette, who has taught me the value of women laying down their lives and pouring their life experiences into one another as we're instructed to in Titus 2:3–8. By simply living her love for God in such a beautifully, vulnerable and transparent way, she has introduced me to the truth that God desires a close and intimate relationship with each of His girls.

My mother–by–marriage, Clara Nell has taught me so much about raising boys, which I knew very little about when I gave birth to my first son. She's so graciously allowed me to take my place in her son's life, setting for me a beautiful example of a mother–in–law. I plan to follow her godly example by welcoming my future daughters–in–law into our home, treating them as a precious additions to our family.

My sister–by–marriage, and my friend, who is a season ahead of me in life, has greatly impacted the way I mother in wonderful ways gained by simply walking through life with me sharing the issues she has faced with her girls. Without even realizing it, she has sown into me mothering wisdom which God has graciously sown into her. My friend, Mary, has also walked before me setting a godly example of a mothering in which I've drawn helpful ideas from over the years.

I am so grateful for being blessed to walk with my friend, Caryl, in the same season of life. Together, we deal with the day to day issues involved in family life, and they have not only enriched my life, but they have impacted the way I manage my family, my home, and also the way Brad and I parent.

They are the reason I have learned to appreciate the term "it takes a village."

Raising a family is a tough job that can seem so much easier when you have other families walking with you through the same seasons of life sharing a commitment to God with a belief system based on the Word of God.

So many of you are among the special women in my life who have sewn specific qualities into me determined by who they are and where they've been in life. God has used their strengths, talents and life experiences, which are uniquely theirs, to sharpen me, strengthening me and making me better in the various areas of my life.

God wants His girls to walk through life with one another, and when we ask God to send us girl friends who will encourage and sharpen us, He will honor and answer our prayers.

I thank God for the precious girls who meet with me in my home for Bible study and prayer week after week. I enjoy the privilege of spending time with these special God's Girls, as God reveals to us His Word. These women are blessings in my life, which I treasure.

Some friends will be in our lives for a season, while others will walk with us throughout our entire lives. I thank God for the friendships that have been cultivated in my life over the years in Bible study groups, prayer groups, school, work, business, and church…over the years.

I am the woman I am today greatly because of the positive impact of the friends God has divinely ordained in my life. There is a part of every friend I've known in the fiber of who I am. God has used each of my close friends to sharpen me in my journey. He supernaturally multiplies the benefits that come from each friendship, and weaves them beautifully into our lives.

My dear friend, Sharon, stopped by for a visit recently and brought me a lovely little bouquet of deep pink tulips. It wasn't my birthday; she simply brought the tulips just because she loves me. What a great idea!

Throughout the year, you may want to celebrate your friendships by sending each girlfriend a note describing the blessings her friendship has brought to your life. Explain which flower reminds you of her and why and then deliver a bouquet of her special flower along with the note. If you have a flower garden or rose garden, you may want to use the flowers that you've grown yourself to make your bouquets. What a beautiful way to celebrate your friendships.

Although friendships bring great joy and happiness to our lives, they can also bring discomfort and pain. I was sharing in a conversation with my son, L.B., who was seven at the time, about friendships. He wasn't quite sure how he could make new friends without replacing Ben, his best friend.

I shared with L.B. that even grown–ups deal with the 'sharing your friend' issue. What I didn't tell him is that women can be the worst at sharing friends. We can be so silly about sharing those girlfriends closest to us with other women. Go ahead and admit it. I bet every single woman has at least one memory of feeling a bit jealous, or shall we say uncomfortable, when your best friend made a new friend.

Recently, a friend asked me to pray for her concerning some feelings of jealousy she was experiencing towards her best friend. Her best friend had been spending a great deal of time with a new girl friend, and although this didn't affect her friendship with her best friend, she was overcome by this big dark cloud that seemed to threaten this treasured friendship.

Although my friend knew in her heart that this new friendship in her best friend's life was a good thing, she still had to deal with these silly feelings of jealousy.

I shared with this friend that I had experienced these same silly feelings of jealousy with some of my closest friends over the years. It's a girl thing. It's something that many women deal with at some point in their lives. It's a natural emotion, but not a healthy one. God wants us to enjoy many friendships, and as He has shared these women with us, He wants us to openly share them with other women.

During the weeks that followed, my friend thanked me for my prayers, and explained that God had changed her perspective concerning this new friendship. God showed her how this new friendship would work good in the lives of these two women, while having no threat on her friendship with her best friend.

God is so good to His girls. He truly cares about the details of our lives; even girlish emotions that make us feel foolish, silly and immature.

God designed our hearts with many rooms, so many friends can live there. I picture our hearts to look much like a high rise hotel with many little rooms to house many guests at one time. When a friend moves into a room in your heart…that room becomes that friend's own special room in your heart. I just love that, for you see, one friend never replaces another friend. Each friend occupies their very own special room in your heart. I love closing my eyes and visiting each friend's room. Each room is delicately decorated with love notes, special keepsakes, memories, conversations, and special moments shared between myself and my friend.

While my friend, Millie's room is covered with silver Brighton hearts and tailored denim skirts, Michelle's room is filled with leopard print everything…including a leopard print toaster. Each room reflects the uniqueness of each girlfriend.

Before a friend can move into a room, the clutter, both spiritual and emotional, must be removed by God, so the room can be properly prepared for a friend. This is the process in which the Lord begins to make us more like Him. He cleans out clutter such as anger, jealousy, insecurity, selfishness and bitterness, and replaces them with the fruits of His Spirit; love, joy, peace, patience, kindness, goodness, faithfulness, gentleness, and self–control. We must be willing to allow another person to walk into one of those vacant rooms in our heart for *whatever purpose* God may have. If we have given our lives to Christ, we don't have the right to allow hurt feelings to keep us from allowing the Lord to use the rooms in our heart.

God wants us to adopt an "Open Door Policy" towards friendship. He wants us to relinquish our right to control those we allow into our hearts and lives, and trust Him with all of our relationships. At the same time, we are to be wise and "*cautious in friendship*" as instructed in Proverbs 12:26.

God is very interested in the friends we choose to spend our time with. He has a great deal to say to us in the Bible concerning our friendships. He not only cares about who we spend time with, but how we spend that time together.

Proverbs 22:24–25, we are warned to "*keep away from angry, short–tempered men (women), lest you learn to be like them and endanger your soul.*" Proverbs 27:19 also gives us a warning concerning the friends we choose. "*A mirror reflects a man's* (woman's) *face, but what he* (she) *is really like is shown by the kind of friends he* (she) *chooses.*"

It's amazing how a wife will begin to resemble her husband after the two have spent years with one another. They not only look like each other, but they may even act like each other to a certain extent, as well. The same is true of friends. According to Tim McGraw, a well–known country music artist and husband of Faith Hill, "We all take different paths in life, but no matter where we go, we take a little of each other everywhere."

Over the years, some of the characteristics of my close friends have become a part of me. One of the funniest little habits I have acquired was from my sister–by–marriage, Julie. I love her gestures and the special language she uses to describe unique life situations. When her girls were tiny, and they would find themselves in a sticky situation, she would simply look at them with an 'I don't know' body movement and say "Ullll."

I understand this may sound odd on paper, but this little 'Ullll' has become a part of my vocabulary. After hearing me use 'Ullll,' many of my friends have adopted its use, also. It seems to be the perfect response to awkward situations we find ourselves in that *cannot* or *should not* be discussed. My friends and I chuckle when we hear each other use the occasional 'Ullll.' On several occasions, a friend and I have actually responded to the same situation with a simultaneous 'Ullll.'

My husband has noticed that I have picked up certain traits of my close friends. I'll never forget coming home from having lunch with a friend one day, and speaking rather "cocky" to my husband. Actually, my words were down right ugly! Brad looked at me and said disappointedly, "I sure can tell who you've been around today. I know you love her, and so do I, but I don't like how you act when you've been around her. You two just seem to get a little carried away."

He then proceeded, in his loving way, to open my eyes to the fact that I was being influenced by my new girlfriend in a negative way. Needless to say, I felt like a slob. I never want to speak to Brad in a way that is demeaning to him. He's my very best friend in the whole wide world.

After realizing the truth in what Brad had said, I knew that I must share my concern with her. Because my friend and I shared the desire to live for Christ and grow together in our friendship, we agreed that we must be very careful in how we speak and act when we're together. That day we committed ourselves to always strive to sharpen one another, and to never influence each other in a negative way. We want our words and our actions to glorify God, and move each other closer to God.

My friend Becky and I met as a direct result of our individual prayers to God requesting that He divinely place a Christian friend in our lives. He answered our prayers the day we met.

Because our friendship was something we had asked God for, we were committed from the beginning to make God the basis of our relationship.

God created us, and designed friendship for our pleasure, so of course it should be the basis for cultivating friendships.

Becky and I have become the very best of friends, and soul mate sisters in Christ, as well. God immediately joined our hearts and spirits together. I just love it when He does that. His joining is a divine uniting. Becky and I have become so very close, and God has used her to teach me all I know about true covenant friendship between women.

Over the years, we have successfully faced one issue after another together, arm–in–arm, hand–in–hand, and heart–to–heart.

After a time, God began to show us areas in our lives and our friendship that were not lining up with His perfect plan for us, His girls. As He began to reveal Himself to us, we obeyed Him. We made changes in our words, our actions, and our attitudes. Our friendship has been an always evolving relationship.

God has continued to honor our commitment to His will in our friendship by strengthening our marriages, our relationships with our families, our relationship with our Heavenly Father, and our relationships with others. I am so grateful to God for teaching me about His plan and purpose for friendship between women through my friendship with Becky.

You may have a friend that is headed in a dangerous direction, in which you have no desire to follow her. If you find yourself in this type of dilemma, and she is having a negative influence in your life, take it to God in prayer first. Ask Him to provide the perfect opportunity for you to share your concerns with her. A good way to begin the conversation is by simply expressing your love for her, and then proceeding by gently sharing the concerns that are heavy on your heart.

By sharing your concerns, you will have obeyed God and fulfilled your role as a true friend. As your friend responds to your conversation, God will direct you as to what your next step should be. He may have you stay close for a season, to aid in her transition or He may lead you to spend less time with her. Either way, seeking God and listening carefully for His guidance is crucial.

I have felt God *check me* at different times in my life, and directing me to spend more or less time with certain women. When we are walking close to God, talking with Him daily, we will hear the whisper of His Holy Spirit directing us in situations such as this one. We are to use God's wisdom and discernment when choosing who we spend a great deal of time with.

At some point in our lives, we will probably find it necessary to "weed our social garden." I know this sounds cruel for a Christian girl to weed a friend from her life. This isn't cruel. On the contrary, it's very smart. When I say "weed our social garden," I am certainly not advising you to go to your friend, and say, "Excuse me, but I won't be calling to talk with you anymore. I'm weeding my social garden, and you didn't make the cut."

Weeding a friend simply means that we put a healthy distance between this person and ourselves. This should be done in kindness and love, and in confidentiality. No words are necessary. In some instances, God may want you to help this woman grow in a certain area of her life, or simply to help meet a need in her life. He just wants you to use common sense and wisdom to know how involved you should become.

Please understand that I'm not talking about abandoning a friend in need. I'm referring to using God's wisdom and caution when choosing who you will spend a great deal of time with and who you give your soul too because we do become like the women with whom we choose to spend the most time.

Do they approach life with a positive attitude? Do they make their relationship with God the center of their lives? Do they challenge you to grow? Do they speak the truth to you in love or do they agree with your every word just to make you feel good?

Do your closest friends live to shop? Do they spend more time on their physical workout than their spiritual workout? Does their conversation revolve around gossip…or topics that have no redeeming value? Do they have a critical spirit? Do they live a self–centered life rather than striving to live a God–centered life?

Take a good look at your close friends because soon you may be a lot like them. Who we are in ten years will be greatly determined by the people we associate with now.

Michelle and Shari were inseparable friends whose story illustrates the influence one friend may have upon another.

Michelle desired to live a God–centered life. She prayed daily concerning her family and friends. The presence of the Holy Spirit was evident as we shared together and her life consisted of the things of God. Her desire was to grow closer to God and allow Him to guide her life.

Shari was also a Christian who loved the Lord, and attended church regularly. As she neared the age of 40, her outward appearance became a priority in her life. She spent more and more time refining her physical body. She was very dedicated to her six days a week at the local co–ed gym, which was well known for its night club atmosphere.

She had a dark tan from using a tanning bed, and beautiful manicured acrylic nails. She had many surgeries to enhance her physical body. (Please understand, there is nothing wrong with regular exercise, suntans, artificial fingernails, or plastic surgery, unless they begin to have an unhealthy affect on a woman's spiritual, emotional or marital health.) It was very clear that Shari's lifestyle shifted her focus away from God.

These two friends spent time together almost every day of every week including sitting together in church every Sunday. As time passed, Shari began to influence Michelle's life in a destructive way. Michelle grew weaker in her resolve to live for God. Her relationships with God, her husband, and her children began to suffer. In spite of this negative impact on her life, Michelle continued to spend a great deal of time with Shari.

Finally, after dealing with many painful issues in her life that were directly related to Shari's influence, Michelle began to spend less time with her friend. To this day, Michelle is still struggling to recover from the devastating impact her friendship with Shari had upon her life, her marriage, and her family.

We probably all have experienced similar relationships. Looking back, I can definitely see how the Lord redirected my relationships many times. I'm sure this was greatly due to the many prayers of my dear Mother because many times I was unaware that I was being influenced in an unhealthy way, or maybe influencing a friend in an unhealthy manner.

My prayer is that God will *show* me if a friendship is having an unhealthy influence on my life before it gets out of hand. I pray He will then, direct me in dealing with the friendship His way.

In Hebrews 10:24–25, Paul instructs us to "*encourage one another and build one another up, just as you are doing.*" Encouraging means to stimulate, support and inspire with the spirit of hope. I love to encourage my girlfriends, and give them hope in their endeavors. I count it a blessing to receive words of encourage, council and direction from my close friends. The Bible tells us that we are to be considered wise if we "*seek godly council*" when making decisions. I count it an extra special blessing when God leads me to one of my closest friends to receive that godly council.

Our responsibility in friendship doesn't stop with encouragement. Paul tells us in Hebrews 10:24–25, to "*consider one another to provoke unto love and to good works*;" Though the word provoke sounds strong, it is to stir us up purposely; to urge to action; to cause mild anger; to strongly encourage.

As a friend, we are called to encourage each other, but a true friend will go even a step further. A true friend will provoke her friend to strive to live a godly life, and make healthy choices.

God has intended that we enter into friendships for the primary purpose of sharpening one another. We are to hold each other accountable. In Galatians 6:1–2, Paul says, "*Dear Brothers, if a Christian is overcome by some sin, you who are godly should gently and humbly help him (her) back onto the right path, remembering that the next time it might be one of you who is in the wrong. Share each other's troubles and problems and so obey the Lord's commands*."

When we hold one another accountable, we do not simply agree with everything our friend says or condone her actions just to make her feel better. A true friend commits to 'rock your boat' a little with the raw truth when necessary, even though it might not be what you wanted to hear.

A true friend will never speak words of unkindness intentionally but will strive to wait for the Holy Spirit to open the door for her to share her concern with you. She will speak the truth in gentleness and love. When she realizes that she has slipped and spoken words that she should not have spoken, she will immediately ask forgiveness from God and her friend.

If our desire is to have trusted friends, we must commit to being trusted friends. If we want friends that will sow good things into the fabric of our lives, then we must begin to sow good things into their lives. Receiving is always found in giving ourselves to others. In Suzanne Siegel Zenkel's book, THAT SPECIAL Friend, she writes, "The greatest wonder of friendship is that the more you give, the richer you grow."

God is very clear in His purpose for friendship. As we look at what God says concerning friendship we see that as God's girls His desires become our desires if we fellowship with Him daily. We glorify God as we obey God.

Obedience to God is the spiritual umbrella under which all areas of our lives must exist, and this includes our friendships. Our focus must remain on God and His purpose for the friendship; not on the friendship itself or even the feelings of our friend.

When we allow our focus to shift from God to a friend or her life circumstances, our perspective and judgment can be clouded. This may lead us to give our friends advice based on our protectiveness and sympathy as a close friend, rather than giving godly instruction that will bring health and healing to their lives.

God uses friends as sand paper in our lives to smooth our rough edges. Consider a sheet of double–sided sandpaper. On one side is a very fine sandpaper which represents encouraging a friend. The other side is very course and rough which may be used when provoking a friend to hold them accountable.

Consider the process of refinishing a valuable piece of antique furniture that has deep chipping in the many layers of paint and varnish that have been applied to it over the years. The craftsman would first use a rough sandpaper to do the heavy duty sanding to remove the layers and layers of coating and imperfection. Then, he would use the fine sandpaper to give it the finished smoothness.

Without the application of the rough sandpaper, the craftsman could not effectively get to the original wood. The rough sandpaper represents the sometimes painful process of *sharpening* and *holding accountable* in friendship. On the other hand, the fine sand paper is so necessary for smoothing minor rough edges of one's life.

When applied to a life by a committed loving friend, encouragement and edification become a life changing, life preserving, winning combination.

It's pretty easy to encourage, but it takes a deeper commitment to hold someone you love accountable to Christ. Many people don't want to be held accountable. They'd prefer simply to be encouraged, patted on the back and pampered. For this reason, many relationships remain in this beginning phase, never evolving into true covenant friendship, as described in Proverbs 27:17. It is not a bad thing for a woman to have friendships that do not grow into covenant relationships because not all friendships are meant to be covenant friendships. In a covenant relationship, two friends commit themselves to be friends for life…enduring all that life may bring…committing to sharpen one another. There are many types of friendships with different ground rules, each unique and special in their own way…serving a specific purpose in a woman's life. While many casual friendships bring joy and fulfillment to our lives, we must not overlook the important role that covenant friendship is to play in our lives.

We must decide if we will be courageous and obedient and accept God's challenge of true friendship. When we enter into a friendship agreement we are openly asking our friends to encourage us and hold us accountable, at any cost. There is a real seriousness involved in entering into a friendship.

Friendships are like people. They are works in progress. When two friends commit their friendship to the Lord and His purpose, He ordains or establishes it. Establish means to bring into existence; to set on a firm basis; to institute permanently; to put beyond doubt. Wow! God promises to establish our friendships, if we will commit them to Him. This establishing is His refining process for our friendships. Just as He promises to mold us into His image, He wants to mold our friendships, as well.

In 1988, I began to ask God to bring Christian women into my life who would walk with me through life, and strengthen me to live for Christ. I never imagined that God would bless my life with so many beautiful friendships.

In God's Word, we see how God intended for women to walk through life together. Mary, the Mother of Jesus, was so close to her cousin, Elizabeth. They were so close that God confirmed that Mary was carrying the Son of God, by actually moving the baby inside of Elizabeth's body.

I've received confirmation concerning important issues in my life through those closest to me. My husband and my very closest friends have come to me, from time to time, with something God had placed on their heart, and to my surprise, God had spoken the same message to me. When two people, dedicate their relationship to God, He will do super natural things in both lives. God desires to unite His girls together.

His perfect plan for us is that we walk hand in hand, connected in spirit, encouraging and strengthening one another to become the wives, the mothers, the women He created us to be. He wants to divinely connect our hearts, and bring us into life enriching friendships He has for us. Mencius describes friendship as "one mind in two bodies." This describes unity between two friends in its truest form.

This song written by Gloria Gather and Phil Johnson, so beautifully describes His girls asking Him to unite them in purpose, heart and spirit.

Make us one Holy Father
Make us one
So the world will know that You have come
Make us more like one another
As you make us like Your Son
Make us one, Holy Father
Make us one

Years ago, my Mother gave me a tiny little book containing selections from *Of The Imitation Of Christ* which scholars believe was written by Gerard Groote. I found on it's pages these words of wisdom which sum up God's design for friendship. "In Me the love of your friend ought to stand; and whoever seems good, and very dear to you in this life, ought to be loved for My sake. Friendship apart from Me is of no value, and cannot last; nor is that union of love genuine and pure which is not knit together by Me."

God's purpose for friendship is to sharpen by encouraging and edifying, and His design for friendship is that it take place only 'in Him.' That's pretty simple.

As a little girl, I remember saying "I love you" was very common in our home. My Mother taught me to express my feelings of love to the people I love. Because of this, I have always found it easy to tell my friends and family that I love them.

I tell all of my girlfriends that I love them. I want them to know that I treasure who they are and feel blessed to have them in my life. I decided a long time ago to express my love and appreciation to others by saying, "I love you." God says to "love one another," so why do we often find it so hard to tell others that we love them.

Recently, I came across an e–mail that my husband had received on February 28, 2000 from his cousin. The e–mail message included the following poem written by author Henson Towne.

Around the Corner

Around the corner I have a friend,
In this great city that has no end,
Yet the days go by and weeks rush on,
And before I know it, a year is gone.
And I never see my old friends face,
For life is a swift and terrible race,
He knows I like him just as well,
As in the days when I rang his bell.
And he rang mine
if, we were younger then,
And now we are busy, tired men.
Tired of playing a foolish game,
Tired of trying to make a name.
"Tomorrow" I say "I will call on Jim"
"Just to show that I'm thinking of him."

But tomorrow comes and tomorrow goes,
And distance between us grows and grows.
Around the corner!—yet miles away,
"Here's the telegram sir"
"Jim died today."
And that's what we get and deserve in the end.
Around the corner, a vanished friend.

At the end of the poem, Brad's cousin had written a personal message to all of her friends prior to e–mailing. Her message read, "Remember to always say what you mean. If you love someone, tell them. Don't be afraid to express yourself. Reach out and tell someone what they mean to you. Because when you decide that it is the right time, it might be too late. Seize the day. Never have regrets. And most importantly, stay close to your friends and family, for they have helped make you the person that you are today. Pass this along to your friends. It could make a difference. The difference between doing all that you can or having regrets which may stay with you forever."

What touched my heart the most about finding this e–mail was not only the penetrating words of love and wise advice that she had sent to all of her friends and family, but I was moved the most when I realized that she sent this message just days before she died in a tragic car accident.

His cousin was 38 years old when she sent this message to her family and friends, and when she died. Today, I am so thankful for her words of wisdom, and her example of expressing love to those she loved. This is a life and death lesson from which we all can learn. I encourage you to make the most of your time here on earth with your family and friends. Don't pass up a single opportunity to tell those you love that you love them.

In our home, we give our family and friends a gift every single day. When a friend's daughter was leaving for her first year at college, I prayed with Her before she left, and I promised her I would pray for her every single day. The morning after she left I awoke about 4:00 a.m., and realized the importance of my promise to pray for Her daily. I asked God to help me remember to pray for her every day. My next thought was to develop 'prayer board.'

I could see it in my mind. I went to L.B.'s bedroom and quietly removed the unused dry erase board from his wall. I hung it on the kitchen wall and listed our friends' and families' names on it. Each morning as we hold hands in our kitchen and pray, we ask God to bless, protect, and draw close to each of our friends listed on our prayer board.

The gift of prayer is a precious and powerful gift and a true gift of love to each of our friends. When we have guests visit our home, often times they will request that we put their names on our board, and, of course, we do. Creating a prayer board in our kitchen has impacted our family's lives, and the lives of our friends in a divine way.

Several of the children whose names appear on our board have had attempted abductions in the past several years and we feel certain that our daily prayers for their protection helped to spare them the horrific experience of being kidnapped.

Friends have enjoyed renewed relationships in their marriages and relationships, while many other prayers for help and healing have been answered, as well.

It's not unusual for new friends visiting our home for the first time to request that their names be placed on our prayer board, and we are quick to oblige. The power is not in the one praying; we can take no credit. The power comes from the One in which we pray to...God Almighty. To God Be All the Glory For All Answered Prayers!

Dear Lord, thank you for the gift of friendship. Thank you for designing our hearts with many rooms. Thank you for being patient with us as we surrender our lives and our hearts to you and allow you to bring women into our lives and hearts. As we celebrate the friendships God has brought into our lives, let's surrender our hearts and lives once again to the Lord to be enriched, stretched and strengthened by the call of friendship. Help us to be good stewards of the friendships you've blessed us with by sowing good things into the lives of our friends. May we make the most of every opportunity to celebrate the gift of friendship you've designed for us all just because you love us. Thanks, God. We love you. Your Girls.

We need not set out in search for a friend...rather, we must simply set out to be the friend Christ modeled—anticipating the needs of others, wearing ourselves out at giving. Jesus died doing it.

—Joy MacKenzie, Friends Through Thick and Thin

— 13 —

Taking Control of Busyness

Remember how short my time is...Psalm 89:47

Walk in wisdom toward them that are without, redeeming the time. Colossians 4:5

Recently, I watched the movie 'Step–Mom' starring Susan Sarandon and Julia Roberts. The movie is based on a true story about a divorced mother of two elementary aged children who finds out she has cancer, and only a short time to live.

During the days leading up to her death, she takes a close look at what is important to her and what is not so important. She begins to simplify her life, so she can spend her remaining days doing the things that matter the most to her which was spending time with her daughters.

This story deeply moved me in my heart, my emotions and my mind. I immediately began to evaluate how I spend the minutes of every day in comparison to how I would spend my days if I knew I had only a few left to live.

My friend and I walked out of that movie theater with teary eyes and a reviewed appreciation for life.

Despite most circumstances, *life* in itself is something to be cherished and never spent carelessly or taken for granted.

Although, we never really die if we know Jesus, our physical life on this earth will come to an end. During the moments before we walk across the bridge that connects earth to eternity, I imagine that many of us may have the opportunity to review our life choices. I want to put forth the effort that it takes to evaluate my daily life, and make changes that will decrease the amount of regret I will face during those last minutes of my life on earth.

Life on earth is but a season, and passes ever so quickly. As I read the following poem entitled, 'How Do You Live Your Dash?', I was greatly impacted by the realization that the tiny dash which separates the birth and death date on a grave stone represents a person's entire lifetime.

Wow! The only similarity that the *tiny dash* and *life* could possibly share is their short length.

How Do You Live Your Dash?

I read of a man who stood to speak
At the funeral of a friend.
He referred to the dates on her tombstone
From the beginning...to the end.

He noted that first came her date of birth
And spoke the following date with tears,
But he said what mattered most of all
Was the dash between those years. (1934–1998)

For that dash represents all the time
That she spent alive on earth...
And now only those who loved her
Know what that little line is worth.

For it matters not, how much we own;
The cars...the house...the cash,
What matters is how we live and love
And how we spend our dash.

So think about this long and hard...
Are there things you'd like to change?
For you never know how much time is left,
That can still be rearranged.

If we could just slow down enough
To consider what's true and real,
And always try to understand
The way other people feel.

And be less quick to anger,
And show appreciation more
And love the people in our lives
Like we've never loved before.

If we treat each other with respect,
And more often wear a smile…
Remembering that this special dash
Might only last a little while.

So, when your eulogy's being read
With your life's actions to rehash…
Would you be proud of the things they say
About how you spent your dash?

—Author Unknown

Life is short, so we must cherish it by spending the hours of each day wisely. David reminds us to cherish our time on earth in Psalm 89:47, "*Remember how short my time is*." In Psalms 39:4–7, David prays, "*Lord, help me to realize how brief my time on earth will be. Help me to know that I am here for but a moment more. My life is no longer than my hand! My whole lifetime is but a moment to you. Proud man! Frail as breath! A shadow! And all his busy rushing ends in nothing. He heaps up riches for someone else to spend. And so, Lord, my only hope is in you.*"

Today is Wednesday, September 26, 2001, and it was only two weeks and one day ago that our great country of America was invaded and attacked by terrorists, killing thousands of people. In a matter of a minutes four airline jets had been overtaken by terrorists, who steered the aircrafts into each of the World Trade Center towers, the Pentagon and (accidentally) a field in Pennsylvania, tragically killing all of the people in the planes, and thousands of the people who were trapped in the buildings.

I imagined these individuals began Tuesday, September 11th in a very normal fashion much like they would have any other day, never dreaming that their lives on earth were about to come to an end that very morning. May God bring peace and comfort to their families who are adjusting to life without them.

None of us know the hour or the exact moment in which our spirits will leave this earth, but we do know that Paul tells us in Hebrews 9:27, "*Just as man is destined to die once, and after that to face judgment.*" While we realize life is a gift from God, we must also understand that death on this earth will come to each of us at the time which God has appointed.

Death isn't something to fear, it is simply the natural end of life on earth when our spirits are transported from earth to eternity, and if you had accepted Jesus Christ into your heart while on earth, you will hear our Heavenly Father welcome you into the gates of heaven.

Fearing death is a natural, physical response to the unknown, however when you trust

God and His Word that assures us a place in heaven when we accept Him, fear can be diminished. Although fear is a natural response to the unknown, there should be only one valid reason to fear death, and that is for those who do not have a personal relationship with God. Jesus speaks clearly of this in Matthew 7:21–23, "*Not everyone who says to me, 'Lord, Lord,' will enter the kingdom of heaven, but only he* (she) *who doest the will of my Father who is in heaven. Many will say to me on that day, 'Lord, Lord, did we not prophesy in your name, and in your name drive out demons and perform many miracles?' Then I will tell them plainly, 'I never knew you. Away from me, you evildoers!'* Have you invested the time with God that it takes to cultivate a personal relationship with Him? Will He recognize you because of the many moments you've shared together, or will He say 'I'm sorry, depart from me, for I never knew you?'

When I view life as hours and minutes given to me in the form of days and years, it seems to be more precious than ever before.

A woman once had a dream that an angel was giving her this message: "As a reward for you virtues, the sum of $1440 will be deposited into your bank account every morning. This amount has only one condition. At the close of each day, any balance that has not been used will be canceled. It won't carry over to the next day or accrue interest. Each morning, a new $1440 will be credited to you."

The dream was so vivid, she asked the Lord to show her what it meant. He led her to realize she was receiving 1,440 minutes every morning, the total number of minutes in a 24–hour day. What she did with this deposit of time was important, because 1,440 minutes per day was all she would ever receive!

Each of us has a similar account. At the close of each day, we should be able to look over our ledger and see that these golden minutes were spent wisely. God gives us minutes each day to redeem the time, by spending it with Him and sharing Jesus Christ and His love with those around us. How are you spending the 1,440 minutes God has given you? Are you redeeming the minutes for the cause of Christ, or do they somehow slip away into the busyness we permit in our lives? The way we choose to spend our time today greatly determines what our life will be tomorrow.

I invite you to join me in a little exercise that may help you determine what you need to change in your life so you will spend your days more wisely. At the top of a blank piece of paper, write the following:

LIFE IS TO SHORT TO…

1. ______________________________

2. ______________________________

3. ______________________________

4. ______________________________

5. ______________________________

6. ______________________________

Begin the exercise by listing everything that comes to your mind when you complete the sentence LIFE IS TO SHORT TO… For me, life is to short to complain, spend a lot of time on the telephone, clean house and do laundry on Saturdays instead of play with my family, have a spotless house before inviting friends for dinner, commit my time to committees and organizations that I don't feel 'called' to be a part of, attend every party, meeting, event, workshop, retreat, class, or field trip I receive an invitation to attend, scrub dirty pans, watch a lot of television, listen to gossip, allow hurt feelings to linger and wallow in self–pity, hold grudges, allow bitterness to grow inside of me and work during the hours my boys are at home.

LIFE IS TO SHORT NOT TO…

1. ______________________________

2. ______________________________

3. ______________________________

4. ______________________________

5. ______________________________

6. ______________________________

After you finish your 1st list, begin your list consisting of things that you feel LIFE IS TO SHORT *NOT* TO DO. My list would include things like…LIFE IS TO SHORT *NOT* TO tell the people you love that you love them, sit and relax a moment or two each day, enjoy your job, enjoy a quiet, relaxing bubble bath, *hang out* at home with your family *without* doing something productive at the same time, enjoy lunch or coffee with a close friend, go on weekly dates with my husband, and lay on my son's bed and listen to him talk about whatever.

My LIFE IS ALSO TO SHORT *NOT* TO send cards and love notes to people I care about, eat healthy and be active, live in clothes that I love wearing, turn the phone off after school and focus on my boys, set a relaxed atmosphere in my home by lighting candles and playing a Kenny G CD every afternoon, play with silly string and squirt guns, jump on the trampoline with my seven year old son, play catch with my ten year old son, slow dance in the kitchen with my husband, get enough sleep, go to a late movie with a girlfriend after putting my boys to bed, get up in the morning and get going, and put in every area of my life, enjoy being crazy–in–love with my sons openly and passionately..

Now that you've completed your two wish lists, consider them to be your personal 'To Do' List. If it is within our means, why would we not work on making our wishes become reality.

Since I made my first *'Life Is'* list about five years ago, I can proudly say that I've worked very hard and my wishes have all become realities. Because of this, I am not the same girl I was five years ago, and my life is definitely not the same life.

My *'Life Is'* list was just the door I needed to walk through to help me begin this process of un–busying and simplifying my life. I addressed one wish at a time on my 'Life Is' list and worked diligently to make it a reality in my daily life.

Realizing that busyness is a choice, and I could choose to succumb to busyness or I could begin to take specific steps that would unbusy my life, impacting my life and my families lives in a life changing positive way.

As I began to tackle the unnecessary busyness in my life by implementing my to–do–list, I began to notice that most women respond to the simple question, "How are you?" by telling you how busy they are. It's unbelievable how many women tell other women how busy they are in an exasperated tone of voice. If they would say, "Yippee, I'm so busy and I love it," I would be happy for the contentment they had found in their busyness, but that is usually not the scenario.

I have to admit that I, at times, have been guilty of describing 'how I am doing' in this same manor. I've realized that emphasizing 'how busy I am' only reinforces and emphasizes the busyness in my life. I want to encourage you to do what I did. Conduct your own private experiment. Casually, without prompting, ask five women the simple question, 'how are you doing?' Take note of their responses. I bet you will find that, at best, four of the five will reply with details describing 'how busy they are.'

I, along with many women, had simply surrendered to busyness, accepting it as a fact of life instead of a choice. Once I became aware of this tendency, I became very careful with the words I chose to describe the state of my life when asked the simple conversational question, 'how are you?'

While we cannot deny the reality of necessary daily tasks in life that can lead to a full schedule, we can be selective in our choice of what items we include in our day. We can actually reduce the state of busyness in our lives simply by choosing not to over–emphasize busyness through the words we speak. I call this 'controlled busyness.'

We live in a society which openly advocates that women adopt the busyness lifestyle as the preferred lifestyle of choice. Because busyness is proudly spoken, encouraged, applauded and rewarded in daily life in these times in which we live, women are faced with the obstacle of overcoming the strong pull to surrender to busyness.

Paul instructs us in Romans 12:2, "*Do not conform any longer to the pattern of this world, but be transformed by the renewing of your mind. Then you will be able to test and approve what God's will is—His good, pleasing and perfect will.*" Paul is telling us that we are to live in the world but not be conformed to the accepted lifestyles and habits of the world, instead spend time in prayer and in the Word of God because this is how you will become renewed and transformed in mind and spirit by the power of the Holy Spirit of God."

Many of us are in danger of becoming desensitized to the fact that busyness is not a healthy way of life, but rather a result of following the example of the world. Hearing busyness constantly spoken by ourselves and those around us talk will only reinforce busyness in our lives.

Let's stop emphasizing busyness in our lives and in the lives of the people we love.

After acknowledging that busyness is a choice, understanding the damaging impact that busyness can have in our lives and the lives of our families is the next step in the process to control the busyness in our lives.

Busyness can distract us from the most important roles in life which can eventually lead to disconnection to those we love. My dad used to say,

"If the devil can't get you to sin, he'll settle for keeping you busy; too busy to spend time with God." Dad was right.

In Don't Sweat the Small Stuff with Your Family, Richard Carlson refers to simplified living as 'Voluntary Simplicity." He says, "As the name suggests, it involves simplifying one's life by choice rather than out of need. Simplifying your life frees up time, money, and energy so that you can have more of each for yourself and for your family.

At some point, we get so busy that it prevents us from enjoying our lives. It seems that virtually every minute of every day is scheduled and accounted for. We rush from activity to activity, usually more interested in 'what's next' than we are in what we're doing in the present.

As I continued on the road to simpler living, I bought the book *Simplifying Your Life* by Elaine St. James. Prior to reading it, I read over it's table of contents which consisted of one hundred simplifying life ideas. I wrote 'ok' by the ideas I was already applying to my life, and I placed a check by the ideas I wanted to implement into my life.

I first read the chapters with the ideas that I had already successfully worked into my life. Then, I read the chapters which I had checked, and committed to incorporate into my life.

This tiny little book has had an enormous impact in my life and my family. As I read each chapter, I not only received encouragement to make change, but I felt empowered to stop doing some of the things that it seems so many people think we have to do in life.

Things like 'not answering the telephone just because it's ringing,' 'drop call waiting' and 'just say no' have been instrumental in helping me feel such a sense of freedom from these assumed activities.

I strongly encourage you, as I have many of my friends and colleagues, to purchase this powerful little book which I believe will help you free yourself from too much stuff in your life. As you read through the list, write 'ok' by the ideas you already do, and place a check by the ideas you want to incorporate into your life. As you make positive changes, you will be empowered by recording your progress.

As you succeed at working each one into your life, draw a line through your check and make it an 'X.'

This book is a perfect example of how one woman can impact another woman's life for good. Ms. St. James has truly made a difference in my life by following the call on her life to share these simplifying life ideas. By doing so, she is sowing simplifying life seeds into the lives of others.

One afternoon while I was standing in my kitchen sharing my '409 skate–mopping' idea with a girl friend, my five year old son ran through the kitchen using my bra for a sling shot. I chuckled in surprise, and said, "We're simplifying so much in our home that we're finding dual purposes for everything."

By the way, my '409 skate–mopping' is a simplified way to mop your kitchen floor when you're short on time. I discovered it out of sheer necessity one day when I only had one hour before our dinner guests arrived. I had to choose between mopping my kitchen floor, and playing outside with my nine year old before he departed for a week of church camp.

Spending a few extra minutes with L.B. was much more important to me that having a freshly mopped spotless kitchen floor. That day I made a conscious decision to begin creating housecleaning short–cuts, so I could spend more time doing what really matter the most to me.

My 409 skate mopping short–cut involves putting on a favorite CD, spraying 409 on the major areas of the floor, tossing an old towel down onto the floor, and skating my floors clean. Skating with sneaker shoes on rather than bare feet works better for tough to clean areas. Even my boys enjoy skating through the house with me. It's not only a short cut to mop your kitchen floor, but it serves as an aerobic workout containing lateral conditioning, as well.

If you're sitting there in disbelief that a woman could actually attempt to mop the floor of her family's home in this pathetic manner, relax in knowing that this doesn't have to influence you in the least bit. You can mop any way you feel necessary, and I'll do the same. Isn't that a freeing way to view simplifying ideas. Choose what works for you, and begin to simplify.

Something else that I found works for me on those days when I have been working diligently on something all day and I realize it's already 2:45 p.m., time to pick my sons up at school, and I haven't even had a shower, combed my hair or put on make–up.

My quick fix solution that has made my life tons easier is to quickly slip on my running shorts, a t–shirt, and my running shoes. Then, put on my baseball cap, my sunglasses, and last but not least, my lipstick. It's simple. A ball cap, sunglasses and lipstick can get you to school pick–up on time feeling put together, while taking nothing away from the project you've spent your morning working on.

I was sharing with a friend about this little problem I was continuing to have when picking my sons up after school. Word of caution: If you happen to be one of those women who keeps a spotless car at all times no matter what, then you might want to skip the next two paragraphs.

It never failed that as my son's teacher opened the car door to deliver my boys, to my horror, the floor of my car would be trashed, and some days things would actually fall out of my car. Yes, things; things like empty water bottles, a plastic plate, shoes, or trash. I know, such a thing never happened to you, right? Well, if you can relate to this situation, do read on my sister.

As I explained my reoccurring situation to my friend, Sharon, she assured me that she had the solution that would relieve me of fearing the embarrassing cluttered state my car somehow finds itself in. (At this point, some of you are thinking, "Just clean your car out more often, girl.")

Well, my friend, confidently whispered in a secret–like manner, "Susan, while you're waiting in the pick–up line, simply glance back at the car floor and gather together everything you see and move it into one spot. Then, all you need to do is keep a bath towel or a blanket in your car, and simply toss it over the pile of clutter. And there you have it, clutter free, stress free after school pick–up."

I was thrilled with my friend's non–condemning, understanding advice to me, which has proven to be just the quick fix solution I needed as I worked hard at balancing work and family, and simplifying...all at the same time.

I've always been project oriented, and my friends have described me as goal oriented and even driven. My husband has been known to refer to me as super woman because I have always worked professionally, managed our home and devoted myself to areas of ministry, as well.

For many years, I was proud of the fact that I could do many things at one time. This is exactly what our society encourages women to do in life. We are encouraged and challenged to work professionally as a career woman, make a hefty income, raise healthy children, manage a home, exercise to look great, have numerous plastic surgeries to give you the perfect body, dress impeccably well, serve as a school room mother, host great parties, cook delicious, gourmet meals for your family, maintain a perfectly clean home, volunteer for community fundraisers, garden and grow beautiful roses, wild flowers, and your own herbs.

We're told that we can teach Sunday School, plan family vacations to historical places, play on a tennis team, own pets, shop for groceries daily if necessary, enlist your children in never–ending after school activities to ensure exposure to a variety of activities, look sexy at the end of a full day, sit on the local junior league, garden club or other civic boards and transform into a 'Pamela Sue Anderson' sex goddess when making love with your husband.

One day, as I was sharing with Brad my description of one of the main differences between men and women, I was surprised with what God revealed to me through the gentle, concerning words of my husband. I was explaining to him how life is much like a chest of drawers, and while the majority of men only open one drawer at a time, most women are capable of opening several drawers at the same time.

For example, when a man goes to work he easily closes the 'home' drawer, as he opens the 'work' drawer. While at work, he focuses on work, giving no thought to the school activities the evening may hold.

Unlike the man, when most women go to work, they not only open their 'work' drawer, but they keep many other drawers open, as well. Important drawers such as, 'dinner preparation,' 'school activities,' 'doctor's appointments,' 'grocery list,' 'birthday plans,' seem to remain open all the time.

In a joking manor, I told my husband, "A woman can cook dinner, do laundry, write a grocery list in her head, plan a birthday party, review her presentation for work, and have sex all at the same time." Brad looked at me and commented, "You know, I used to think that your ability to do lots of things at the same time was a good thing, but I've come to believe differently."

Brad explained to me that although I had made a great deal of progress tackling my physical busyness, I needed to focus on un–busying my thoughts, as well. He shared with me that it made him feel less important in my life when I would allow myself to become distracted by thoughts of numerous other issues while in a conversation with him.

For my husband, who is like many men in that he doesn't enjoy reflecting or sharing his heart, to tell me that my behavior makes him feel unimportant in my life, was just the wake–up call that this girl needed.

I love my husband more than any other human being in the whole wide world, and I only want to treat him in a way that proves how much I love, honor and respect him. This loving comment from my husband helped me to acknowledge not only the unnecessary busyness in my daily schedule, but the unhealthy busyness in my mind.

I immediately made a list of the pros and cons of bring able to open multiple drawers at one time, and this is what it looked like.

PROS

1. I feel like I get a lot accomplished

2. I add variety to my day

3. I can satisfy more people; touch more lives

CONS

1. I increase craziness in atmosphere of the home life and work life because I work on several projects at the same time when I multi–task

2. I increase stress levels: Internally which is mental and: Externally which affects family, friends, people around me; clients, patients, etc.

3. I never completely focus on one thing, so nothing and no one ever ends up getting 100% of my attention at any one time; leaves people feeling unimportant

4. I do not finish conversations concerning one topic before rushing into a conversation concerning another topic

5. I tend to become so engrossed and preoccupied with my own activities and ignore others

After considering this comparison of pros and cons, I was convinced that my ability to do many activities at one time was not the strength that I had considered it to be, instead I had allowed it to become a weakness that needed my immediate attention.

As I began to address the busyness in my *mind*, I made a commitment to focus on one thing at a time, instead of several. I work on my computer during the day hours while my boys are in school, and I designated our after–school hours to my family. This completely erased the mental and verbal conflict between my work and my family in the evenings.

My tendency to work on multiple things at one time was not an easy habit to break. I expressed my desire to change in this area, asking God to show me *what* I should be working on and *when* I should work on it.

I remember times sitting at my computer, feeling very unsettled inside because I should have been doing something else at that moment instead of working on the computer. After experiencing this unsettled feeling several times, I recognized that this was God's way of gently reminding me that I really should be focusing on something else at that very moment.

God continues to whisper in my ear, sometimes using that same unsettled feeling, as to say, "My dear daughter, there is something of higher importance that you should be doing right now. Think about it. Choose wisely how you spend these next minutes." He never fails to make that something known to me, and if I'm tuned in to Him, I'll hear Him gently direct me through my thoughts.

Designating work time and family time not only decreased the stress that came from being interrupted while working, but also the guilt that resulted from working while my boys were home. Separating work and family time enabled me to feel good about giving my best to both work and my boys.

To help me relax and slow myself down physically and mentally, I began to play a relaxing CD immediately after arriving home from school with my boys, instead of allowing the TV to blare throughout our home. I always have my kitchen candle burning to set a relaxed tone in our home, along with a small rock fountain that I run continuously in our family room.

These small changes may seem insignificant in themselves, but when implemented on a regular basis into our home, they have made an enormous impact by setting a relaxed tone for our family.

Most afternoons, between the hours of three and five, I don't answer the telephone. This allows me to give my sons my complete attention during their transition from school to home. I can tell a huge difference in my mental state, and my boys, when I removed the television and the telephone from our lives for those two hours.

My friend Kim found that she needed to remove the telephone from their lives beginning each night at eight o'clock. In their home, they do not except phone calls after eight o'clock to ensure their family focuses on their family, instead of being distracted by outside issues.

Because the woman in a home sets the atmosphere of her home, I realized that my emotional state definitely affects my family. A woman is the 'heart of the home', and most men are simply not wired the same way. Myself and my family are two great reasons for my decision to learn to relax, slow down and unbusy my life and my mind.

I'm a shower kind of girl simply because a bath takes too long. Never the less, I committed to relax in a hot lavender bubble bath one night a week, playing soft music, and filling my bathroom with candles. Over time, I have grown to appreciate and enjoy the soothing affect that relaxing in a hot bath has on my mental and physical self.

Another change I made to help me slow down and learn to relax was to create a quiet place for just me. I created my own special place in my living room complete with all of my favorite things. I selected my most favorite chair in our home to be my quiet time chair. It's a very old bedroom chair that was given to me (used) years ago, which I had covered in a raspberry red and cream toile fabric.

Beside my chair sits a fairly large two tier raspberry red antique lamp table. On the top, I place my favorite framed photos of my family and closest friends, my favorite tea cup, my Bible, a favorite flower arrangement, and a hurricane globed candle.

On the lower shelf, I stacked my most favorite books and devotionals written by women who have become my mentors through the written word.

Between my chair and lamp table, I place my basket filled with goodies. It holds my journal, my prayer list, a box of tissues, pens, pencils and a high lighter, sticky notes, my favorite stationary and postage stamps.

I have grown to love and cherish this special spot because I know that I can just sit and be quiet when I am in that chair. This special place is where God and I enjoy wonderful times together, sometimes sitting and sometimes kneeling.

Sometimes, I feel God drawing me to my quiet place to be with Him, so He can quiet my spirit, my mind, and my body. The addition of my special place has been a life changing one which has helped me immensely in my journey to slow down and unbusy my life

I'll never forget the day I sat down on my living room sofa and began to cry. I was overwhelmed by attempting to work full–time as an assistant manager for a women's wellness center, manage my home, and be a mommy to my three year old son, L.B., and my new born son, Blake. I knew something had to change, and my husband realized this too. He has learned that when I am moved to tears, something important is about to take place because I am a fairly strong woman who doesn't become overwhelmed easily.

I found myself in a moment of crisis; torn between my profession, my passion for helping women live healthier, happier lives, and cultivating a life for my new family. My life had changed immensely as I entered into this new season of life, and my priorities changed along with it. My passion for helping women had not diminished, however, my role as wife and mother became my primary passion in life. My God–given calling was to nurture and care for my family first and foremost.

Deep within myself, I knew this was God's way of moving me to a new place with a new focus. It was time for me to make some changes in my life. That day I surrendered my life once again to my Lord. I surrendered my position at the wellness center, my community services, and ever other activity in my life. I sat them at the feet of Jesus, and asked Him to show me what needed to be altered because I knew that He was the only One who really knew what was best for me in this lifetime.

I prayed Proverbs 3:5–6 that says, "*Trust in the Lord with all thine heart; and lean not unto thine own understanding. In all thy ways acknowledge Him, and He shall direct they paths.*"

As I began to sob aloud, expressing my frustration, Brad held me in his arms and prayed for me. He thanked God for sending me into his life, and he asked God to direct me in the way that was best for me and our family.

Brad has always encouraged me and completely supported me in all of my endeavors. After God, Brad is the wind beneath my wings, and a precious blessing in my life. He is my safest place on earth, and I can rest assured that he truly wants me to do what I want to do in life. I've never met a man with more character in my entire life. Whether I felt lead to work professionally full–time or part–time, or work only at home, Brad has always supported my decisions. He only wants me to do what God places in my heart for me to do. I am truly blessed to have been given Brad Dantzler to live with and walk with during this lifetime. For this man, I am truly thankful.

I knew right away that I needed to cut back on my hours at the wellness center. At first, I went from forty hours plus to thirty–two hours. Over the course of several years, God lead me to drop down to twenty hours a week at the wellness center, while bringing to my attention all of the little changes that I needed to make in my life and home to continue this process of gaining control over the busyness.

Last November, after feeling lead to resign my position at the wellness center, I asked God to make it very clear to me if I was to quit my job.

I wanted to know for sure that this was what He wanted me to do. If the truth be known, I was reluctant to give up my profession all together. Not only because I had a desire to help women, but because I took pride in helping women.

A few weeks following my request to God, it was announced that the hospital would be closing the wellness center. This would be a very clear sign to me that 'yes,' I was to quit my job and move on to the next season of my life.' God knew He had to do something drastic to make His point clear to me, and that's just what He did.

During the weeks following the closing of the wellness center, I went through a separation process. Although I was certain that this was God's perfect will for my life at this time, I experience feelings of failure, disorientation, disappointment, and lostness, due to my professional title being stripped from me. I felt profession–less, pay–checkless, and professionally naked to be honest. I had held a professional position for all of my adult life. How would I function without a career, professional recognition and (last but not least) a paycheck?

This transition was not a natural transition for me, and I'm sure the devil jumped in to enhance this horrifying picture of me not working, but staying at home. Maybe, he suspected that God was about to do some amazing things in my life; things that could only be accomplished after I was freed from my present position at the wellness center.

During this period in which I was beginning to adjust to my new 'unemployed' state in life, my family and I had gone to the beach. I began to ask God once again to show me what my days should consist of, what direction He wanted me to take. I felt torn in the transition of one season and the next.

As I was sitting on the beach reading, I glanced down at the magazine I was reading and read this in the margin. Coming in June, 'Peeling Off the Labels, Wife, executive, svelte size 6: Losing an identity can be a dizzying blow–or the beginning of freedom.' That's it, I thought. I haven't lost a title, I've gained my freedom.

From that moment on, I knew that God was wanting to free me up before leading me into the next season of my life.

A woman caring for her family, and growing children into adults is the most important role, and at the same time, the least acknowledged role in the entire world. The Bible clearly states that God's first call on the life of a woman is her God, husband, children, and home. I was simply experiencing a bit of culture shock.

I had been feeling drawn to my home in my spirit in a very strong way. I knew that for many reasons I was to give up my job at the wellness center. I had peace in the midst of this change, and my peace came from trusting God to do what was best for me.

According to Henry Blackaby in Experiencing God, "Intimacy with God is the single most important thing in my life." I love that! Somewhere along the way, I confused 'service to God' with 'intimacy with God.'

In addition, I read a selection from Oswald Chamber's daily devotional, My Utmost for His Highest where he states, "Service to God is the greatest competitor to intimacy with God."

As God began to work this truth in me, I began to see how I had allowed church work, programs, service opportunities, study groups, and ministry projects to take the place of my intimacy with Christ. It makes perfect sense to me, now. It's much easier to be busy serving than it is to be still, quiet, and vulnerably intimate with a Holy God.

A prime illustration of this truth may be seen with Mary and Martha, which is found in the book of Luke. Jesus came to their home for a visit. Mary did nothing but sit at the feet of Jesus, while Martha, worked her fingers to the bone in the kitchen in preparation for the meal. Wait a minute! Did I get that right? Let me try again! Mary sat at the feet of Jesus, while Martha allowed herself to become distracted with the busyness of the moment? When Martha brought this to Jesus' attention, His reply addressed the issue of service verses intimacy. In Luke 10:41–42 the Lord exclaims, "*Martha, Martha, you are worried and upset about many things, but only one thing is needed. Mary has chosen what is better, and it will not be taken away from her*." Jesus makes it very clear that intimacy with Him should always take priority over service to Him. Joanna Weaver, author of *Having a Mary Heart in a Martha World,* so beautifully compares the busyness of Martha's Kitchen to the Intimacy of Mary's Living Room. Martha's busyness in the kitchen will never produce the precious living room intimacy that Mary enjoyed with Jesus. Martha's busyness distracted her from being with Jesus. Busyness breeds distraction. It was Martha's eagerness to serve Jesus that caused her to almost miss the awesome opportunity to know Him. It is so easy to get caught up in serving God, trying to please Him, and prove our love for Him, that we rush right past the intimacy of the living room. In the end of life when we see Him face to face, *will we know Him, really know Him…and will He know us*? The world sends us the message, "Do more, do more!" God is gently whispering to His girls, "Come sit with Me, and be still and know that I am God."

The Bible tells us that our service to God is important, but it should never come before our time with God. Our service to God should flow as a result of our time with God. James 2:17 declares just this, "*Faith by itself, if it is not accompanied by action, is dead. But someone will say, 'You have faith; I have deeds.' Show me your faith without deeds, and I will show you my faith by what I do.*"

I'll never forget my conversation with Miss Natalie, a sweet elderly woman, who had walked with the Lord for more than 50 years. It was obvious that He was the love of her life. After I had shared some exciting things in which I had been involved at my church, she walked over to me. She gently took my face in her hands, and said, "Honey, God does not care about what you do for Him, He just cares about who you are to Him."

All of a sudden, it seemed like God was sending me so many messages that all pointed to the fact that He wanted to spend time with me. Imagine that! The God who created the whole wide world wanted to be with me, a simple girl from Shelby, Ohio. I fell on my knees and apologized to God as I realized that for most of my adult life I had been living in distracted busyness. As I asked God for His forgiveness, I also pled for Him to show me how to "un–busy" my life in order to make more time for intimacy with Him.

Step–by–step, and ever so gently, God began to shed light on all that needed to be removed from my life. A few weeks later, the hospital administrator announced that the entire wellness center would be closing. Now, that's what I call clear direction!

I resigned from my position as director of the women's ministry at my church, alone with several other adult oriented ministry commitments, but continued my commitments to the children's ministry. I placed everything in my life in God's hands, asking Him to show me what should stay and what needed to go. I ask Him to be very specific with His direction because I didn't want to do any one thing out of my own will or simply because it was for a worthy cause.

After asking God to show me if He wanted me to continue the Bible study for women which I had been facilitating in my home, I could hardly believe His crystal clear and immediate answer. Within about two days, there were 26 women from different churches, wanting to attend the study on prayer. The really neat part is, I didn't even advertise for this study. I told a few girls, and God took it from there. It was another very clear message.

As I was jogging one morning talking with God, I explained to Him that there seemed to be a thick fog separating Him from me. I could almost see the fog between us. I began to pray, "Lord, I can't see you because of all the good stuff in my life. There's so much good stuff and God stuff filling every minute of every day that it seems to be somehow keeping me from You."

I pleaded with God to help me clear this fog because I just wanted and needed to see Him. I asked Him to remove all the things from my life that were keeping me too busy to be with Him. I knew God was near me, but I just couldn't see Him because of the fog.

It was similar to the feeling you get when you're driving a car in a very thick fog. You know the road continues in front of you, but you just can't see it because of the fog.

I told God that all I wanted to do was to hold His hand and walk beside Him. I knew He was on the other side of the fog of busyness, so I pictured myself racing in faith through this fog and running towards Him…in hopes that He would take my hand and pull me safely to His side. That is exactly what He did over the course of the months that followed. He would bring to my attention items that needed to be removed from my daily life schedule, and each time I obeyed Him it was like I would take another step through the fog moving closer to Him.

One day last week, I went for my morning jog in spite of the thick fog that was in the air. The fog was so blinding I could hardly see the houses in my neighborhood, and the sun was no where to be found.

Although I couldn't visibly see the sun, I was confident that it was just on the other side of the thick layer of fog. As usual, I began to pray while I jogged through my neighborhood that morning. Often, I will pray through the Lord's prayer, praying in detail each phrase, and sometimes after thanking God for everything I can possibly think of…I'll pray for each neighbor's family as I jog by their homes.

About fifteen minutes into my run and my prayer time, I began to see the faint light from the sun, which was sitting right on the other side of the fog. As each minute passed, I continued praying, and the sun continued to shine until it seemingly broke through the fog.

Finally, the fresh sunshine of the new day was bathing my face with warmth. As I began to thank God for the sunshine that morning, I realized that this is exactly what happens when we discover a thick wall of fog seeming to blind our view of the 'Son.'

No matter how thick the fog of life might be, we know by faith that the 'Son' is waiting faithfully on the other side. As we pray without ceasing and obey what God leads us to do, the fog will eventually fade away and our vision of Jesus will be clear once again.

This story of the fog helped me to see how service to God can easily keep us from God. Service to God is not why we were created. We were created simply to spend time knowing and worshiping God. As we make spending alone time with God our first priority, He will then show us what tasks He would like for us to include in our days.

Task oriented personalities, which I happened to be, may find that it is very easy to not only permit the fog of busyness to settle in one's life, but to allow your task oriented behavior to add to the creation of the fog, as well.

Within several months, my life had completely changed. I continue to pray, "Lord, please keep out everything that will cloud my view of you. It's like there is a fog of so many man written rules standing between You and me. It seems as though man–made laws have made it so complicated to get to You. I just want to really know You; not programs, processes or traditions; Just YOU."

Today I am thanking God for revealing to me that this task oriented fog of busyness had indeed formed, distracting my view of Him, and helping me to realize that all of the good things that I was involved in doing for God had taken the place of my private time with God.

Because of our activity oriented lifestyles, it may be difficult for some women to understand how good works for God could possibly keep them from Him. It is very simply. Good works done for God are just that; good works. They are acts of service that we do for God because we love Him, but they are not moments alone with God getting to know Him in a very personal intimate way.

Relating this topic to my relationship with my husband helps me to better understand that service to someone can never replace intimate time with that person.

I wash Brad's laundry, iron his pants, clean the garage, cook his meals, make him a turkey or ham sandwich for lunch every day, along with so many other acts of love that I do because I love him. However, not one of these should or could replace the intimate one–on–one time that God designed a husband and wife to share for the purpose of enjoyment and the uniting of two spirits.

I can only imagine my husband coming home from work suggesting that we spend intimate time alone that evening and to his surprise I reply, "Oh Honey, I loved you all day long as I was cleaning the garage for you because I know how much you detest that job." Most husbands might be thinking, "What in the world does cleaning the garage have to do with having sex tonight? I don't get it."

Just as my cleaning the garage cannot possibly serve the same purpose as intimate time alone with my husband, service to God cannot replace intimacy with God. It's plain and simple.

It's very easy to confuse the two because love is the reason for both, and those who love God want to please Him with acts of service. James 2:18b–26 explain that our service to God is a deliberate reaction to our faith in God which is strengthened by spending time with God. "*I will show you my faith by my works. For as the body without the spirit is dead, so faith without works is dead also.*"

Putting service to God before intimacy with God is taking things out of the order in which God intended and will cause our efforts to be made in vain.

Recently, I read the book God Catchers. Throughout the entire book, the author, Tommy Tenney, uses his relationship with his daughters to describe God's relationship with us, His children. It was exactly what God had been speaking to my heart.

He just wanted to be my Heavenly Father, and for me to be His daughter. God has used this book in my life to free me from living in a manmade box! This was a box that I helped to create. It was a box that I thought God somehow wanted me to live in to please Him. Guess what, girls? God doesn't endorse boxes or busyness that can keep us from intimacy with Him. He didn't created them, and He never intended for His girls to be bound by them. His plan for us was to run free with Him, enjoying His company in this beautiful world that He created just for us.

Today, Praise God, I am so grateful to Him for not only revealing to me the truth that uncontrolled busyness can distract me from the most important thing in my life; time with God, but also holding my hand and gently guiding me through what was just the beginning of the deepest spring cleaning that this girl has ever experienced.

It's amazing how God sees everything in our lives, and is very sensitive to reveal the things He wants to change in us little by little as we are ready instead of just all at once. He's so patient with His girls, showing us tender mercies and loving kindness on a daily basis.

Today, I am enjoying a more calm, more centered life with more peace than I did just a few years ago, and I pray daily thanking God for the progress I've made, and asking Him to help me continue to get back to the basics and enjoy the blessings that He meant for me to enjoy from the beginning of my creation.

As God's Girls, let's commit to live each new day remembering that it's a gift from God, cherishing every moment, grasping every God–given opportunity, and controlling busyness tendencies, placing intimacy with God before service, and choosing wisely how we will spend our dash.

"Father, give me the grace today to take time. Time to be with you. Time to be with others. Time to enjoy the life you have given me. Help me remember that today is the day you have made. May I rejoice and be glad in it! Amen.

—Luci Swindoll, *Joy Breaks*

— 14 —

Free! Free To Be...God's Girl!

It is for freedom that Christ has set us free. Stand firm, then, and do not let yourselves be burdened again by a yoke of slavery. Galatians 5:1

Thou art worthy, O Lord, to receive glory and honor and power; for thou hast created all things, and for thy pleasure they are and were created. Revelation 4:11

...we are able to hold our heads high no matter what happens and know that all is well, for we know how dearly God loves us, and we feel this warm love everywhere within us because God has given us the Holy Spirit to fill our hearts with His love. Romans 5:4 (LB)

As the oldest of three girls, I was raised in a middle class Christian home in Shelby, Ohio and I was a text book first child with a choleric personality and the biblical Martha tendencies. In short, I was a people pleasing, service oriented, church–going girl, who would find herself in desperate need of an authentic intimacy with her Heavenly Father.

My parents raised us in church. When I say *in* church, I mean *in* church. Our family went to church Sunday morning, Sunday evening, Wednesday evening, and every other time the church doors were open. Many women have painful memories of being raised in a strict Christian home.

I must admit, however, although our family was not perfect (whose is?), I didn't turn out emotionally handicapped from my childhood experience.

Actually, I have very good memories of my involvement in church. I believe it had a lot to do with the fact that both of my parents were always actively involved in our Christian education. My mother always taught one of our Sunday school classes, and my dad volunteered as the youth pastor.

Our whole family would get involved in church projects that would impact the youth of our church and community. While my Dad was the spiritual head of our home, my Mother was truly the heart and soul. My parents established the rules in our home based on what they believed God's Word said, and I respect them for their commitment.

My parents gave me a strong sense of faith in God. My husband, Brad, once said, "Your faith in God is amazingly strong, and is such a natural instinct for you to just believe and trust God." He said, " It's like the Word of God has been woven into the fiber of who you are."

What a great gift a parent can give to a child: an introduction to Christ and a foundation for a strong faith in God. I am truly grateful for this gift that my parents worked into my life.

Although I remember my Dad reminding my sisters and I that God created us for fellowship with Him, it has only been recently that I have begun to understand the beauty in knowing that God created me so He could spend time with me.

In Kevin Lehman's, The New Birth Order Book, he describes the first born's typical traits as follows: leadership ability, aggressive, compliant, perfectionistic, organized, driver, list maker, logical, scholarly, care–giver, strong–willed, reliable, serious, goal oriented, well organized, people pleasers, believers in authority, self–sacrificing self–reliant and conscientious. Whew! Put those altogether, and there I am, the typical first born child.

Dr. Lehman states that first born children can be entrusted with a great deal of responsibility. "They are careful and calculating and usually sticklers for rules and regulations," he explains, "The other side of the coin for the first born, however, is that all that attention, the "ooh–ing" and "ahh–ing," the spotlight, and the responsibility add up to—PRESSURE!" Dr. Lehman highlights the first born's memories of what he used to hear from Mom or Dad when he was a child as:

- I don't care what he did—you're the oldest!
- What? You don't want to take your little sister with you?
- Fine—stay home!
- Couldn't you keep your little sister out of trouble?
- What kind of example is that?
- Will you please act your age?
- When are you going to grow up?
- He's littler than you. You should know better!

Reading these comments, I chuckled as I remembered hearing some of these same comments from my own parents. A seriousness came over me, however, as I realized that I had said some of these same things to my oldest son recalling how tough it is being a first born child.

Now that I'm a parent, I better understand how easy it is for a parent to automatically place pressure on their oldest child without being aware of it. It's easy to see how these pressures can lead to the development of the "people pleasing" disease.

Looking back, I now see that most of my life I lived somewhere between striving to please my parents and setting a good example for my two younger sisters. I was far from perfect, but I did make safe, sensible choices, most of the time. Many students at my high school viewed me as a goodie–two–shoes, I'm sure.

Sometimes, I would picture myself as Olivia Newton–John's character, Sandra Dee, in the movie 'Grease,' the good girl, who would transform into the sophisticated, risk–taking, Sandy. I'd give up my pale yellow conservative dress for those sleek, tight black pants, off the shoulder black fitted halter, black studded leather biker jacket and 4 inch candy apple red Candies shoes.

There was only one problem. Susie Slone was not a risk taker, and in my heart of hearts, I really didn't want to be the 'wild one.' Most times, I played it safe and sensible. That's me, alright, safe and sensible still to this day.

I usually made decisions based on pleasing my parents, pleasing God and setting a Christian example for those around me. It's a natural for a daughter to want to please her parents whether earthly or Heavenly. By no means are these unhealthy reasons for making decisions, I simply got carried away by allowing myself to begin trying to please everyone else in my life. What a silly and unrealistic idea!

Recently, I shared in an interesting conversation with a teenage friend, as she expressed how disappointed she was to find that many of the teens in her youth group she had been attending seemed to judge her simply because her life didn't exactly mirror theirs. To her, it felt like they were judging her commitment as a Christian based on how her day–to–day choices concerning church attendance and many other issues may or may not line up with what they believed to be the acceptable Christian behavior. She said, "It's like they are measuring me with their own measuring stick and it's just not right."

I understood too well what my young friend was describing to me because not only had I been unfairly measured by the measuring sticks of other Christians, but without realizing it I too had inflicted my perspectives and opinions concerning the Christian life on others as I measured them by my own measuring stick.

Our life circumstances and experiences play a huge role in the development of our opinions and belief systems, which are at the core of the measuring sticks we use to measure ourselves, and many times, others. Recently, an extremely intelligent, highly educated gentlemen friend of mine, who is in his sixties, acknowledged this very fact when he admitted, "You're right, Sue. It's not fair for me to measure anyone else by my measuring stick because my measuring stick isn't necessarily the measuring stick that someone else lives their life by."

As I pondered his comment, agreeing with his point that we should never judge another human being by imposing our measuring stick opinions and beliefs upon them because that is exactly what they are...our opinions and beliefs, I needed to see what the scriptures had to say concerning this idea of 'measuring one another.' In Philippians 2:12, Paul instructs the early Christians to be concerned about their ***own*** salvation when he says "*—work out* ***your own*** *salvation with fear and trembling; for God is at work in you, both to will and to work for His good pleasure.*" (RS)

In James 4:11–12, James, thought to be the brother of Jesus, firmly addressed this issue of judging others when he says, "*brothers do not slander one another. Anyone who speaks against his brother or judges him speaks against the law and judges it. When you judge the law, you are not keeping it, but sitting in judgment on it. There is only on Lawgiver and Judge, the one who is able to save and destroy. But you—who are you to judge your neighbor?*"

Now here's a scripture that is direct and to the point, and presented in a way which I can truly appreciate. I can almost hear James saying, "God is the only judge, so who do you think you are young lady...that you can judge your neighbor by your own opinions concerning the Bible?" That basically clears up the 'judging others issue' for this God's girl; God's the judge and I am not, making it extremely clear that...I need to simply be concerned with Susan's relationship and life walk with God, and overcome the temptation and tendency to measure or judge anyone else's.

As I explained to my teenage friend, I shared with her that living a Christian life originates in the heart of each individual after receiving Christ, evolving as a very personal life walk that takes place between God and His child. Although many Christians mean well by sharing their interpretations and opinions of the scripture, due to the natural human tendency to judge others, they may sometimes go too far, unfairly judging other Christians for not adhering to the exact Christian lifestyle they have grown to believe is the most Biblical.

God has permitted me to experience the critical judgments of others upon my Christian lifestyle as a route to reveal to me just how painful judgment from another Christian can be. It's so painful to be unfairly judged, but I needed to feel the pain of the offense before I could understand the pain that I may have unintentionally inflicted upon others.

I'll never forget the comment that a husband of a girlfriend made just weeks after they were married. He had suggested that she not spend much time with me, eluding to the fact that I couldn't possibly have a real relationship with God because I didn't worship the way he believed to be Biblical. Feeling insulted, unfairly misjudged and simply hurt, I learned a lesson that I could have learned no other way. I thank God for allowing me to learn this painful yet valuable lesson because now I am very, very cautious to not judge other Christians by my measuring stick.

There is only one measuring stick in which we each are to measure everything in our lives and that is God's measuring stick, which is the Bible, the inspired Word of God. Henry Blackaby says, "It is critical that you measure everything you hear against the Scriptures. Trends in psychology and philosophy come and go, but God's Word is timeless.

Whenever you share an opinion in counseling someone else, make sure that it comes from the Scripture and not merely from your best thinking. As long as you base your life choices on the Word of God, time will be your defender and will validate the wisdom of your choices."

Now I know, it's impossible to please everyone, and accepting this fact of life was key to me learning to let go of my desire to please others. The more time I spend with the Lord, praying and reading the Word, the more He reveals to me deep within my spirit that He is all that matters, and I need to keep my eyes firmly focused on Him with my ears stubbornly tuned in to Him.

I was taught as a little girl to set a Christian example for my sisters and others around me, and that is what I set out to do. For most of my life, I have worked diligently, striving to set a Christian example for those around me. I tried to have my devotions every day, attend church regularly, be involved in church programs, stay away from any habit that might lead another into temptation, keep the ten commandments, help others, be kind, honest, humble, patient and thoughtful. I'm tired just thinking of how hard I have been working to humanly produce a Christian example out of my life.

All this time, I was relying on my human natural power and abilities to set a Christ–like example, trying to do all the right things that I thought God wanted me to do to be more like Him. I was trying to be righteous and holy by my own natural means.

Isaiah 63:6 talks about righteous acts, "*All of us have become like one who is unclean, and all our righteous acts are like filthy rags; we all shrivel up like a leaf, and like the wind our sins sweep us away.*" The very best I can humanly do to make myself righteous is like filthy rags compared to the righteousness that comes from heaven.

Matthew 6:1 warns, "*Be careful not to do your 'acts of righteousness' before men, to be seen by them. If you do, you will have no reward from your Father in heaven.*" Righteousness means to be "in the right" in relation to God. Paul dedicates the third chapter of Romans to the topic of righteousness.

Romans 3:20 –23a says, "*Therefore no one will be declared righteous in his site by observing the law; rather, through the law we become conscious of sin. But now a righteousness from God, apart from law, has been made known, to which the Law and the Prophets testify. This righteousness from God comes through faith in Jesus Christ to all who believe.*"

We can't read the Bible enough to make ourselves righteous. Righteousness only comes from God through faith in Jesus Christ. How do we increase our faith in Christ? By getting to know Him intimately, we will increase our faith. Matthew 6:33 sums it us for me, "*But seek first His kingdom and his righteousness, and all these things will be given to you as well.*" How do we seek God? We seek Him by spending time alone with Him, getting to know Him intimately. A close intimate relationship requires intimate time alone.

Consider a husband and wife relationship. They may spend a great deal of time with their friends and family, but if they never spend intimate time alone, focusing only on each other...will they ever experience an intimate relationship? No. The same is true concerning our relationship with Christ. Attending corporate church services was never meant to take the place of intimate time alone between a girl and her God.

We are instructed in the Bible to gather together with other believers to worship God, but group worship was never intended to replace intimate time alone with Him.

After all of these years, little did I know that all I needed to do to set a Christ–like example was to spend more time alone with Christ Himself. I didn't need to attend more church services or Bible studies; I needed to take more time to be alone with God. It's a true fact that we become like the people we spend a great deal of time with, and this is true with Christ. The more time we spend in His presence, the more our lives reflect Him.

Can you believe the Christian life could be such a simple plan? Well, it is. God made it simple, and man has made it seem so difficult. God's plan is simple, but the road isn't always easy.

When I spend time with God, focusing on Him, He fills me up. Then, as I walk through my days doing whatever the day may hold, the overflow of Jesus in me is what sets the Christian example for others. There's nothing more beautiful than to witness the changing power of Christ written on the transformed lives of His girls.

At some point, I placed 'trying to please God above '*knowing* God,' but now I know that as my focus is on knowing my Heavenly Father, He will work in me what naturally pleases Him.

I couldn't have been further from the truth to think that God would love me more if I was a good girl, and He might love me less if I was a bad girl. Acts 10:34 says, "Then Peter began to speak:" I now realize how true it is that God does not show favoritism but accepts men from every nation who do what is right." God has no favorites; He loves us each the same.

As I pondered the thought that 'there is nothing I can humanly do to earn God's love, forgiveness, mercy or salvation,' I asked myself several questions. If I could earn God's love, then it wouldn't be unconditional love, would it? If I could earn God's forgiveness, mercy and salvation by doing good deeds, then Jesus didn't need to die on the cross, did He?

Isn't it interesting that the first song that most children learn in Sunday school is "Jesus loves me, this I know, for the Bible tells me so"...and the first Bible scripture that many of us learned as children was John 3:16, "*For God so loved the world* (His girls) *that He gave His Only Begotten Son that whosoever believeth in Him should not perish but have everlasting life*." (KJ)

That little song and scripture sum up our entire existence. God loves us so very much that He sent His only Son to die for our sins so we all wouldn't have to pay that painful price.

When I think about what kind of love would cause a Father to sacrifice His Only Son to be brutally nailed to a cross with big rusty nails, I am humbled and honored and so aware of my unworthiness of this precious life price that was paid so that I could know God.

Adam and Eve's sin destroyed the bridge connecting us to God, and Jesus death and resurrection restored that bridge, so that you and I can walk across without having to even pay a toll...and cultivate a relationship with our Heavenly Father; a relationship that is the sole purpose we were created.

Although God does keep a record of our lives, He's not sitting up in Heaven with a great big clip board just waiting to record my sins and good deeds. Quite to the contrary, our Heavenly Father is waiting for His girls to turn their hearts and thoughts towards Him. He's waiting for His telephone to ring because He longs to visit with us, revealing His heart to His girls which is what He's wanted to do since the very beginning of the world.

I think of our miniature dachshund, Little Bit, who when reprimanded for leaving a little stinky gift for us on the carpet, slouches to the floor putting his tail between his legs, slowly creeps away from me barely peeking back at me in a very guilty and shameful manner.

When Little Bit is praised for making a good choice like relieving himself in the grass instead of on the carpet, he struts around so proud of himself, basking in his brief little moment of glory, knowing that he has pleased me.

It's very obvious that Little Bit wants to please us and he feels so badly when he doesn't, but he simply accepts his discipline, then jumps up into our arms again focusing on being with us. Unlike my Little Bit, who jumps into my arms immediately forgetting the bad choice he just made, I would allow the guilt that I experienced from bad choices and sins that I committed to consume me. When I would make a good choice, my spirit would strut much like Little Bit, but when I'd make a bad choice my head would hang low and I'd waste days punishing myself for letting God down.

Looking back, this is exactly how I lived much of my life, being preoccupied by desperately wanting to please God that I totally overlooked the best part…knowing Him and His unconditional love.

I grew up hearing the word 'grace' being used often, so it isn't an unfamiliar term to me. However, only recently have I begun to truly understand what the gift of God's grace means in my life.

The word grace is defined by Tyndale as 'totally undeserving favor extended to man from God.' Grace is a love gift from God that we do not deserve and cannot earn. God loves us unconditionally, and there is simply nothing we can do in our lifetime that will make Him love us more or less. We cannot earn His love or His grace; we simply receive it as His gift to His girls.

God's love for His girls is much like the healthy, unconditional love of a parent towards a child.

Often, I find myself reminding my sons that there is nothing they could ever do to make me love them less. I want them to know that their actions don't regulate the degree of my love towards them. I tell them that I love them simply because they are my sons, when they make good choices as well as when they make bad choice.

Looking at unconditional love from a parents point of view has enabled me to better understand God's unconditional love towards me. He loves me with the unconditional love of a Heavenly Father for a daughter. When I make good choices and when I mess up, He loves me the same.

He took my hand and began to reveal to me that He loves me…not matter what…He loves me. Can you believe it! God loves me when I'm good just as He loves me when I bad.

The only aspect of my relationship with God that my behavior directly effects is the intimacy level of the relationship itself. When a child respects and honors her parents, the relationship can grow to a healthy level of intimacy that is not possible when the child behaves disrespectfully, dishonoring the parent and refusing to give them their rightful place in their lives.

Psalms 103:8–13 is a beautiful example of God's loving kindness and tender mercy towards His girls. "*He is merciful and tender toward those who don't deserve it; He is slow to get angry and full of kindness and love. He never bears a grudge, nor remains angry forever. He has not punished us as we deserve for all our sins, for His mercy toward those who fear and honor Him is as great as the height of the heavens about the earth. He is like a father to us, tender and sympathetic to those who reverence Him.*"

He loves me, then He loves me, and then He loves me some more.

As I read this passage, I think of Hebrews chapter 11, often referred to as "*God's great hall of faith.*" God chose to use people like Abraham, Isaac, Moses and even Rahab, the prostitute, who in spite of their human–ness, exemplified a strong faith in God.

As we read the names of these individuals, we know that they were very much human living human lives which were not perfect. God deliberately chose to emphasize their strong faith instead of their weaknesses or failures.

This is exactly what God always does when He looks at us, His girls. He doesn't expose our weaknesses continuously, but instead He recognizes our strengths, while gently leading us to grow to spiritual maturity in all areas of our lives.

As I began to understand this truth, I realized that God, my Creator, truly loves me and created me solely for His pleasure which is clearly shown in Revelation 4:11, "*Thou art worthy, O Lord, to receive glory and honor and power; for thou hast created all things, and for thy pleasure they are and were created.*" His primary desire for my life is to passionately enjoy an intimate relationship with Him. This is what brings God pleasure.

My family and I were on our boat in the gulf off of Marco Island, Florida recently. It was so peaceful with a clear blue sky and crystal blue ocean as far as my eyes could see. Three dolphin were swimming along side of the boat.

There we were just our little family and God. It was as though I could hear God saying, "I love you" through the calm breeze, the waves and the seagulls. There were no phones, programs, time schedules, clients, meetings…just God surrounding us with His great big sky and ocean. I felt so hugged and so loved by Him.

Our family spent Easter Sunday on the Isle of Capri this year. We attended the Island's annual Easter Service. It was outdoors under a big white tent. The pastor's message was preceded with the song, "God Loves People More Than Anything."

The pastor spoke about how God loved us so much that He chose earth, over all of the other planets, for us to live on. He said, "God made earth and then by placing us on it, He was saying 'I love you more than anything.'" He pointed out that many people love the gift of the earth. Some love the earth more than anything; more than the One who gave them the earth.

The pastor explained that there are people who God blesses with gifts of nice houses, boats, cars, success, and money. Many times instead of loving the giver of these wonderful gifts, people end up loving the gifts more than the giver. With every blessing and every gift God gives us, He is saying to us, "I love you more than anything."

As I was jogging one morning, I asked God to reveal to me something new in His Word, and would you believe that's just what He did. He brought Psalm 3:5 to my mind, we are instructed to *acknowledge God in all of our ways*. I realized that this is the key to stepping closer to God and beginning to get to know Him more intimately.

We cultivate intimate friendships by first acknowledging the other person and proceeding to spend time with them on a one–to–one basis getting to know them. Since spending time together communicating grows friendships with people, it makes perfect sense that spending time communicating with God will grow our relationship with Him, as well.

How do we begin to cultivate our relationship with our Heavenly Father? We simply begin by acknowledging Him in every circumstance of our lives. "In all thy ways acknowledge Him" simply means to acknowledge God in every situation in your life whether it be good or bad. To acknowledge God in all your ways means to respond and communicate with Him concerning every little and big issue that occurs in our lives. He cares about every detail of our lives.

We are to thank Him and give Him the credit for every good thing in our lives. James 1:17 says, "*Every good gift is from God,*" so shouldn't we thank Him instead of giving all the credit to His delivery man.

For example, after having surgery several years ago, I was telling an acquaintance how thankful I was to God for the success of the surgery, and she corrected me saying, "You should be thanking the doctor, since he performed the surgery?" I politely explained that I was grateful to the doctor and I certainly thanked him for his services, but first and foremost I thanked God. I explained that the doctor was the vehicle God chose to use to bring this gift to my life. The doctor was simply God's delivery man.

We also need to thank God for the good things that He will bring through the bad circumstances in our lives. Paul addresses this in Romans 8:28 when he says, "*And we know that all things work together for good to them that love God, to them who are called according to His purpose.*" (KJ)

No matter how bad or painful a situation or circumstance may be, trusting God to keep His Word and work something good out of a bad situation is what we must commit to do. He wants His girls to take Him at His Word.

Before we know it, we will be talking with God throughout every day because every where we look there is something to thank Him for in our lives. We can thank Him for the sunshine, our health, money for food and a home, friends, and family, fellow believers, His presence and His promises, and the list never ends because without Him nothing would exist.

Since I can remember, my mother has met alone with God, kneeling quietly on her bathroom floor with her Bible and prayer list every morning and every evening without fail. In Psalm 92:1–2 David tells us to do just as my mother does. "*Every morning tell Him, 'Thank you for your kindness,' and every evening rejoice in all His faithfulness.*"

There is nothing more precious to me than snuggles from my little guys, and the unwritten rule in our home is that first thing in the morning mom gets early morning snuggles, and last thing at night, she gets bedtime snuggles. Of course, mom reciprocates the snuggles, while openly giving them throughout the day.

I treasure these precious snuggles with my little guys, and I've asked them to never stop even when they grow older. I explained how important these times are to me, and how healthy they are for all of us.

As I thought about how I treasure and look forward to these daily snuggle times with my children, I realized that God must look forward to snuggles from His children in much the same way.

I believe that is exactly what God is speaking through David in Psalm 92:2. He's talking about giving God our first moment of every day in early morning snuggles, and our last moments of every night in bedtime snuggles.

After realizing that God loves snuggle time with His children too, I began to remind my boys as they approach me for snuggle time each day, to say good morning or good night to Jesus and tell Him that they love Him. The more we acknowledge God in the minutes of every day, the closer we become to Him.

God never moves away from His girls. If there seems to be distance between you and God it can only be because you have stepped away from Him. This can be a conscious decision or unconsciously initiated by choosing a lifestyle that separates you from God.

The really great news is...you only need to whisper His name to begin stepping closer and getting to know Him again. It's easier than picking up the telephone and dialing long distance number, for you see, God's always waiting on your phone line...there's no need to even dial.

Rest assured He's got your number and He's waiting on the line just to hear His daughter's voice. Hmm. That is so sweet and so difficult to comprehend, that God Almighty is truly our Heavenly Father, who created us and placed us in this world for the sole purpose of cultivating a relationship with Him. That is one truth that absolutely blows me away.

I'm so glad that my Verizon phone bill doesn't include my long distance calls to Heaven because I'd surely be broke these days. The Lord has become much more to me than simply a Sunday phone call, but more like the oxygen that I need to sustain my daily life. God's presence is so magnificent and preciously peaceful that it leaves me wanting more. The more I know Him, the more I desire to know Him.

I talk with Him about the details of my life and He's showing me that He knows and cares about every little detail in the lives of His girls. Let me share a beautiful example of how much even our simplest thoughts mean to God.

Last year I wanted to buy a pair of $90 GAP denim overalls, but decided that I really shouldn't spend that kind of money on them, so I bought $29 Old Navy overalls instead. Well, I ripped my Old Navy overalls beyond repair, and once again began to entertain the idea of buying the GAP overalls.

Over the course of about three months I continued to talk myself out of driving all the way to Orlando to pay $90 for a pair of GAP overalls. Not getting them was definitely not life threatening. I just didn't feel right about paying so much money for these overalls, when I really needed to spend my money in predetermined areas of our family budget.

During this time I didn't tell anyone about my crazy desire to buy these GAP overalls, and I certainly didn't pray about them. Not that I shouldn't have or couldn't have, I just didn't feel like it was that important.

One evening while on my way to work at the wellness center, I once again decided against driving to Orlando to buy these overalls because I would have had to use my grocery money. Imagine me explaining to my family that we will be eating peanut butter and jelly this week in our lunches and bologna sandwiches for dinner because Mom really needed to buy these $90 GAP overalls. Yeah, right. That would go over really well, not to mention how good it would make me feel inside.

So, once again I decided that I would make the right decision for me at this time and postpone buying the overalls. You'll never believe what happened when I walked into the wellness center. My fellow staff member and friend, Lori, walked up to me greeting me in her usual cheerful manor, and said, "Hi, Susan! Hey, come into the office a minute. My nail tech gave me this brand new pair of size 8 GAP denim overalls which she just bought, but she doesn't really like the way they fit her. She thought I might know of someone who could use them, and I thought they might fit you. Would you like them?"

With tears beginning to roll down my cheeks, and a huge smile growing on my face, I shared with Lori how God had used her to let me know that even though these GAP overalls were not a life and death situation, and even though I hadn't even prayed for them, He heard my thoughts and read my heart. He just wanted to give His daughter a gift, letting her know that He truly does care about every little detail of my life.

Not only is God showing me He knows even my thoughts, but that He cares for every single one of His girls and every detail of our lives. That fact just WOW's me every time I think about it!

I pray each morning asking God to empty me out and fill me with more of Himself, so that all I do and say will bring glory to Him. As we walk through each day together, I sense His Holy Spirit abiding in me, walking with me and working through me.

There's nothing more precious in all of life than to know the presence of the Holy Spirit of God. Oh Lord, Please breath into me your presence and your power fresh and new every day I walk on this earth.

When we begin to acknowledge the presence of God it becomes as natural as breathing in oxygen. God doesn't simply live in buildings and wait for His girls to visit Him on Sundays. He lives in the hearts of His people, and therefore, wants to be an active part of every minute of every day. He's waiting for us to call on Him, inviting Him into our hearts to be as present as the oxygen we breath.

Over the past several years, I have grown so close to my Heavenly Father, and I am beginning to recognize His guiding hand concerning the daily issues of my life. Whether His message to me is to send a note, or cook a meal, whatever it may be, I'm learning to just confidently obey Him.

As I began to include God in the course of my days, I began to hear Him speaking to my Spirit, not in an audible voice, but His gentle guiding presence that I've grown to recognize and cherish.

I'll never forget the day I sensed God directing me to stop by and visit an old acquaintance, and deliver a specific message concerning God's interest in my friend's life. I told God I would go to his office during his busiest time, and if he was not busy with patients then I would know that I had heard God correctly.

As I drove into his office parking lot the electricity went off, preventing him from seeing his patients, so there was my sign. I joined him in his office, shared with him what God had placed on my heart concerning him and said a friendly good–bye.

You're going to love what happened next. The moment I stepped out of the office door to go to my car the electricity mysteriously powered up. My friend looked at me in disbelief, and I said, "God's in control, isn't He?"

I could tell you story after story of how God has enlightened me to His active role all around us...as we get to know His heart. I love Psalms 91:1, "*He THAT dwelleth in the secret place of the most High shall abide under the shadow of the Almighty*." My desire is to live in the secret place of the most High, and I'm just now beginning to understand how precious, holy and safe that place is.

My dear friend and mentor, Millie, has recently experienced a new sense of freedom in her spirit that has been derived from her intimate relationship with her Heavenly Father. I met Millie about thirteen years ago when I attended a Bible study she was teaching for a diverse group of women.

It was through Millie's anointed teaching of the Word of God in that cozy living room that began a spiritual growth spurt in me that helped me to begin to move closer to God and desire to know Him in a more intimate way.

Millie is a beautiful woman of 62 years, and she is married to Frank. Frank, the big strong athletic type guy, used to serve as the lay chaplain for several professional baseball teams; the Cleveland Indians, the Boston Red Sox and the Kansas City Royals over the years.

Frank is now confined to a wheel chair as a result of numerous strokes. For a while Millie cared for Frank on her own, but now she has full–time in–home care for Frank, as she continues her position of English Department Chair and teacher at Winter Haven High School.

During this season of her life which consists of countless unexpected circumstances, she has reached a newly found place of freedom where her soul sings and flies through each and every day. I love how Millie describes this free place that God has brought her too.

"My times were dramatically changed three years ago when my once very take charge and athletic husband of 41 had a serious stroke that left him spending his days in a wheelchair and his nights in a hospital bed. This has surely not led to the retirement years of travel and enjoyment that we had long anticipated. Though I would not have chosen this path for our lives, nor would I wish it upon our worst enemy, these have become some of the richest years of my life which I would not have missed for any thing in this world.

Because in one twenty–four hour period of time, my world as I had known it changed forever, I found myself having to trust in God like never before. Needless to say, most of the busy things have been stripped away from my life. As time has worn on, I have become so very thankful for the peace, calm and quiet that now reign. What at first may have seemed to bind or to keep me from doing those things I loved doing have now actually served to set me free to fly higher with Him.

The intimacy that has resulted in a total dependence upon God is something I never dreamed possible. When I kneel down in front of the little blue wing back chair in my bedroom and enter His presence, it is as if He has pulled back a beautiful bridal veil and welcomed me in saying, 'Oh, I am so glad you are here; I just love it when you come to spend time with me. I will spend the rest of your life showing you how very much I love you.' During those moments, nothing else matters as I share the deepest longings of my heart with the God of the universe, and He whispers His love to my spirit.

How is it possible for a human spirit to be in touch with the spirit of God? How does He fulfill His promise in Isaiah that He will be my husband? Only He can answer those questions, but there has never been a time in my life where I have known such utter and complete joy, peace, comfort, freedom and the awareness of His presence…not just some of the time…but every hour of the day. Truly, "*God has caused me to be fruitful in the land of my affliction.*" Genesis 41:52b"

Millie has written many beautiful poems as the words seem to flow easily out of her during her intimate moments spent with Him. One of my favorites in "Behind the Veil."

Behind the Veil

Oh, for the joy that was set before Him
He endured the rugged cross that day,
So that we may enter His presence
in a new and exciting way.

No longer kept from the throne room
By the veil that had stood between,
It was ripped from the top to the bottom
Nevermore our entrance to screen.

He's been waiting down through the ages
For us to look full in His wonderful face
and to realize that what He has given
Was to invite us up into His PLACE.

As we enter to kneel down to worship
Our presence to Him is a thrill.
For the joy that was set down before Him
He died all our longings to fill.

He invites us to come always higher,
Higher than we can possibly know
And to see that His love and desire
For us He'll continually show.

He delights in His obedient children
As we expectantly visit with Him.
He wants us to know that not ever
Will His thrill at our visits grow dim!

Oh, Jesus we'll never get tired
Of seeing your sparkling eyes
as we come into your very Presence
and to know that your love never dies.

Oh, thanks for your standing invitation
To spend time in your own special Home
And that for us you'll always be waiting
To gather us close to your throne!

—Millie Farthing, author

As I read the words that my precious friend and mentor uses to express how she feels about her Heavenly Father, it was as though she had taken these same words right out of my heart.

At night after tucking my sons into bed, I sit down with my Bible, a cup of hot tea, and I'm ready to enjoy quiet time with my Lord. I always begin by thanking Him and praising Him for Who He is and for the many blessings He's so graciously brought into my life. I'll read passages from the Bible as I feel lead, and I'll just begin to share my deepest thoughts with Him.

During these precious moments, I feel God's presence so close that it's almost as though I'm laying my head on His lap, as He ever–so–lovingly holds me close just as a loving father would hold his daughter. I pour out my heart before Him and expose every area of myself, keeping nothing hidden from Him. I surrender my family, my friends, and my will.

Oh what treasured moments spent in the presence of the Most High God, feeling His love surround me and fill me is truly the most priceless treasure in all the world. Not only does God snuggle close to me in the quietness of my candle–lit living room, but He has become my running buddy too.

I used to love running several times a week with my close friend, Karen. We'd share our deepest thoughts during those late night runs. We'd laugh and cry together. One time we even joked about bringing a note pad to make lists while we were running. It was so much fun.

What a blessing to treat our minds, bodies and spirits in a forty minute run. As our families' schedules began to change, however, we found it nearly impossible to run together. Running with Karen was such a gift. How could I possibly go back to running by myself? I was dreading those lonely runs. I had never enjoyed running alone. I remember praying, "Who am I going to run with now, God. Please show me your plan."

My first morning running alone, I truly missed Karen, but I found out what was better than running with a close friend who loved God. It was running with God, Himself. When God met me on the street to run that first morning out, I knew I had met the ultimate running partner. I love the way His plan just comes together.

Each morning after kissing my three guys good–bye, I just can't wait to go running with my Lord. As I begin to run along the lake, I say, "Good morning, Lord." I thank Him for the breath of a new day. I feel so free out there just Jesus and me. As I inhale the fresh morning air, it's as though I hear God say, "Good morning, my dear."

I thank Him for the gentle breeze, the clear blue sky, the cheerful birds and the sunrise. I just take it all in like never before in my life. Each morning, as the warmth of the newly risen sun envelopes my body, I can almost hear God say to me, "I love you, my daughter. I love you so much." As I feel His love cover me, my eyes fill with tears, and I reply to Him, "I love you back, Lord. I love you, back."

At the close of every e–mail, note or conversation, I usually say, "I love you," to my friends, and one friend began to reply with, "I love you back." What a wonderful way to return love to someone who has just expressed their love to you. It feels good to have someone reciprocate your love, by saying, "I love you back."

I'll always remember my run with God that day. When I felt Him say to me, through the sunshine, "I love you," the truth jumped out at me. It was so clear to me. All these years, God wasn't wanting to hear about what I had done for Him or only what I needed from Him. He longed to hear me simply say, "I love you back."

When I was in third grade, I experienced my first crush on a boy named Jimmy, and I played the silly little game that many young girls used to play with daisies. I plucked each white petal from the daisy very slowly, one at a time, alternating the phrases… 'he loves me,' 'he loves me not.' And I truly believed that the phrase of that very last petal would tell me if Jimmy loved me…or not.

Well, Jimmy didn't love me, but someone else sure did. And that someone is my Heavenly Father, who, I believe, created daisies especially for His girls to enjoy. I imagine God whispering gently and most lovingly, with the pluck of each petal, "I love you, I love you more, I love you always, I'll love you forever"…and on and on He loves us. No matter what He loves His girls…and that means you and me.

God has brought me to a new place where my spirit runs free. It is a place where I can feel like a little girl again despite my age; His little girl. In this new place, I am experiencing freedom like never before deep within my spirit.

This new place is where God and I walk hand in hand, and my feet feel like they aren't even touching the ground. There are no chains, boxes or man–made rules that bind my soul or quench my spirit in this new place. This is where He wants all of His girls to live. It is a place where God says He loves me, and I say, "I LOVE YOU BACK, GOD!"

These days, no matter where I go or what I do…in my spirit, I am a little girl twirling freely in the middle of an endless field of beautiful white and yellow daisies. Just my God and me. It is true, and now I know. God created you and me, so He could spend time with us.

He loves us more than anything. He cares more about who we are, than what we do. Yes! God loves us more than anything. He has helped me learn to fly in a world where many of His people have forgotten they can fly, and He wants to do the same for each of His girls.

Dear God, Thank you for making me free. I am finally…FREE! FREE TO BE GOD'S GIRL!!!

Free, I long to be free

Come and Fill my Heart with hope
Come and fill my life with love
Come and fill my days with dreams
Empty me of all the empty things
That I hold onto
Come and fill my heart with you

Come and Fill My Heart
—Written By Grant Cunningham–Matt Husemann
—Performed By Avalon

Appendix A

Take Your Wellness Temperature

1. ***Life Is How You Change It***

"*Your attitudes and thoughts must be constantly changing for the better. Yes, you must be a new and different person, holy and good.*" Ephesians 3:23–24

Life on earth is brief. With life comes change, and changing for the better on a daily basis is an important part of God's perfect plan for His girls. He wants us to not merely tolerate change, but to welcome change with excitement in our hearts. Change is not a curse, rather a gift of opportunity. Change is God's invitation to His girls to join Him in the designing process of our lives and futures. Change always begins in the heart, and as the heart changes and grows the woman changes and grows. Wellness is about taking small steps every day towards healthier, more balanced lifestyle which God has intended for His girls.

Bible References for "Change"

Psalms 139:23–24
Isaiah 41:10
1 Corinthians 6:10–20
Ephesians 3:17
Hebrews 12:1
Philippians 3:13–14
John 10:10
Romans 12:1–2

2. ***The Five Dimensions of Wellness***

"Let us strip off anything that slows us down or holds us back, and especially those sins that wrap themselves so tightly around our feet and trip us up; and let us run with patience the particular race that God has set before us." Hebrews 12:1.

God gave His girls the Bible to use as a step–by–step instruction manual to direct us safely and successfully through life. God promises health and success in every area of our lives when we treasure His words and direct our hearts and minds towards His wisdom. After we invite Him to take up residency in our hearts, He begins to strip each room in His temple (that's us), and transform them to reflect Him. This process involves acknowledging the chains that bind us, detaching the chains, healing and adapting to life without the chains, and living victoriously with the scar of the chain. The spiritual dimension of our lives (God's intended temple) acts as the entire foundation and structure of the life of a woman, while the other four dimensions are represented by rooms in the temple.

"*Haven't you yet learned that your body is the home of the Holy Spirit that God gave to you, and that He lives within you? Your own body does not belong to you. For God has bought you with a great price. So use every part of your body to give glory back to God, because He owns it.*" 1 Corinthians 6:19–20.

As caretaker of God's temple, I encourage you to walk through this Wellness Temperature, inviting you God to walk with you and reveal the specific changes that He desires for you in each area of your life. I encourage you to pray Psalm 139:23–24 as a prayer inviting God to join you in this task. *"Search me, Oh God, and know my heart; test my thoughts. Point out anything you find in me that makes you sad, and lead me along the path of everlasting life."*

3. **Evaluate your wellness by using the following rating scale. After evaluating yourself, highlight the Helpful Ideas which you feel will help you improve your state of wellness in each area.**

5 = living well–balanced wellness lifestyle to it's fullest

4 = living balanced wellness lifestyle–making great progress to celebrate life

3 = learning to live a balanced wellness lifestyle–desiring continued growth

2 = making progress towards improved wellness

1 = contemplating improvement and growth in this area

A. Physical Wellness: Physical Activity

"*She sets about her work vigorously; her arms are strong for her tasks; she is energetic and strong.*" Proverbs 31:17.

Because of the pressure that the media places on women through their standard of perfection, it is imperative that women spend time looking into God's mirror, to gain His perspective on their lives, both the physical and the spiritual. The health of the body is important to God and this is the reason Paul teaches that both body and spirit are to glorify our Lord. God is not as concerned with what we do for exercise, but why we exercise. He wants us to care for our physical bodies for the purpose of glorifying Him and not ourselves. From season to season, as our families grow older, our lives will change, and so will the nature of our physical workouts, and we should not limit ourselves to what we've always done or what someone else is doing, rather take an unlimited approach to fitness as we travel through life's seasons. Our bodies are precious gifts that God has given to us, His girls, and the quality of care we provide for it is our gift back to God!

How do you feel physically? On most days, do you feel energized? Do you accumulate at least 30 minutes of physical movement during the course of most days?

Evaluation _____

Bible References for "Physical Wellness"; Physical Activity Component:

Proverbs 31:17
3 John 2
1 Timothy 4:8

Helpful Ideas:

- — Change your attitude towards physical activity
- — Recognize the importance of physical activity in your daily life and accept the responsibility to provide it for the body God loaned to you.
- — Be thankful you are able to move and do the best you can, as often as you can
- — Get out and get moving; walk alone; walk with a friend; walk a pet; play with a child.
- — Put more energy into housework and yard work
- — Buy a headset and...dust, sweep, rake, and mow the lawn to music
- — Make a 10 minute commitment; then 15; then 20; then 25; then 30, etc.
    - Discover an activity you enjoy
    - Schedule a realistic time for your workout and keep your appoint as you would an important doctors appointment.

B. Physical Wellness: Healthy Eating

Everything is permissible for me–but not everything is beneficial. Everything is permissible for me—but I will not be mastered by anything. 1 Corinthians 6:12.

The good man eats to live, while the evil man lives to eat. Proverbs 13:25.

God created His girls with amazingly complex physical bodies designed with many intricate systems working together to support and sustain the body by healing and repairing themselves. From the beginning of creation, good health was, without a doubt, part of God's perfect plan for His girls, and the secret to good health is to live in a way that will actually promote the healing and repair processes of the body, rather than hinder them. When we eat to live rather than live to eat, we will gain a healthier approach to nutrition. Eating healthy most of the time and indulging on occasion is a healthy and realistic approach to healthy eating.

Do you eat healthy most of the time and feel free of guilt to indulge on occasion? Do you enjoy meal time with friends and family? Do you know what foods make you feel good both physically and mentally?

Evaluation _____

Bible references for "Physical Wellness"; Healthy Eating Component:

Proverbs 13:25
1 Corinthians 6:12
1 Corinthians 10:31

Helpful Ideas:

— Learn to eat the foods that will help your body function at it's best; both physically and mentally
— Eat protein for a quick energy boost
— Eat high fiber foods for stress relief
— Make water your drink of choice
— Pack a thermal lunch box every day…in case you need healthy snacks
— Pre–bag veggies in single serving baggies…they're easy to grab
— Hard boil 6–10 eggs at beginning of week…add to recipes, veggies, or just eat as protein snack
— Share a restaurant meal
— Share dessert
— Eat healthy most of the time and DON'T FEEL GUILTY to indulge on occasion!!!
— Do not go on a diet

C. Emotional Wellness: Trusting God

I will say of the Lord, He is my refuge and my fortress; my God: in Him will I trust. Psalms 91:2.

Trust in the Lord with all your heart and lean not on your own understanding; in all your ways acknowledge Him and He will make your paths straight. Proverbs 3:5–6.

Don't let your heart be troubled. Trust in God; trust also in Me. John 14:1.

Emotional wellness involves developing healthy stress management skills that will enable us to successfully deal with the stress of daily life. Stress is basically neutral; it's the way we choose to react to stressful situations that determines if the stress becomes negative or positive. Understanding that nothing can happen in our lives unless God permits it to happen is very important information when responding to life's stressful situations and issues. We can find strength and comfort in knowing that nothing can take place in our lives unless God personally authorizes it. The key to emotional wellness, the way God intended for His girls, is to trust God despite unpleasant life circumstances. No matter what happens, we must commit to say, "I WILL TRUST YOU, LORD!!"

How do you feel emotionally? Are you taking control of your emotional health are situations controlling you? Are you taking responsibility for your reactions to stressful situations or do you blame others?
Do you worry often? Have you learned to truly trust all situations in your life to God?
Do you allow stress to become negative or do you commit to make it positive? Do you spend time relaxing on a daily basis?

Evaluation _____

Bible References for "Emotional Wellness"

Psalms 29:11
Psalms 118:24
Proverbs 27:12
1 Thessalonians 5:17–18
Proverbs 19:11
Philippians 4:4–7
Proverbs 15:15
Proverbs 17:22
Romans 5:3–4
Psalms 5:3
Psalms 91:2
Proverbs 3:5–6
John 14:1

Helpful Ideas:

— Take responsibility for your reactions to stressful situations and don't blame others
— Commit to make stress positive by reacting positively towards stressful situations
— Believe the Bible is the Word of God…and what it says is TRUE
— Trust God with everything (live by Proverbs 3:5–6)
— Acknowledge God in all things in your daily life
— Read, study and apply the wisdom found in the Book of Job
— Learn to relax
— Set aside time each day for relaxing; at least 5 minutes
— Take a hot bath while listening to relaxing music
— Drive slower and listen to relaxing music you enjoy while in the car
— Turn off the TV
— Don't answer the phone just because it's ringing
— Rethink your buying habits
— STOP being a slave to your day planner
— Just say NO
— Resign from any organization whose meetings you dread
— Don't Sweat The Small Stuff
— Get up an hour earlier (ok, maybe only 30 minutes earlier)

D. Intellectual Wellness: Wisdom, Knowledge–Understanding

Through wisdom a house is built, and by understanding it is established; and by knowledge shall the chambers be filled with all precious and pleasant riches. A wise man is strong, yea, a man (woman) of knowledge increases strength.
Proverbs 24:3–5.

God loves His girls so much that He has given us the gifts of His knowledge, His wisdom and His understanding, and placed them in the Bible. When we read God's Word, the Holy Spirit will unwrap the gifts of knowledge and wisdom, and we will never be the same. By His knowledge and wisdom, will we gain His perspective and better understand all of life's issues, while improving our intellectual health. As we draw knowledge and wisdom from His Heavenly well, we will hear Him saying often "Heads Up, Girls," steering us safely through life by making us aware of who our enemy is and how to overcome him.

Do you read the Bible on a regular basis? Do you spend enough time reading the Bible and talking with God that you're experiencing Him revealing His wisdom to you?
Do you challenge yourself intellectually by reading and learning more to increase your knowledge? Are you trying to look at situations from other perspectives? Do you desire to increase in wisdom, knowledge and understanding, so you can change and experience personal growth in your life?

Evaluation _____

Bible References for "Intellectual Wellness"

Proverbs 24:3–5
Philippians 1:9
Proverbs 29:2
2 Peter 1:5–10
Isaiah 33:6
Ezekiel 3:15
John 13:34–35
1 Corinthians 15:10

Philippians 2:3–4

Helpful Ideas:

— Buy a translation of the Bible which you can easily understand
— Read, study and apply God's Word daily
— Read a daily devotional (ask God which one is best for you)
— Don't be quick to judge others
— Know your personality strengths and weakness; and work on the weaknesses (read a personality book and take the assessment test inside)
— Keep a journal
— Read at least one book each month
— Get up an hour earlier(ok, maybe only 30 minutes earlier)
— Record milestones in each area of your life
— Set goals for personal growth
— Become a good listener

E. Social Wellness: Healthy Relationships

As iron sharpens iron, so one friend sharpens another. Proverbs 27:17.

God created women with the hope that they would enter into friendships with one another. Women bring unique gifts into the lives of other women; gifts that a man cannot bring. As women, we are called to cultivate relationships with other women, and doing so we will fulfill God's purpose for friendship. His purpose for friendship is to encourage, strengthen, and sharpen one another. Women are to complete one another instead of compete with one another. As God's girls, we need to be good stewards of the friendships He has blessed us with by sowing good things into the lives of our girlfriends. May we make the most of every opportunity to celebrate the gift of friendship you've designed for us…just because you love us.

Do the friends and family you choose to spend time with have a positive influence on your life? Do you need to "weed your social garden?" Do you really enjoy your friendships? Are you a good friend to others? Do you know what the Bible teaches about friendships? Have you ever asked God to bring a friend into your life that would be a healthy influence?

Evaluation _____

Bible References for "Social Wellness"

Proverbs 27:17
Hebrews 10:24–25
2 Corinthians 9:2
Galatians 6:1–2
Hebrews 3:13
1 Thessalonians 5:11
Ecclesiastes 4:9–10
James 5:16
Proverbs 22:24–25
Proverbs 27:19

Helpful Ideas:

— Find out what the Bible teaches about friendship
— Ask God to reveal to you who you should spend more time with and who you should spend more time with
— Take time to be with those people that are closest to your heart
— Let your friends know that you value their friendship
— Spend time with people who make you better; those friends who strengthen you
— Reach out and give the gift of yourself…spend time with others
— Spend time with those friends that you serve as a "caregiver" too
— Have lunch, coffee or a chat with a friend at least one time each week
— E–mail your friends
— Send a note of encourage someone once every week
— Go out of your way to be kind to someone every day
— Just be yourself
— Be quick to forgive

F. **Spiritual Wellness: Getting to Know God More Intimately**

I am the vine, ye are the branches; He that abideth in me, and I in him, the same bringeth forth much fruit; for without me ye can do nothing. John 15:6.

He that dwelleth in the secret place of the Most High shall abide under the shadow of the Almighty. Psalms 91:1.

The spiritual dimension of a woman's life serves as the foundation and basic structure of her entire existence. The physical, emotional, intellectual, and social dimensions are greatly impacted by the condition of her spiritual health. God created His girls with a God spot that only He can fill, and He waits like a gentleman to be invited into a life. When we invite Christ into our hearts and lives, it's as though we invite Him to ride in our 'car of life.' It's only when we ask Him to drive our car, rather than ride as a passenger, that He truly fills His intended place in our lives. Realizing that life on earth isn't about us, but all about a great big God, will bring a new freedom to a girl and open the door that leads to the secret place of the Most High, where intimacy with Christ begins.

Do you spend time alone with God on a daily basis? Do you sense the presence of God in your life? Do you know God in a personal intimate way, as your Heavenly Father, or would you describe your relationship with Him as more formal, maybe even distant? Do you make your spiritual workout priority on a daily basis? Do you understand that the quality of your spiritual wellness directly affects every other area of your life? Do you really desire to know God more intimately?

Evaluation _____

Bible References for "Spiritual Wellness"

Philippians 1:21
Psalms 91
Jeremiah 18:1–6
John 1:1–3
John 15:1–7
Mark 12:30
Psalm 104:34

Helpful Ideas:

— Read, study and apply the Word of God on a daily basis
— Participate in a Bible study for women
— Find a church to worship and grow in

- — Spend time with other women who make their spiritual health priority
- — Make your spiritual workout priority every day
- — Decide when you will spend time alone with God, and protect it!
- — Set–up a special place just for you and God to meet together; a special chair, your Bible, devotional book, prayer guides, prayer list, candle, favorite photos, books, writing paper, tissues, blank note cards
- — Read a daily devotional
- — Talk with God all through the day about the events of your days
- — Seek out a spiritual mentor; someone whose beliefs and spiritual walk you respect

Dear Reader,

After writing this book, I have a new appreciation for God's unconditional, never ending love for His girls. His beautiful expressions of love towards me continue to 'Wow' me day–after–day. He continually makes His presence known to me in ways that confirm He truly is in control of every detail of my life.

I hope you have enjoyed reading God's Girls as much as I enjoyed writing it. My prayer also is that God has used it to reveal Himself to you, His girl, in new and wonderful ways.

I'd love to hear about your story and how God is working in the details of your life. While I will try to answer every letter, I would count it a privilege to pray for you. I love to inspire women by sharing God's Girls topics at retreats, seminars–conferences, so feel free to contact me at:

Susan Slone Dantzler
P.O. Box 2372
Winter Haven, Florida 33881

In His Love,

Susan

Printed in the United States
753300003B